THE
FACES OF
POVERTY
IN NORTH
CAROLINA

The Faces of Poverty in North Carolina

STORIES FROM OUR INVISIBLE CITIZENS

Gene R. Nichol

THE

UNIVERSITY

OF NORTH

CAROLINA

PRESS

*This book was published with the
assistance of the* BLYTHE FAMILY FUND
of the University of North Carolina Press.

Designed by Richard Hendel
Set in Utopia, Aller, and Bunday Sans
by Tseng Information Systems, Inc.
Manufactured in the United States of America

The University of North Carolina Press has been
a member of the Green Press Initiative since 2003.

Library of Congress Cataloging-in-Publication Data
Names: Nichol, Gene R., 1951– author.
Title: The faces of poverty in North Carolina : stories from our
invisible citizens / Gene R. Nichol.
Description: Chapel Hill : The University of North Carolina Press, [2018] |
Includes bibliographical references and index.
Identifiers: LCCN 2018021266 | ISBN 9781469646527 (cloth : alk. paper) |
ISBN 9781469646534 (ebook)
Subjects: LCSH: Poor—North Carolina. | Poverty—North Carolina. |
North Carolina—Economic conditions—21st century. | North Carolina—
Social conditions—21st century.
Classification: LCC HC107.N8 N57 2018 | DDC 362.509756—dc23
LC record available at https://lccn.loc.gov/2018021266

For my girls—

Glenn, Jesse, Jenny, Soren, and Belle

CONTENTS

TABLES, MAPS, AND GRAPHS

A PREFACE FROM THE WOODS OF HICKORY

It's hard not to be taken with Hickory, North Carolina, at least on first blush. Nestled in the foothills of the Blue Ridge Mountains, west of North Carolina's urban piedmont, Hickory's 40,000 residents can boast of broad avenues, a quaint city center, impressive museums, welcoming neighborhoods, massive and well-attended churches, a fine private university, tranquil country roads, and an appealing natural environment with endless outdoor recreational opportunities. Sheltering mountains typically produce moderate winters and cooler summers. Prices are modest.[1] Hickory has the look of an older, easier Carolina. Even the name appeals.

Hickory has been repeatedly recognized as an "All-American" city. The town website notes that *Reader's Digest* designated it one of the "ten best places" in the country to "live and raise a family." *Money* magazine has posted similar accolades. *Forbes* praised its decidedly low cost of doing business. Hickory casts itself as the banking, commercial, and medical hub of a 350,000-person metropolitan area famed for its furniture and hosiery industries. More recently, telecommunication powerhouses have helped produce much of the world's supply of fiber-optic cables. Its hopeful slogan is "Life Well Crafted."[2]

Hickory has also, in the last fifteen years, experienced immensely trying economic times.

The pressures and alterations of global trade have hit hard. Furniture and textile jobs, much of the core of Hickory's economy, disappeared with velocity after the North American Free Trade Agreement took hold. The *Washington Post* would write in 2009 that "global trade has overwhelmed this manufacturing (hub) beside the Blue Ridge."[3] The region has lost more jobs to international competition than just about anywhere in the nation.[4] Mills closed, the number of factories dwindled, and even newer fiber-optic plants experienced massive layoffs. The harsh tides of the Great Recession then piled on with a vengeance. In 2000, Hickory's unemployment rate was a scant 2.8 percent—well below state and national averages. By 2010, it had soared to a breathtaking 15.5 percent—the steepest rise in North Carolina and one of the four or five sharpest municipal unemployment increases in the nation. Over the same period,

Hickory's poverty rate almost doubled (from 11 to 20 percent). Its median income dropped precipitously.[5]

In 2011, a Wall Street publication listed Hickory as one of ten cities that would take more than a decade to recover from the recession.[6] *USA Today* later deemed it the "eighth worst city in America to try to find a job." *Business Insider* included Hickory on its purported listing of the "most miserable cities" in the nation. A Gallup Poll in 2014 reported even more demoralizing results.[7] Great numbers of residents lost their jobs, their savings, their homes, and, it seems, their prospects. A small, bucolic manufacturing mecca had become an economic disaster zone. And while some indicators have improved in recent years, the crisis remains substantial.[8]

For the first time, in the last decade homelessness has become a daunting problem in the small North Carolina city. The Salvation Army Shelter of Hope is pressed well beyond its capacity. As a result, some 200 to 250 wounded souls live in the woods surrounding town. They patch together makeshift cardboard lean-tos and dilapidated tents, keeping a wary eye for police and complaining neighbors. Some camp setups are simple, little more than a milk crate for seating and a tarp to fend off the rain. Others string together more intricate, if feeble and often porous, designs. Many campers gather in groups, though the safer course, they indicate, seems to be huddling in smaller, less attention-provoking numbers.

In summer, the camps bear the oppressive markers of the South: intense heat, draining humidity, sudden rainstorms, relentless mosquitoes, yellow jackets, gnats, and snakes. In winter, snow and frost pose distinct and direct dangers. More than one homeless struggler has perished against the cold.[9] About a third of those "living out" are women. Some are kids—though their parents, fearing abuse and neglect proceedings at the hands of the state, work hard to hide them. All share conditions and perils that are deplorable. Their circumstances make it hard to remember Hickory is an "All-American City" and even tougher to recall that the United States is the richest major nation on earth.

Roger Cornett and the fifteen or so volunteers of the Open Door Homeless Relief Project—run out of the basement of a tiny Baptist church in nearby Conover—spend much of their days and nights, and almost all of their resources, trying to keep people living in the woods of Hickory whole, safe, well, warm, and alive. Cornett is a sixty-four-year-old retired businessman who suffers from the debilitating neuromuscular disorder myasthenia gravis. Some days his illness makes it hard for him to leave the house, or even the bedroom. Particularly on those days, his wife, Janice, works enthusiastically to fill the gap. But on most, Roger Cornett joins early mornings and late nights, tapping a remarkable reservoir of energy and stamina. He doesn't look the part of the heart-on-the-sleeve-do-gooder as he crisscrosses the county in a battered pickup, NRA sticker prominently displayed. But Cornett and his seemingly fearless cohorts venture into often-dangerous campgrounds distributing tents, tarps, food, cookstoves, utensils, propane cylinders, blankets, trash bags, clothing, portable heaters, and even dog food. "I never took well to retirement," Cornett explains. "I couldn't believe people were being left to live like animals in my own home county."

"God calls us to do what we can," Cornett allows; "I'm no angel." Campers, as Cornett prefers to call those he serves, often refer to him as "Chaplain Roger." And the New Testament is never far from his words or thoughts. Still, he explains, "I'm no Bible thumper." People who live in the woods "don't like to be thumped."

As I learned over multiple visits to Hickory from 2012 to 2017, the stories of those living in the camps are tough to hear.[10] A young pregnant woman indicates she's living in a tent until the baby comes. Cornett says he has "four pregnant women in the woods now (summer, 2015)—we try to help with medicine and transportation to the doctor or the hospital." In an August heat near 100 degrees, before one of my visits the same year, he spends much of a day getting fresh water and an ice cooler to a difficult-to-locate young woman living with two children. A thin man in his thirties, Bill Stock, explains he's been homeless off and on since 2009. A "lot of us would be dead out here without Roger and his people." You "learn not to look vulnerable," he reports. A "woman has to get with a man or she'll get hurt."

Making the point, Cornett introduces me to a lesbian couple living along the wood lines. Janet Teal (not her real name) was raped, beaten, and stabbed two days earlier. She shows us thirteen stab wounds. The sight is sickening. Cornett and one of his friends had helped subdue the assailant. "I don't know how long we'll last" out here, Teal concedes.

A disheveled man in his mid-twenties, Chuck Strand, describes losing his parents, his home, his job, his car, and his moorings, all in ten months. He just couldn't handle it, he explained. There was nowhere to turn. He concedes he "hasn't found [his] way yet." He tells me he thinks there are about 125 camps in and around Greater Hickory. A "lot of people have crashed like me."

Randy Jacobs, forty-eight, reported that his life wasn't always such a disaster. He went from successful trucker to homeless desperation in four years. "All thanks to a traffic accident that left [me] disabled and then unemployed. I'm not a bum," he says with an edge. "My life just fell apart." Robert Noe explained to one of my colleagues that the loneliness can be worse than the horrifying conditions. His only company, some days, is a cat apparently set out near his campsite. The feline's company can "lift his spirits." Noe also prays a lot when he's down. "God's got a plan for me, I just don't know what or when."[11]

Dorothy Edwards, who has worked closely with Cornett for years, speaks of a young couple in their early thirties—Mark and Christina Stern—she still can't get out of her mind. They both lost their jobs when their respective employers closed in the middle of the recession. Eventually they sold their cars and lost their apartment. When they could no longer afford even the cheapest motel, they had to go to the woods. Christina, in tears, explained to Mrs. Edwards, "This is new to me, please don't pay attention, I'm sorry for the blubbering. . . . I know I've got to get used to it, but I've never even been camping before."

Another regular Open Door volunteer explains he's "convinced that a lot of us are just a couple of tough turns" away from the bottom. "I drove a truck for over twenty years, then I had a heart attack," he indicated. "Fortunately, I was able to live for a while with a friend." Otherwise, "I'd be in the woods myself," he says. "We started this program with no money at all. . . . We do what we do in faith," he assures. "Jesus walked among the poor; I'm convinced he'd be out there in those woods," he says.

As we visit campsites off Lenoir-Rhyne Boulevard, near Tate Boulevard, behind the Texas Roadhouse restaurant, and near the offices of the *Hickory Daily Record*, Cornett explains: "I wish the high and mighty around here would realize, with this economy, there is no typical homeless person." Some have worked for twenty years. They "come from all walks of life; some had decent jobs six months ago." Cornett says, "I'd guess about a third of the people we help have significant mental health challenges, a third have substance abuse problems, and another third have just had the economy trample them." And then a few troublemakers just come out to prey on the vulnerable.

We need "more help from the community and less looking down their noses," Cornett concedes. Dorothy Edwards adds, "The campers look for jobs; they don't want to be here." Often they "can't get work because they don't have an address." They "can't fill out an application because they can't say where they live—there are carpenters, plumbers, some with college," she says. Folks for whom the bottom fell out.

Another Open Door volunteer says, "You can't really categorize the homeless people seeking refuge in the woods of Hickory. . . . They're all individuals and they all bring their own issues to the table." But "there is such great, surpassing need here." We can't "get enough support to do this work." A few small churches do their best to help Cornett's ministry. But the larger Hickory churches have generally been slower to warm to the effort. Though they spend tens of thousands on missions to Haiti and impoverished third world nations, "they usually don't want to hear about hardship in their own backyard," Cornett explains.

Cornett's Open Door Homeless Relief Project operates on a shoestring budget, typically ranging from $10,000 to $20,000 a year, depending on donations and the challenges of the economy. A local realtor's association has been making a generous annual contribution, won over, in part, by Cornett's persistence and, in part, because it learned Cornett takes no salary for his prodigious labors. Cornett points to a cadre of donors who consistently demonstrate "how amazing hearts can be." Of course, as conditions worsen and need expands, money usually gets tighter. Most folks here are "scared of the poverty in their own community," Cornett says. "They prefer to pretend it's not there," he says. Cornett also sees it as part of his mission to take community leaders into the camps to witness the hardship firsthand. But most refuse to go, citing safety concerns or personal discomfort.

"My faith teaches me that Jesus didn't say to avoid looking down into the abyss. Jesus taught me that you've got to get down in the hole with people and make friends with them," Cornett explains. "We've got to quit turning a blind eye." Cornett practices, daily, what he quietly preaches.

When we talked, Marcia Stimson (again, not her real name), forty-seven, reported that she was then living, briefly, in the Salvation Army shelter—for the third time. "I'm one of their best bell ringers, a top producer." But "you have to leave after three months and I haven't been able to make enough money to eat and afford a place to live." So she may be homeless again, any day. "I've come to expect the worst," she sighed.

"You know when you hear people say, if it wasn't for my spouse, I'd be poor? That's me." She spoke with precision, but without emotion. "I was self-employed, doing pretty well, working in finance. My business crashed in 2009. I lost my job, my income, my apartment, eventually my car."

"I don't fit the norms; I'm not in the right categories," Stimson explained. "I don't have any addictions. I don't drink. I don't smoke. I don't do drugs. I don't have any children. I'm not pregnant. I don't have any medical issues. I don't have a mental illness. I've been advised to act like I'm crazy, but I won't do that. There's no funding for someone like me. I'm almost fifty. It's bad now, but I worry what it's going to be like when I'm older."

Stimson has lived in the woods surrounding Hickory for months at a time. "I'm self-sufficient," she said; "for ages, I wouldn't apply for food stamps." She found it too embarrassing. But she recounted a hard cycle: "I work and save a little money. Then I try to get housing. Like I was working at Healthy Home Market in Hickory. But it closed up and I lost my apartment. So I was homeless again. I didn't have any transportation, so I couldn't go to one of their other stores. They said they'd hire me. I'm a good worker. But I couldn't get over there. I'm unlucky with employers, I guess. There's no job stability here."

Stimson's description of life in the woods was chilling. "At first I liked the thought of living outside. I always enjoyed camping." But, she quickly learned, you have to be secretive all the time. If people find out where you are, they "call the cops, or they'll steal all your stuff, or worse." By "worse," she explained, she "was very scared of being raped." A "lot of women get raped out there."

She lived, most of the time, with a friend, Dave. So other men would generally leave her alone. But even then, she didn't feel safe. "To tell you the truth, in the middle of the night I find raccoons really frightening," she said. And "the hygiene is terrible." You've "got to go to the bathroom" and "the mosquitoes and bugs and snakes are horrible."

Stimson packed all her belongings in a trash bag each morning and took them with her, so "no one would steal them." When she'd return in the evening, she felt the most vulnerable. When "I'd come back, I'd have to sneak past the mobile homes near the road where I came into the woods." If they saw her, they'd report her to the police. The morning wasn't as bad. An early riser, she'd "get out of the woods by 5." Then you don't have to worry so much about being seen.

Stimson told me she'd spend a lot of the day in the library. She fit in there "more than most." She "knew how to use computers" and she likes to read. The whole time, though, she "was always looking for jobs. . . . I'm not picky," she said. She had a "seasonal job" at Walmart packing boxes, but it ran out. She was a barista at Java Journey for about six months, "but they closed up too. . . . I keep meeting the wrong employers." If she had a decent job, she "could do it on [her] own . . . that's what I want." But how do you get by on minimum wage or if the job's part time or, "like a lot of them, it's the third shift, when you have no transportation?" At $7.25 an hour, "you can't get both rent and food," try as you might.

Like several folks I spoke to, Stimson said "it's best to live in a small group." The more people you get, "the more drama . . . the more chance of getting hurt or robbed, the more chance of drugs being around." But it's lonely, and "the winter bothers me, I'm scared of hypothermia." One night she was traumatized, at about 3:00 A.M., when a sudden and torrential rain washed her tent and campsite down a hill. One of Cornett's "camp captains" (she called him Papa Smurf) rescued her before daylight, bringing another tent and blankets. After he managed to calm Stimson down, he left with a simple "God bless you."

Stimson's reference to hypothermia reminded me that, after having visited the camps several times with Cornett, one January morning when I arrived, the atmosphere was much altered. Snow had begun about 10:00 A.M., and the temperature had already dropped to the mid-teens. The upcoming night, all feared, would be brutal. The entire Open Door crew was decidedly on edge. Cornett was in hyperdrive. His cell phone rang incessantly. He rushed heaters, tarps, and blankets to a half-dozen sites. He seemed to fret even more over others he couldn't get to. Cornett has no apparent fear of personal danger. But he was terrified that people were going to freeze to death before morning. Life is always on the line in the Hickory camps, but never so much as in the hard throes of winter.

Stimson said she was "shocked when [she] first came to Hickory. . . . There were hundreds of people living in the woods, hundreds the shelter couldn't help out, lots of folks living in their cars, a lot more couch hopping, going from place to place." There are "some amazing people here, like Roger Cornett and the Open Door folks," but mostly folks "can't stand the sight of homeless people," she explained; "we give them the creeps."

Stimson has lived at the edge since 2009. The existence wears, debilitates, and disables. It also dehumanizes. In words I haven't been able to forget, she explained it this way: "When you've lost your job and lost your savings and lost your home, and your car, and then I even lost my cat—who was very dear to me—it may sound funny, or stupid, but losing my cat hurt me deeply—when you lose everything, you lose your sense of being a person. You lose your own independent identity. Your own space to fill in the world. It's hard to remember you're still a human being. That you have a chance at a decent life, or that you even deserve one. That you are worthy of existence."

The woods of Hickory haunt.

They teach as well.

They teach of a hardship existing today, in North Carolina and the nation at large, that is more potent, more wrenching, and more brutal than the great bulk of us likely realize. Poverty, and the ancillary deprivations, barriers, and indignities it triggers, I'll argue in the pages that follow, is North Carolina's greatest challenge.

The woods of Hickory also reflect a poverty that cannot be squared with the silence of both public and powerful private institutions and communities that, too commonly, effectively deny its existence. No political leaders, or almost none, acknowledge or inveigh against North Carolina's burgeoning poverty. More readily, they protest that there is no real poverty or hunger or undeserved economic hardship within the state's borders.[12] Anyone following the discussions in our corridors of power, today and likely for decades, would become convinced, at least by default, that poor people in the Tar Heel State simply don't occur. Or if they do, they should be the targets of derision and discipline.

It is also true, as the work of Roger Cornett and the Open Door Homeless Relief Project hints, that in locales across North Carolina, selfless volunteers, civil servants, philanthropists, and humanitarians give generously of their time, resources, and overstrained capacities to come to the aid of people hard-pressed by poverty and circumstance. It can be difficult, in my experience, to wrap one's mind around such generosity and commitment. This seems especially true of heroes such as the Open Door stalwarts, who themselves often don't have two dimes to rub together, yet who dedicate almost the entirety of their lives to aiding those whom they see as even unluckier or more constrained than themselves. Driven by a furiously engaged sense of community and an acute, often religion-based commitment to the plight of others, they fight, beyond tirelessly, to lighten and enrich the lives of their fellows.

Still, as Cornett's work also reminds us, charity cannot fill the unbridgeable chasm that exists between our needs and our capabilities. As Augustine put it, "Charity is no substitute for justice withheld."[13] In fact, even with such wondrous efforts, each month, on most fronts, we likely lose ground.

And perhaps the most telling, the harsh and unyielding deprivation of the Hickory wood lines is completely invisible to most of us.

In an earlier life, it was my singular fortune to do political work with the late U.S. senator from Minnesota Paul Wellstone. Paul explained that, in every corner of the nation, our greatest shortcoming as a people was a growing willingness to "turn our gaze away from those locked at the bottom of American life." I always thought that what he meant by that was, perhaps, that our kids were doing well, and our folk and our friends, and their children, and their children's children. The horizon bodes optimistic as far as the eye cares to see. We understand life might be tougher for others, and in some quarters maybe even impossibly so. But those burdens appear only across the tracks or across town or on the other side of the state or the country. We suspect the hardship. And maybe if we saw it up close, we'd even deem it unacceptable, incapable of being squared with the American promise. But we aren't forced to face it. We simply avert our eyes to more congenial and more tolerable terrain.

This book, briefly put, seeks to live in this chasm—a chasm many of us would prefer to avoid. It looks pointedly and purposefully at the people and places of one state, my own, North Carolina. It seeks, sometimes uncomfortably, to help press our gaze back, to crane the neck, to recapture a broadened and more complete vista. In so doing, I hope that we might return the conditions, the prospects, and the possibilities of the bottom economic third—the poor and the nearly poor—to our shared and urgent public agenda. In the process, the wounds of body and spirit visited on our sisters and brothers by wrenching poverty might be ameliorated. At the same time, I hope we might draw closer to the type of state, and nation, we constantly claim we seek to be.

THE
FACES OF
POVERTY
IN NORTH
CAROLINA

1

POVERTY, EQUALITY, AND NORTH CAROLINA'S GREATEST CHALLENGE

Even here in eastern North Carolina, with all its challenges and its hard history, people think, unless you see a child actually starving or a homeless family literally on the street corner, or unless that's actually occurring in your family, then poverty's not really a problem. In an affluent country like the United States poverty is mostly hidden. It's hidden here too. You have to be willing to seek it out, to go and try to understand it. You also have to be willing to look at it from the broad sweep and the historical perspective. Most people aren't interested in doing that. Entrenched poverty affects everything. It is layered, generation after generation. Most poor people in this county (Wayne) have never had a real chance.—Shirley Edwards, 72, community and civil rights activist, Goldsboro, North Carolina

We speak much for equality in the United States. Our first statements as a nation attested to a "self-evident truth" that all "are created equal." President Abraham Lincoln reminded us, at Gettysburg, that we were "conceived in liberty and dedicated to the proposition" of equality. Our central nationalizing constitutional amendment guarantees, to all, "equal protection of the laws." We pledge daily allegiance to an assurance of "liberty and justice for all." Lyndon Johnson, in his most noted and eloquent speech, went so far as to claim that "this was the first nation in the history of the world to be founded with a purpose." The "great phrases of that purpose," such as that all are created equal, "still sound in every American heart."[1] We talk a great game. But what we do has little in common with what we say.

The statistics of American poverty are straightforward and demoralizing. Almost 13 percent of Americans, over 40 million, fall below the federal poverty threshold, about $24,339 in 2016 for a family of four.[2] Our poverty is skewed sharply on the basis of race. Twenty-two percent of African Americans and 19.4 percent of Hispanics are poor, compared with less than 9 percent for whites and 10 percent for Asians.[3] It is also skewed by sex and age. Fourteen percent of women live below the poverty threshold, compared with about 11 percent of men. And the youngest among us, the most vulnerable, are typically the poorest. Eighteen percent of

American children live below the poverty threshold; thirty percent of our kids of color do.[4] Children represent 23 percent of the overall population but 33 percent of those in poverty.[5] In the 2014–15 school year, we had 1.3 million homeless schoolchildren.[6]

In 2016, 41.2 million Americans, 12 percent of households with about 13 million children, were reported by the federal government to be "food insecure"—experiencing significant hunger in their day-to-day lives.[7] Unsurprisingly, given our national economic prowess, we now have the greatest income inequality, the largest gaps between rich and poor, since 1928. The top 1 percent takes 24 percent of our national income, while the bottom 90 percent secures only 50 percent.[8] Wealth disparity is even more pronounced. The top 1 percent of Americans holds 39 percent of our country's wealth; the bottom 90 percent claims, shockingly, only 23 percent.[9] The richest 400 Americans have more wealth than the bottom 150 million put together.[10] We've been on this intense separating trend for forty years.[11]

International comparisons are bleak, and telling.[12] We countenance greater levels of poverty and child poverty than most other advanced industrial democracies.[13] In fact, we consistently rank at or very near the bottom of poverty listings with peer nations. We have the worst levels of food insecurity among the advanced countries.[14] And we have decidedly steeper income disparity than our peers.[15] To find our match in income inequality, perusing the list of nations, you have to move past the European nations, of course, and the other New World nations, past India, past Turkmenistan, down to our colleagues at the bottom of the registry: Mozambique, Saudi Arabia, Singapore, Togo, and South Sudan.[16] In every meaningful sense, we've become the richest, the poorest, and the most unequal advanced nation in the world.[17]

In North Carolina things are worse. Over 15 percent of us—more than 1.5 million—live in poverty.[18] About 650,000 Tar Heels live in deep poverty, with income levels less than half of the traditional federal poverty threshold.[19] Very large numbers have no health insurance. The median household income nationwide is $57,617. In North Carolina it's only $50,584.[20] The state has, reportedly, the second highest percentage of low-wage employees in the nation.[21] Nearly half of the state's counties suffer poverty rates over 20 percent.[22] The federal government reports that ten eastern North Carolina counties demonstrate "persistent poverty": Bertie, Bladen, Columbus, Halifax, Martin, Northampton, Pitt, Robeson, Tyrell, and Washington. That means at least 20 percent of county residents have lived in poverty for the past 30 years.[23] In most of those counties the national authorities could as easily have said 150 years—tracing a line directly back to slavery.[24]

Fourteen percent of men and 17 percent of women live below the poverty level in North Carolina.[25] Women make 82 cents on the dollar, compared with men.[26] About one-third of female-headed households live in poverty.[27] Twenty-two percent of Tar Heel kids statewide are poor—almost 500,000 of our children.[28] Nearly one in ten of those under eighteen lives in extreme poverty, on an income of around $12,170 a year for a family of four.[29] Forty-two percent of Hispanic kids and 38 percent of black children and Native American children are classified as poor.[30] Over a third of North Carolina babies, middle-school students, and teenagers of color are plagued by the challenges and barriers of wrenching poverty. And income inequality has risen very dramatically in North Carolina over the past forty years.[31] Over that period, inequality mushroomed in 97 of North Carolina's 100 counties. From 2010 to 2014, 65 North Carolina counties markedly expanded the trend.[32]

Race, it seems, is never far removed from poverty in North Carolina. African American, Latino, and Native American poverty rates are two to three times those of whites. Minority unemployment rates are routinely double. Racial wealth disparity is massive. For every dollar of wealth held by North Carolina's white households, African American and Latino families retain merely six and seven cents, respectively.[33] Such disparities can be so extreme they are hard to even comprehend. The Great Recession, nonetheless, reportedly made them worse.[34]

North Carolina has one of the country's fastest-rising poverty rates. A decade ago, it was twenty-sixth among the states, a little better than average. Now it is twelfth, moving past the competition.[35] It also has the twelfth highest rate of child poverty.[36] A recent national report named Roanoke Rapids and Lumberton two of the three poorest cities in America.[37] Over 1.5 million Tar Heels, 15 percent, participated in the food stamp program (Supplemental Nutrition Assistance Program, or SNAP) in 2016.[38] Vance and Robeson counties, in the eastern part of the state, had among the highest food stamp participation rates in the country.[39] Almost 1.8 million Tar Heels are classified as hungry, one of the nation's highest rates. Nearly 560,000, about one in four, of North Carolina kids didn't get enough to eat last year.[40]

In 2014, Professor Raj Chetty and his colleagues at the Equality of Opportunity Project concluded that Charlotte, North Carolina's richest metropolitan center, had the worst economic mobility of any major city in America.[41] If you are born poor in Charlotte, in other words, you are more apt to stay that way than anywhere else. About the same time, the U.S. Census Bureau announced that North Carolina had, over the last decade, experienced a greater rise in concentrated poverty (census tracts where 20 percent or more of residents are poor) than any other state. When the numbers were peeled back, experts found that four of the ten American cities with the sharpest increases in concentrated poverty were located in North Carolina. Winston-Salem was ninth; Greensboro, sixth; Charlotte, fourth; and Raleigh, third.[42] As economic engines revved in Charlotte and Durham, isolated neighborhoods there experienced mushrooming child poverty rates, sometimes exceeding 80 percent.[43] Families scrambled to survive, almost unseen, even by their neighbors, without access to electricity, sewer systems, and clean water. The Charlotte-Mecklenburg school district reported over 4,000 homeless students in 2016.[44] North Carolina now forms America's leading edge in concentrated poverty.

North Carolina is, on this front, reflective of its region, the South. Each year, the Census Bureau reports demonstrably higher poverty rates for the South than other regions of the country.[45] Most of the country's fifteen poorest states are southern. Though about one of seven Americans lives in poverty generally, in Mississippi and Louisiana the rate soars to one in five. In Texas, South Carolina, Alabama, Arkansas, Georgia, Tennessee, Florida, Kentucky, Oklahoma, and of course, North Carolina, the rates are markedly higher than national averages.[46] All of the states with child poverty rates over 25 percent are southern. Of the eight states with over 10 percent of children living in extreme poverty (with household incomes less than half the federal poverty standard), six are located below the Mason Dixon line.[47] The former confederate states set the gold standard in American economic deprivation.[48]

But bad as they may be, these statistics are only the numbers. Dry, bloodless, repetitive numbers. Bound for some dusty bookshelf. Ripe for the forgetting. Poverty, though, isn't a number. It is a draining of the body, a wound to the soul, an injury that divides and diminishes, as it rejects. The numbers alone miss that. They fail to touch the face of hardship in North Carolina. An even partially accurate portrait of this state's poverty has to press beyond the trends and tables of census and income reports, unemployment levels, health insurance patterns, and economic impact estimates. The challenges, barriers, and exclusions of wrenching hardship and deprivation and their accompanying heartbreaks can look quite different up close. There's much more to see closer to the ground. And it can sear.

Poverty statistics alone fail to tell the story of some 1,100 low-income Tar Heels waiting in line all night long, some for over forty hours, outside the massive civic center in Fayetteville, hoping to receive free dental care in a remarkable all-volunteer medical mission when the doors opened the next morning. Some folks had traveled, often great distances, usually to have simple procedures, such as having teeth extracted that had long caused intense pain. When my students and I asked, repeatedly, when had they last seen a dentist, most would answer that it was ten or twenty or thirty years ago. "Sure it hurts, it hurts a ton," a sixty-year-old black woman told me, "but who can afford to see a dentist?" A middle-aged white man who had recently lost his job said his "tooth was killing him." But when he went to see the dentist, they told him taking it out would cost $3,000. "I just got up out of the chair and walked out the door," he said. A young mother added, "I've got a daughter; if I spent money like that on myself, my girl wouldn't be able to eat. You've got to make sacrifices when you have a kid." Still, in the end, hundreds of those who waited in the mammoth line couldn't be seen. There simply wasn't the capacity. And although in some previous years, ten or more such miraculous "missions" had been held in North Carolina in a single year, more recently the heroic organizers have only been able to manage three or four, or fewer.

North Carolina's hunger statistics are haunting, but they speak little of the terror appearing in the voices of parents struggling mightily to merely feed their kids. Nothing tears at a parent, they say, like the words "Mama, I'm so hungry." Those words make you feel "like the worst kind of failure." We might have been poor when I was young, they explain, but we always had food to eat. "Now I never even really know where the next meal is coming from." Those standing in line at the food pantries can also surprise. They aren't, officials explain, the ones people assume would be there. They are not the folks on the side of the road asking for handouts. "They're our neighbors, the ones who wait on us or take care of our kids or sit down the row at church on Sunday." They are usually employed. They are almost always embarrassed. Frequently, they once had better jobs. But now they work longer hours for poorer wages and with fewer benefits. Their stories can crush. Parents willingly sacrifice their dignity, their health, and their well-being for their kids. Children are robbed of the ability to thrive and the joy of life by the ravages and the fears of hunger. These are folks who make choices daily that shouldn't have to be made in a nation of surpassing resources. They are forced into choices that most of us cannot readily contemplate. I know I can't.

And mere numbers don't convey in Charlotte, North Carolina's corporate mecca, the feelings of hundreds lining up each morning by 5:00 A.M. at Crisis Assistance Ministry, in the shadows of the great banking towers, at the edge of "uptown" near Interstate 277. The fearful and weary faces rise early to try to keep their families from being forced to live on the streets. Many of those I met in line were working, most had children, and almost all struggled to pay for food, rent, utilities, health care, and transportation on minimum-wage or near minimum-wage jobs in an expensive city. They often worked more than forty hours a week. Still, they couldn't keep their heads above water. Trying to survive and support their kids was an all-consuming job. They explained, over and over, that the assistance they hoped to receive is crucial, indispensable, and decidedly appreciated. But what they really wished would happen was that their employers would pay them a wage that somebody could live on in Charlotte. "They know that I work hard, but you can't get by on eight dollars an hour here." So, they say, they have to beg for help. But "if I could make a decent, humane wage, I wouldn't have to worry about food stamps or electricity vouchers or bus passes or rent subsidies." Then they would be able to make it on their own. They wouldn't be forced to ask for handouts.

More ominously, health care statistics can reveal a lot, but the figures don't match the power or the heartbreak of the words of wives who have lost their husbands and of children who have lost their parents because they couldn't afford the tests and screenings and procedures essential to modern health care. The statistics alone don't reveal the angst of those unable to see an essential specialist or to deal with life-threatening symptoms because they don't have the dollars or the insurance necessary to pay the fare. The numbers don't explain the horror felt by an idealistic young doctor who treated a low-income waitress for months for free—a young woman without insurance and without a strong and healthy heart who died "because we couldn't get the medical device that she needed." A patient who, the same doctor reports, "would be alive today" if she was able to secure health care coverage. Instead, she was allowed to die, or was forced to die, simply because she was poor. The young doctor's words echo those of a rural North Carolina practitioner with thirty years' experience: "For decades, I've watched my patients with no insurance pay a terrible price. I've seen women die of invasive breast cancer when they couldn't afford mammograms. I've hospitalized patients who stopped their medicines so they could pay other bills. I've seen the slow death by invasive colon cancer of patients who couldn't afford a colonoscopy and diabetics who couldn't pay for insulin."

A similarly vivid and wrenching portrait of poverty in North Carolina, especially the poverty of its children, comes from Title I schoolteachers whose children face "the harshest challenges of extreme poverty." The teachers speak of children who dread long weekends, school holidays, or snow days, unsure of what, if anything, they'll have to eat until classes resume. Teachers see the trauma of students coming home to the eviction notice or hear that they couldn't do homework because the electricity had been cut off. Some students have scarcely traveled out of their neighborhoods or gone to restaurants or seen an interstate highway or been to the mountains or the coast. Many of their students are from single-parent households where the mother or, less often, the father works long hours or the night shift, so that even third- and fourth-graders go largely unsupervised and may be required to care for even younger siblings. There are children who have been up all night because of brawls and gunshots in their buildings, who have no access to books or computers and yet are expected to perform proficiently on standardized tests. These are students whose very lives refute the notion that equal educational opportunity can be separated from debilitating poverty.

Affordable housing data triggers alarm, but it can be more telling to see some 300 Jacksonville residents lined up all night long against the winter's cold, hoping to get on the waitlist for federal housing assistance at the Eastern North Carolina Human Services Agency. Standing in the line was necessary simply to secure a spot on the waitlist, not to get housing itself. Housing might come, if at all, only many months or years later. More likely, it won't come at all. "People were camped out, in freezing weather; they came with their blankets, their coffee thermos, their heated tea, to help make it through the night," the agency director reported. "We tried to get the elderly and the disabled inside, but there wasn't enough room in the building," she said. For over twenty hours they learned of neighbors facing choices between paying bills and putting gas in the car to get to their daughter's cancer treatments; of folks selling their blood to get clothes and food for their children; of evictions and layoffs and denials of unemployment compensation. Eventually, of course, the line became too long and had to be closed off. And all of this occurred in a city whose state representative had famously said, some months earlier, on the floor of the General Assembly that there is no extreme poverty in North Carolina.[49]

Again, in Fayetteville, where the federal government's official point-in-time count finds over a thousand local homeless souls, a remarkable policewoman—tough as nails or tougher—says her work with the homeless community "was so heartbreaking at first that I almost couldn't bear it." She explains that "the first body I ever found was a vet, like me—I thought, this is no way for a veteran to die, on his military cot, out under a wood line." She reports seeing scores of folks living, day after day, week after week, in peril under the bridge at Person and Water streets downtown. She told me that when she started coming across families with kids—mom, daddy, baby—she thought that it would be considered abuse and neglect. But she was informed by her superiors that it's not. There is a "mother living with a baby under six months old right now in a vacant house a few blocks from here," she explained. Things are much worse than when she started nine years ago. "We have a lot of working homeless people now—working at McDonald's and Taco Bell or doing landscaping; they can't possibly afford rent and day care." She performs patrols early in the morning: "hitting my areas in the morning, to make sure they're still alive." People "need to take their blinders off," she explained. "I never dreamed this could be happening in my home town."

Notations on the shortcomings of public housing in deeply segregated communities of eastern North Carolina can be powerful, but they are tepid compared with the tears of a mother who, despite working full time continuously for many years, is forced to see her children live in projects so dangerous that they can't safely play on the front porch or run through the yard or walk to the bus stop, even early in the morning, to get to school. These are Wayne County housing facilities where kids have seen other children fatally wounded while walking down the street, etching memories, she knows, they will never manage to lose. Other residents spoke of apartments without adequate heat or security but with and more than adequate infestations of rats and insects—projects that are so fear-inducing that most local residents, understandably, won't go anywhere near them. But young children are expected to live here, routinely, in gratitude and optimism, while a broader world enjoys comfort, safety, protection, and security that these kids can never contemplate. As a shelter director explained, "Most people in Goldsboro don't see the hardship our clients endure. They just get slapped around by life. . . . This shelter is the safest place in Wayne County for most of them."

Studying only the numbers also masks the character of tense and guarded conversations with health care workers in one eastern North Carolina city who reluctantly reveal to us that they bend the rules to place oxygen in the homes of their incapacitated and impoverished patients in order to make it tougher, under state law, for the utility companies to shut off the water and power their clients can scarcely afford. It is impossible not to admire the struggle, the candor, and the commitment of such determined caregivers. And there could be no doubt that they sought, in bold insistence, to put the interests of their endangered patients decidedly above their own. Their dilemmas and their patients' hazards are unrevealed and unexamined in the naked statistics of the databank.

And the numbers miss the actual strains of East Spencer, a small, historic, mostly black town in Rowan County, where over 50 percent of the community lives in poverty. East Spencer has no high school, no library, no commercial district, and no grocery store. It is what the scholars call a "food desert." Ironically though, the national corporate headquarters of the massive Food Lion grocery chain is found just a few thousand yards over the bridge in neighboring Salisbury. Residents also point to a huge food distribution center, for the ALDI network, located smack in the middle of East Spencer itself. It apparently sends food-laden trucks across the region, everywhere, perhaps, except down the street into the community where it resides. So the residents of East Spencer, often without any available transportation, public or otherwise, pay exorbitant prices for the extraordinarily poor selection of foods to be found in the local convenience store. This situation reveals in stark terms that the massive commercial food distribution system that works so readily and effectively for most of us silently casts others aside, and that the isolation of poverty separates, degrades, and wounds, as it marginalizes.

None of these examples matches precisely the desperation of thousands of young, undocumented, immigrant Tar Heels who have lived in North Carolina almost all of their lives; who have mastered, against all odds, their grade schools, middle schools, and high schools; who embraced the remarkable work ethic of their parents, often accumulating records of academic distinction; and then who are effectively barred from the state's community college and public university system—and thus any meaningful access to higher education. These children have scarcely ever been to Mexico or Central America or their parents' country of origin, but they are then culled from their lifelong friends and colleagues and relegated to trying jobs that quash their talents and their opportunities under an outspoken torrent of "illegals" bashing. "The place where I had lived my whole life, and where I had given everything, and tried to be a good kid, said that, unlike all my friends, I couldn't go to college, and it wanted to kick me out," one of the young hopefuls reported. As a result, his buddies with poorer grades and less impressive records headed off to strong schools and bright futures as he began washing dishes in a local restaurant, relegated to an underclass, denied the opportunities that, for others, mark the promise of a nation.

Perhaps more pointedly, more singularly, North Carolina's daunting poverty statistics don't capture the fears of a brilliant young black mother from Halifax County who graduated from the University of North Carolina (UNC) at Chapel Hill, moved back home as she and her family had long planned, lost her position in a business closing, and eventually lost her housing and almost all of her sense of hope. But as she explained, she was actually terrified that she was also losing the far more crucial battle with her nine-year-old son, against peer pressure, on the importance of education in the first place. As he would put it, "How can you prove going to school does any good by what's happened to you, mom?" She worried, through tears, that she had no acceptable answer to the most crucial question from the most important person in her life. And in that hardship and despair, tragically, she is not alone.

In the chapters that follow, then, I will try to outline the structure, demographics, and broad characteristics of North Carolina poverty. But I will try to touch its particulars as well, to put faces to the numbers. I won't claim the portrait is systematic or encompassing. Our poverty is too great, too varied, too impactful, too determined, and too hidden for that. Still, even when narratives are individualized, they can be revelatory. If one of our most potent societal shortcomings is that we are frequently unaware of the intense challenges experienced by our fellows, the words of those living in poverty can, perhaps, help lift the veil and pierce the invisibility that shields the hardship of so many. That, at least, is my premise.

In candor, I approach the challenges of poverty in my home state more as an equality lawyer of forty years than as an economist, demographer, ethnographer, urban policy analyst, sociologist, public health scholar, education expert, or racial theorist. American constitutional law works at the intersection of aspiration, of officially declared commitment, and of a frequently value-transgressing reality. It explores—or at least it should—both what we profess and what we allow to occur, what we say and what, in reality, we do. It seeks a corrective when our practices veer too wildly from our declared promises. It triggers a remedy when undergirding presupposition hides cruel violation, when promises of full membership go consistently and pervasively unsecured. The chasm that sometimes exists between our collective social boasts and our acceptance of marginalization and exclusion can frequently be best illuminated through the jarring stories of our sisters and brothers.

I will often explore the intensity of North Carolina's poverty categorically, with chapters on hunger, education, and access to health care. I'll also report on groups of particularly hard-pressed Tar Heels: children, immigrants, low-wage workers, and the structurally and long-term unemployed. And since race and poverty seem to be eternal companions here, racial economic disparity and subordination will be repeated themes. I will also focus on geography, looking at the wrenching, isolating, chronic poverty of eastern North Carolina and some of the distinct but related challenges of hardship in the mountain west, where chronic and deepened poverty is apt to be accompanied by confederate flags, Donald Trump signs, and the challenges of opioid addiction. I will look hard, too, at what have often, against expectation, become the most intense pockets of economic deprivation in the state: isolated but burgeoning areas of concentrated poverty in the midst of Charlotte, Raleigh, Durham, Greensboro, and Winston-Salem. It is also impossible to spend significant time in poor communities in North Carolina without learning, in amazement, of those thousands of selfless souls who defy ease, odds, and self-interest to lighten the fates of their impoverished neighbors. These Carolinians apparently believe that they are, in fact, their brothers' keepers; they insist that the greatest American value is that we're all in this together. I will do my best to write accurately, if too briefly, of them as well.

But I won't end with these descriptions. I should explain why.

My goal is not strictly or only academic and expository. I have lived in North Carolina a long time. It is my chosen home, my favorite place on the planet. I am also convinced that wrenching poverty amidst plenty is, by a wide margin, North Carolina's most potent problem, its greatest sin against defining democratic promise. Yet rarely does it meaningfully appear in our political discourse. Scarcely a word about poverty is uttered in the halls of our General Assembly, as leaders debate the policies and enact the standards that will govern the state's future. Recent North Carolina governors have almost never mentioned it, regardless of political affiliation. No electoral contests meaningfully explore poverty's challenges or turn on poverty-alleviating proposals. Even when activists request that major candidates focus on issues of intense economic deprivation, the silence remains nearly complete, in an odd truce whereby all comers ignore the unseemly elephant in our collective space. If North

Carolinians listened only to their politicians, they would have no idea that poverty exists. Poverty crushes, but it has been thought, apparently, well and safely ignored. The discordance between poverty's impact and its responding attentions is perhaps the most extreme in our public deliberation and discourse. I seek to change that.

Still, there's more.

North Carolina has undergone a transformation in partisan political control since 2010. Both houses of the General Assembly have been dominated, for the first time since Reconstruction, by the Republican Party. During most of the last seven years, North Carolina has had a Republican governor and a heavily partisan and reliably activist Republican state supreme court as well. National commentators have regularly (and accurately) characterized the state as having rapidly moved from a modestly progressive political posture to, at the least, becoming firmly planted among the small cadre of the most politically conservative states in the nation.[50] And the legislative changes embraced span a wide array of economic, social, and political fronts. It is no bold exaggeration to say that, politically, North Carolina is a significantly different state than it was a decade ago.

That transformation has not meant, of course, that poverty has now become a potent focus of electoral discourse or legislative deliberation. Intensely contested statewide races for the governorship and a U.S. Senate seat in 2016, for example, again almost completely ignored the plight of the poor. But legislative decisions since 2010—restricting Medicaid and other health care services, dramatically cutting unemployment benefits, eliminating the state earned-income tax credit, turning back proffered federal funding for poverty programs, restricting traditional access to food stamps and legal services, paring back housing and day care subsidies for low-income residents, eliminating pre-K prospects for at-risk children, while raising the tax burden on poorer residents to dramatically reduce the tax rates of wealthier ones—have had a profound impact on impoverished North Carolinians. The results echo in the stories they tell. So it is impossible to explore the challenges of economic hardship and disparity in North Carolina without also taking a focused look at these measures, which, I argue, are rooted in a broader political calculus that mirrors the invisibility of poverty highlighted throughout these pages. Here poor people, too often, simply don't count. They are effectively eliminated from the constituency. Their interests make no entry into North Carolina's political calculus. As a result, an ample segment of the polity is decidedly and intentionally denied full dignity and membership. Two million poor Tar Heels, living in or near the edges of poverty, become excluded, disqualified. Their challenges are augmented and exacerbated; sensible remedies for their hardship are foreclosed. And their voices are rarely heard. I explore these policy challenges extensively in a final chapter, concluding with a call for a politics of full membership, recognizing that poor North Carolinians are, in the phrase of constitutional adjudication, "entire citizens" of the commonwealth in which they reside.

2

POOR KIDS, EDUCATION, AND HARDSHIP IN NORTH CAROLINA

The brightest and most privileged kids are brighter than ever. Our poor kids are poorer than they have ever been. It used to be that being poor just meant you didn't have money. Now that is only the tip of the iceberg. It is much more complicated than that.—Angela Scioli, twenty-four-year veteran teacher, Raleigh public schools

It is embarrassing to admit, but in the United States and in North Carolina, our poorest citizens are our youngest ones. In the nation at large, as I've indicated, almost one in five children lives in poverty. The rates grow worse the younger a child is; poverty levels are highest for kids five and under. Many millions of children live in extreme poverty nationwide, and over a million kids are reported to be homeless. For the first time in our history, now more than half the children in public schools live in or near poverty.[1]

Internationally, as ever, we are the outlier. Despite our staggering economic prowess, the United States ranks near the bottom of the thirty-five Organisation for Economic Co-operation and Development (OECD) nations in child poverty.[2] We have a higher infant mortality rate, the Centers for Disease Control reports, than all but four of the OECD nations, and we are last among the wealthy European countries it uses in peer comparisons. A baby born in the United States is nearly three times as likely to die during her or his first year of life as one born in Japan, Iceland, or Slovenia.[3] Even so, our excruciating child poverty and health comparisons rarely stir meaningful political comment in American public discourse. We allow the greatest—or nearly the greatest—percentage of our babies to live in poverty, and we seem untroubled by the result. Child poverty is an American epidemic, self-inflicted.

In North Carolina, childhood poverty, childhood extreme poverty, and childhood hunger rates soar above national averages. One in four of the state's youngest kids (under age five) is poor. Nine percent live in extreme poverty.[4] Fourteen percent of Tar Heel children now live in concentrated poverty neighborhoods, where very high percentages of residents are poor. More than 55,000 of our kids are homeless.[5] Race dominates child poverty, as it does with adults. Extraordinary numbers of Native American, African American, and Hispanic kids live below the poverty threshold, including about half of those under five.[6]

Many North Carolina counties report breathtaking percentages of child poverty. In Northampton (51.4), Scotland (46.9), Swain (45.3), Robeson (44.9), Edgecombe (43), Bladen (41.8), Chowan (41.5), and Jones (41.5) counties, nearly half, and sometimes even more, of all kids live in poverty. Some counties, of course, fare much better. Only 13.2 percent of kids are poor in mostly suburban Union County, and 10.7 percent live below the federal poverty standard in Dare County, on the coast.[7]

The state also, in recent years, has lost much ground on these measures. In 1990, North Carolina's child poverty rate was in the middle of the pack. That began to change in the 2000s, and now it is fourteenth worst in the nation.[8]

The households in which poor kids live don't always fit the stereotype. Sixty-four percent of families with children living in poverty have at least one full-time worker.[9] About a third of poor kids live with their still-married parents.[10] Over 98 percent are American citizens, and over a third are five years of age or younger.[11]

THE IMPACTS OF CHILDHOOD POVERTY

We also have a strong sense of what these statistics mean, what the impact of poverty on children typically turns out to be. It can surprise no one that poor kids are much more likely to be homeless or to live in dangerous and unsafe neighborhoods. They are far more likely than their nonimpoverished peers to go hungry, to live in food deserts, to be exposed to toxic substances, to be uninsured, to have diminished access to health care and transportation, and to live in substandard housing. They experience worse health outcomes across the board and are more frequently subjected to risky behaviors, crime, and violence.[12] Their mothers are less likely to have received medical attention and adequate nutrition during their pregnancies. Poor mothers' children have, on average, lower birth weights and higher infant mortality rates than other newborns. And poor kids are much more likely to suffer from chronic illnesses, and as adults, they have shorter life expectancies than wealthier children.[13]

Recent scholarly findings suggest, as well, that poverty has a demonstrable negative impact on a child's brain development. Prior studies had revealed that poverty can contribute to compromised cognitive function and lower performance in school.[14] But imaging studies now link early childhood poverty to smaller brain size and less-efficient processing of sensory information. Children who grow up in impoverished households show smaller amounts of white and grey matter in their brains than do the kids of parents of greater means. These diminutions alter the density of nerve connections in the brain. Poorer children also develop smaller hippocampus and amygdala regions, which affect attention, memory, and emotional response.[15] Scholars speculate that increased stress experienced by children living in families where finances are inadequate, and thus parental support and interaction are diminished, may lead to the changes. The causal list may be long and non-exhaustive. But the conclusion is linear and inescapable: poor kids begin to experience diminished life chances almost immediately. As Candice Odgers, associate director of the Center for Child and Family Policy at Duke University, puts it: for kids "the effects of poverty are [often] toxic, they become biologically embedded, they get under the skin."[16]

Volumes could be and have been written on each of these wounds routinely resulting from growing up poor. I want to focus here, instead, on one other haunting correlation: the tight and inextricable relationship between child poverty and educational attainment.

I do so for several reasons.

First, nationally, the impact of poverty on education has been very robustly studied. Stanford's Sean Reardon, the nation's leading expert on the income achievement gap in educational outcomes, argues that not only has the restraining impact of child poverty been repeatedly and amply demonstrated, but it may be the most conclusively demonstrated aspect of our entire education literature.[17]

Second, educational opportunity, of course, is potently linked to any meaningful notion of equality. Many argue, with enthusiasm, that the American commitment to equality assures access and opportunity, but not results. The world, it turns out, is frequently more complex than such stark demarcations might suggest. But even if one accepts and concedes to the potential ambiguities, meaningful educational opportunity surely lives close to the core of our constitutionalism.

Third, remedial poverty programs are, to understate, controversial. For many skeptics, the only acceptable avenue of poverty relief is education. As one who speaks frequently about economic hardship and inequality, I can attest that no small number of North Carolinians (as well as other Americans) protest that an assured educational equality is the only permissible government intervention on behalf of the poor. If impoverished kids lose, systematically, at the schoolhouse door, then they may well lose everywhere.

EDUCATION AND POVERTY

Research powerfully establishes that growing up in poverty tends to put children behind as they begin the formal education process.[18] The most socioeconomically disadvantaged children lag substantially behind their peers in both reading and math skills from their first days of schooling. As a result, studies find, poor children face substantial obstacles to school success. Entering students with wealthier parents demonstrate notable differences in cognitive skills on their first day of kindergarten.[19] Effective communication with teachers and peers, along with other noncognitive skills, reveals substantial gaps as well. The most economically disadvantaged children lag the most dramatically in these less readily quantifiable skills essential to educational achievement. Emma Garcia's and Elaine Weiss's studies have concluded that, across the board, poverty "is the single factor with the most influence on how ready a child is to learn when she first walks through the school's kindergarten door."[20]

And the economic achievement gap dominates American education through graduation. Helen Ladd of Duke University, in surveying the research on child poverty and education, writes that "no one seriously disputes" the fact that students from economically disadvantaged households perform less well in school, on average, than their peers from more advantaged backgrounds.[21] The correlation between poverty and diminished achievement has been repeatedly and fulsomely demonstrated, from the famed Coleman Report of 1966 to the more intricate analyses of the present day. Studies use differing measures of socioeconomic status, such as income-related measures, occupation and education level measures, and free and reduced lunch eligibility standards. Regardless of the methodology, Ladd concludes, "similar patterns emerge."[22] Data from the National Assessment of Education Progress reveals that more than 40 percent of the variation in reading scores and almost half the variation in math scores, across the United States, are associated with distinctions in child poverty rates.[23] Professor Reardon's studies trace the achievement gap between children from high- and low-income families over the last half-century. He concludes that it is potent, large, and growing and now far exceeds the achievement gap between black and white students.[24] The economic achievement gap is 40 percent larger for children born in 2001 than for those born twenty-five years earlier. It is now twice as large as the racial achievement gap. Fifty years ago, the numbers were reversed.[25]

The results are mirrored in international comparisons. Data from the massive Program for International Student Assessment (PISA) shows that among fifteen-year-olds, both here and in each of the thirteen or so nations that outpace us educationally, students of diminished economic status have much lower test scores than their more advantaged homeland counterparts. The Stanford Graduate School of Education and the Economic Policy Institute, after plowing through the PISA numbers, determined that if the United States had an economic composition similar to that of the other leading nations, we would rise from 14th to 6th in reading and from 25th to 13th in math. In other words, we compare so poorly with our international competitors because we allow so many more of our children to live in poverty.[26]

Students from economically disadvantaged families, in short, perform decidedly worse, on average, than their peers from more advantaged backgrounds. This, of course, is the noted "zip code" standard. Little matters as much to a kid's success as the wealth of his family and neighborhood.

In North Carolina, studies by the Public School Forum indicate that the ten wealthiest counties spend almost $50,000 more, per year, per classroom, than the ten poorest counties. The unholy gap results from the variation of property wealth across the state. The richest counties have more than $2 million in real estate capacity per student to support taxation levies. Poorer counties have about $300,000 in capacity for each schoolkid. The gap expands every year.[27]

In 2014, North Carolina launched a controversial public school report card system. Individual schools receive, annually, a grade ranging from A to F. Over 80 percent of the schools where four out of five students qualify for free and reduced lunch subsidies received a D or an F on the card. Over 90 percent of the schools with less than 20 percent low-income students secured an A or a B.[28]

BEYOND THE NUMBERS

Brendan Fetters, thirty-five, has been teaching in high-poverty elementary schools in Raleigh for a decade. He reports, perhaps unsurprisingly, that many teachers flee the high-poverty schools at the first opportunity.[29] But many others, like Fetters, are actually drawn to the often daunting challenge, which he describes as "a calling within a calling." The schools are not the types the superintendents visit, bringing along dignitaries and news cameras. Nor do the politicians who regularly characterize the schools and the teachers as "failing" or "broken" show their faces. Day in and day out, teachers like Fetters deal with what he describes as "the intense challenges of real poverty." It is "a lot to navigate," he explains; "there are hurdles that the general public has no clue about."

Fetters reports that "it is becoming a much greater hurdle to get to the actual instruction—what I do best, teaching the kids." Students aren't going to perform at the highest competitive levels on end-of-grade tests if so many of them haven't had any breakfast or if they were up all night because of fights in the neighborhood or at home. Fetters says, "Last year, one of my third-graders looked really terrible for several days. He'd obviously been up all night over and over again. We finally just started letting him go to the health room and get some sleep. After several days, I called his mother to talk about what was going on. She got really angry, told me it was none of my business, and that I'd better not call her again."

The number of kids in his third- or fifth-grade classes who have to go home, cook dinner, and take care of even younger siblings has astonished him. "A lot of my kids are latch-key, their parents work long hours, or may be stuck in the night shift," Fetters says. It is hard to focus on math or spelling when they are worried about whether their sisters and brothers are going to have enough to eat. They don't ever get the chance to be kids, much less students, he says. "It is not realistic to think they are going to succeed," Fetters believes; "the responsibilities some of these very young kids have are stunning."

Fetters is no longer surprised when his nine-year-olds come up at the end of the day, on Friday, in tears because they are unsure when they will get their next meal. They're worried it won't be until lunch on Monday, he says. And a lot of the little boys, especially, look to him as a father figure. "What many of these poor kids need is attention; what they really want is somebody who cares for them," he reports. Sometimes they just need to talk. "I try to find some time during the day to walk and talk with them," he says. Just walk and talk. Often that's what works best. Fetters's classes used to be comprised of fourteen or fifteen students. Last year (2014), again, he had twenty-three. "I remember how much more I could do when we just had 15." The school district seems to think technology will answer the shortcomings. But "that's nuts," in Fetters's view. "Poor kids need extra attention; having another seven or eight kids in class makes a huge difference." One-on-one time becomes almost impossible.

The Title I (high poverty) schools are "really, really taxing," in Fetters's experience. There are constant challenges many other teachers rarely face. "My best friend teaches in a high-wealth school," Fetters explains, "but he used to teach at my school before he went over there." His friend says the differences are breathtaking. This year, the high-wealth school is apparently going to have, for the first time, one busload of kids from an impoverished community. "They are all bent out of shape about it," he says. Fetters finds it hard to believe his poor kids are getting a fair, much less an equal, chance.

Angela Scioli performs an analogous mission at the high school level. A former Wake County (Raleigh) teacher of the year, Scioli has witnessed significant change over the course of her twenty-four-year career. The brightest and most talented, each year, become ever more accomplished. "Our poor kids," though, she explains, "are poorer than they have ever been." And their disadvantage is not just limited to money.

Scioli describes for me the work she and her colleagues did to try to assure that one of their bright, extremely impoverished students could go to a local historically black university. "How do you fill out a complex financial aid form for a kid who has moved from place to place and person to person his entire life?" The university was great, she reports, flexibly admitting him, largely on promise. He moved into the dorm. No sheets, no towels, no mattress pad, no suitable clothes, no bicycle, no textbooks, no laptop. "We got on Facebook and lots of teachers helped, though they themselves often don't have enough money to comfortably live on," she says. A laptop and textbooks proved considerably harder. It wasn't enough just to ask for donations. But those who teach high-poverty students have become used to sacrificing for their schoolkids. "We also tried to do things like take him to dinner, he'd hardly ever had that experience," Scioli reports.

Still, she explains, "our middle-class notion that if you just get some scholarship money together, things will be ok is a fantasy." A "student has to have people he can predictably rely on, it's more than a question of dollars." Her words are reminiscent of Ta-Nehisi Coates's explanation that "I didn't always have things, but I always had people between the world and me."[30]

Scioli describes a high school girl she became close to. "She was constantly taking care of her siblings; like some others, they largely came to school for food and heat and, in the summer, air conditioning." As graduation approached, Scioli and her colleagues helped the young woman get a job through a local church. "We helped her get an apartment, within walking distance of her work."

Things went well for a time. "But as soon as she got the apartment, people started showing up to live with her—an uncle, a brother, bringing problems with them," she says. She was "always beset." But the truth is, she couldn't possibly be happy in that apartment if she was alone and her family was left out. "She couldn't feel like an independent agent in the world," Scioli thinks. One aspect of white privilege, Scioli has come to think, is that "we don't fully understand the notion of allegiance." We are much more individualistic than a lot of my students are, she says. That doesn't change with a few dollars or a comfortable place to live.

Another young woman Scioli mentors does very well in her courses, including Scioli's honors sociology class. As Scioli has come to know her and her family better, she's realized that poverty in the constant in their lives. It affects every component of their existence, though it is never directly discussed. The mom has several jobs, so she is rarely able to spend time with her daughter. They have an apartment close to school and work because they don't have a car and bus service is spotty. She is single, with three kids. The children are largely required to raise each other. They have moved about twenty times that the student can remember. Every ounce of energy is spent trying to eke by. "Money drives everything," Scioli explains: "Life is an unplanned domino of hard circumstance."

The young student, Scioli says, "is whip smart." She was also holding down two jobs, one at Starbucks and one at Harris Teeter (a local grocery store). She knows that her mother will want to move again soon, and she'll have to decide whether to stay or go. She would prefer to stay, but she worries about her two younger brothers. "Sometimes I think she's required to be the adult in the household," Scioli says. She's already an old soul; "she's never had the chance to be a kid."

NaShonda Cooke has been teaching in very high-poverty Durham schools for almost twenty years. She estimates that last year twenty of twenty-six students in her class came from families facing extreme economic distress. They were, again, kids who often hadn't had enough to eat, who sometimes didn't own coats or who wore the same clothes day after day, and who lived in houses or apartments containing almost no food and little furniture, in dangerous neighborhoods and unsafe buildings.

Cooke's students, too, are kids who know the trauma of coming home to the eviction notice or who explain they couldn't do homework the night before because the electricity had been cut off. They have scarcely traveled out of their neighborhoods or gone to restaurants or seen an interstate highway or been to the mountains or the coast. Many are from single-parent households where the mother or, less often, the father works long hours or the night shift, so that even third- or fourth-grade students live largely unattended.

Cooke reports that the barriers experienced by such children have markedly increased in the last decade, as parents have lost jobs or, more often, begun working longer hours for lower wages. The kids try to hide it. "I'll go on a home visit and there's no food, no couch, no table, no bed—the children say, 'Please don't tell anyone, Ms. Cooke, we're okay.'" But, she explains, "I grew up in public housing myself. I know why they're acting out."

Cooke directs an inspiring program called Men of Honor on a volunteer basis, beyond her regular teaching duties. It provides a different space, a safe haven for kids facing challenging circumstances. "We alter clothes, we wash clothes, we give away clothes, we have a shelf with clothes arranged by size, since so many of our kids don't have winter clothes," she explains. "Poverty drives everything here," Cooke notes.

> We even altered our start time because we didn't want kids standing out at the bus stop without coats waiting for the bus to come.
>
> We really hate snow days and extended vacations. The kids have their eyes on the food bags at the back of the room, after they are delivered to the classroom. They don't know when they are going to get to eat again. We also have a share table at the back of the room. The kids will take anything home. They ask, eyes wide, "Can I take this to my little brother at home." It breaks your heart.

"But my boys don't come in with their heads down," she says. They do their homework. They talk about how to treat girls, about how to deal with the police, about drug abuse, about "their preparation for the world." Grades have improved. Suspension rates have dropped. They do college tours. "I expect you to be here," she tells the students when they arrive on campus. "I'm going to demand it of you—don't tell me your only career chances are in rap or the NBA." Last year, Cooke was invited to high school graduations at four different schools by students who explained they would never have made it except for her impact on their lives years earlier.

NaShonda Cooke admits it is more discouraging now. And some days it can be hard to start it all up again. "But I've got a great reason to put up with it all—these kids," she says. When "they improve, I'm lifted up." Cooke is an eighth-generation teacher. It is, literally, in her blood. "I love working with students who have a tougher path," she smiles. Cooke's father is a preacher. He says it's a calling. She says, "I'm where God wants me to be."

One of my own favorite former students is Jessica Holmes. She is now a young lawyer and Wake County commissioner. Only a little more than a decade ago, though, before she did her undergraduate and law school work at the University of North Carolina, she was struggling heroically with the traumas of extreme poverty in Pender County, on the eastern coastal plain of North Carolina. NaShonda Cooke's story resonates with Holmes. "I had these angel teachers that saved me," she says, fighting back tears. "They never really spoke about it; they didn't make me feel guilty. They acted as if what they were doing for me was just normal. When you come from where I grew up, teachers can be the dividing line between a teenage drug abuser, or a pregnancy, or a committed student." Holmes thinks she had teachers committed to ending intergenerational poverty one student at a time:

> I'm not really so far removed from the life of those high-poverty kids. Five kids, a single mother. Shuffled from homeless shelter to homeless shelter. We changed schools a lot. I didn't know, until I went to college, that some people had showers and air conditioners and central heat in their houses. It was only then I began to learn that people had computers and books to take home, or parents to read to them, or to go to their games, or to give them rides. I'm asked to go to school programs now as a county commissioner. The students always ask me, "What was your favorite book when you were a little girl?" I say, "I don't know, I never had a book."

It was a different world:

> The only attorney I ever met was one dealing with the arrests of my neighbors or my relatives. Our conversations included, "Who got shot in the neighborhood" and "Was there a drug bust next door last night?" Have you ever had helicopters hover over your street? I thought it was normal to come home and have the lights cut out. I knew, in some sense, the D-Boys were doing things they shouldn't, but they seemed like pretty good folks to me. They bought me clothes and something to eat sometimes. They'd get taken away sometimes, but I didn't really put the pieces together.

I had four younger brothers and sisters. I think the pressure was always greater for the older kids. I always thought it was my responsibility to make sure they had something to eat, not my mother's. I was much more worried for them than for myself. At the end of the month, after the food stamps ran out, I'd freak out. How do we make it three or four more days? I felt like it was my responsibility to figure it out, and, if I didn't, I'd failed them.

Jessica Holmes believes her teachers made it possible for her to escape, to become a professional and an elected public official. "It started in the second grade," she says. "My teacher would come around in the morning and put apples and fruit in my backpack," she remembers. Holmes just thought, at first, that the school was a friendly place, that they were giving food to everybody. "I thought that teachers were just really generous people," she says. Later, a high school tennis coach would make sure she had a ride home after practice. And then, when a ride didn't come or things were tough at home, the coach would let her stay at her house. She eventually began "helping me with my classes, checking my attendance, helping me prepare for tests," Holmes says. "She kept doing it when tennis season was over and then, later, so did my drama teacher," she explains. They never really spoke much about it. They didn't want to make a big deal of it or get credit for it. That's just the kind of people they were. "For all the talk about bad teachers," Holmes tells me, "I know that angel teachers saved my life—what's the price tag for a teacher that saves a kid's life?"

CHILD POVERTY AND EDUCATIONAL REFORM

There can be little doubt that education is a powerful tool for fighting poverty. But it is just as certain that poverty is a powerful barrier to meaningful educational opportunity. The troubling correlation between educational attainment and poverty has placed the near-perpetual efforts to reform public education in North Carolina in an exceedingly odd position.

For decades, state leaders have been at or near the forefront in public school reform. Governors in the 1990s and from 2000 to 2010 professed strong rhetorical and often financial and programmatic commitments to marked improvement in K–12 education.[31] In the eyes of many, North Carolina became a national leader in standards-based accountability, supplementing overarching assessment programs with additional early childhood efforts. Achievements were seen by some as uneven, but there could actually be little doubt that the state experienced a profound governmental commitment to public education.[32]

With partisan changes in legislative and gubernatorial leadership in 2010, the proffered tools of public educational reform altered notably. North Carolina significantly expanded its charter school program, adopted an extensive and aggressive tuition voucher system, moved to eliminate teacher tenure, created a controversial school grading scheme resulting in almost all high-poverty schools receiving failing marks, and tellingly reduced teacher and teaching assistant positions in moves that were broadly regarded as foundationally pressing toward school privatization.[33]

It is not my purpose to litigate these opposing policy positions here. My point is a different one. Neither Democratic nor Republican public school reform initiatives, over the last three decades, were accompanied by significant state or local efforts to reduce child poverty. And as I'll explain in concluding chapters, reform endeavors since 2010 have been accompanied by sweeping substantive legislative changes that have worked to notably increase poverty, child poverty, and concentrated poverty. It is not inaccurate to say, therefore, that for more than a quarter-century, North Carolina leaders have sought to "reform" almost every component of the state's public education system except the foundational challenge that academic research and conversations with committed, struggling public school teachers confirm has the greatest impact on student educational attainment: child poverty. It is not possible to have one of the highest state child poverty rates in the nation—one that allows more children to live in poverty than almost any other advanced country—and still have the best, most accomplished school system on the planet. It has never occurred. The data suggests it never will.

3

GOING HUNGRY IN NORTH CAROLINA

We have so many thousands of North Carolinians who don't know where their next meal is coming from, or if it's coming at all. People I talk to are shocked to learn how high the rate of hunger is here. In the last four years, we've quadrupled the amount of food we've delivered through the pantries and we can't come close to meeting the need. A third of people we serve are kids. It outrages most to learn that we've let this happen. Hungry children live in our midst while we tout our position as breadbasket to the world. Is there anything more heartbreaking than listening to a mother say she has to decide which of her children will get enough to eat today? Or looking in the face of a little boy who says, "It's a hard day for me because it's not my turn to eat?" That should never happen in the United States. Never. Hunger is a tragedy that doesn't have to occur. It happens here because we choose to tolerate it. And it will keep happening until we refuse to tolerate it. This is a real crisis. A great urgency. I don't see how people can ignore it. It is totally unacceptable.
—Clyde Fitzgerald, Second Harvest Food Bank of Northwest North Carolina

If you've got food, you may have a lot of problems. But if you are hungry, you've got one problem.—Alan Briggs, North Carolina Association of Feeding America Food Banks

I usually tell folks it's important to sit down before hearing about hunger in North Carolina. The federal government uses the odd term "food insecurity" to measure hunger. It refers to "limited availability of adequate safe food" and the "uncertain ability to acquire acceptable foods."[1] For nonbureaucrats, it means that during the past twelve months there were periods in which your family couldn't get enough to eat.

Other national studies use the modestly more straightforward measure of "food hardship," asking respondents whether "there have been times in the past twelve months when you didn't have enough money to buy food that your family needed."[2] By either standard, daunting numbers of Americans struggle with hunger. Over 41 million of us, nationwide, are designated as food insecure, including almost 13 million of our kids. About one in eight of the whole population and nearly one in five of our children face potent challenges of hunger.[3]

Food insecurity is even higher in North Carolina. In 2007, 12.6 percent of Tar Heels were classified as hungry. By 2015, the figure had risen to 16 percent, some 630,000 households.[4] Over 22 percent of the state's children are food insecure. That is the tenth highest rate among the fifty states.[5] Sixty-one of North Carolina's 100 counties have food insecurity rates over 15 percent.[6]

The highly regarded Food Research and Action Center, in an extensive April 2015 report titled "How Hungry Is America?," found that 21 percent of North Carolinians suffered from food hardship—lacking the resources to buy the food they need—in the previous twelve months. This, too, was found to be the eighth highest rate in the nation. The Greensboro–High Point metropolitan statistical area was listed as the hungriest in the United States, with 28 percent of all residents suffering from recurring hunger in 2015. Number one. By the next year, Greensboro–High Point had dropped to ninth in the center's study, though Winston-Salem had risen markedly, to fourteenth. Charlotte (twenty-sixth) and Asheville (twenty-eighth) also showed alarming numbers.[7]

A separate study a few years earlier had concluded that Winston-Salem was the nation's worst large community for childhood food hardship, among kids five and under.[8] The First Congressional District in eastern North Carolina has one of the country's very highest (of 436 congressional districts) food insecurity rates.[9] But these tragic and humiliating rankings rarely make their way into our mainstream political or public discourse. As Clyde Fitzgerald, the director of Second Harvest Food Bank of Northwest North Carolina puts it: "Our leaders have decided not to talk about hunger or poverty. I don't know why."

Hunger, like poverty in general, is racially tinged. The state's First Congressional District is almost 45 percent African American. The Twelfth Congressional District (pre-2016), encompassing the I-85 corridor from Charlotte to Greensboro, is 49 percent black. In both districts, the food insecurity rate is over 24 percent. In no other congressional district, where the percentage of black residents is at most 23 percent, does the hunger rate exceed 19 percent.[10]

The Food Bank of Central and Eastern North Carolina (FBCENC), established in 1980, serves thirty-four counties through a series of warehouses and about 800 (mostly religious) partner agencies across the Triangle (Raleigh, Durham, and Chapel Hill) and the eastern part of the state. Almost 600,000 Tar Heels are food insecure in its service area and a million live at or near the poverty threshold. Demand for its food assistance has dramatically multiplied in recent years. In 1992, it distributed about 5 million pounds of food. By 2016, the number was nearly 60 million.[11]

The FBCENC knows what it is doing. It has received the Feeding America Networks' top award for excellence, surpassing the nation's other 202 food banks. Still, Peter Werbicki, its CEO, explains, "I've been doing this for twenty years, and I lose sleep worrying about whether we'll be able to keep up the overstretched level of service we do today." He'd like to be more "visionary, but we've been in disaster mode for many years," he says.

Even at present levels, my colleague Dr. Maureen Berner reports, "the need for food assistance is vastly unmet; the system lacks the capacity to meet current and future demands." Werbicki puts it this way: "We distributed over 55 million pounds of food last year in thirty-four counties. But we could have sent it all to Wake County and still not met the need even there."

Clyde Fitzgerald's Second Harvest food bank serves much of the western part of the state. Its writ includes, challengingly, Greensboro, High Point, and Winston-Salem, where food and child food hardship rates soar. Fitzgerald reports that 29,000 schoolchildren in Forsyth County (Winston-Salem) go to school more to find something to eat than to learn. In Guilford County (Greensboro), the number of children is 40,000. You've got to be blind, he thinks, to miss the crisis.

"We've witnessed, in the last decade or more, the worst unemployment crisis in 80 years," Fitzgerald reminds us. "Through no real fault of their own, the landscape has shifted for so many of the people we see," he says. Jobs are no longer there, and for those in manufacturing, they aren't going to come back. High-tech recruiting won't help them, Fitzgerald says; they need basic, living-wage work. And they have almost no prospects for getting it. The "fact that a lot of our clients aren't well educated doesn't mean they don't have strong work ethics," Fitzgerald insists. "They are hard-working folks," he says.

A few summers ago, Second Harvest, which serves 300,000 poor residents, ran out of food. "We sent our trucks out and, given the huge increases in demand, there just wasn't enough food to stock them," Fitzgerald reports. "People I talk to are shocked at the level of hunger we have here." One-third of the people we serve are kids, he indicates. "It outrages folks to learn we've let this happen." Alan Briggs, executive director of the North Carolina Association of Feeding America Food Banks, explains that the challenges have continued well past the purported end of the recession. "Some food banks and pantries across the state have had to cut back their operating hours because they keep running short of food," Briggs explains. "In many ways, we are the private sector's response to the crushing problem of hunger in North Carolina, but, in truth, we can't carry that full burden, we can't possibly keep up."

Asheville's Manna Food Bank Director Cindy Threlkeld has seen the same tension. "Despite general signs of an improving economy," she reports, "there is still incredible demand." The "most startling thing," in her view, is that "child food insecurity still haunts us." The "fact is we're not doing what it takes to make sure children have what they need to eat." The tragedy for kids "has not improved and has actually gotten worse," she notes.[12]

Annya Soucy, who runs the Food Bank of the Albemarle in Elizabeth City, in the state's northeast corner, has had to adjust both expectation and aspiration. Given the towering hunger of the region, "our goal is to reach about half of the people in need in our service area." Communities here just "do not have the jobs that can pay a wage to support a family on." People assume "that the area's beaches produce lots of wealth, but most everyone works in the service industry here," Soucy says. Wages aren't good in the first place. Then, as soon as the tourist season ends, the food bank and the food pantries are crushed. "We'd like to set the bar higher," but it's not possible financially, she indicates. She knows they are only "putting a band aid on an open wound."

Jill Staton Bullard, now former director of the Inter-Faith Food Shuttle in Raleigh and Durham, notes in alarm that "we have more people who don't know where their next meal is coming from, or, really, whether, and when they'll be able to eat again." The challenge is more urgent than it was six or seven years ago. "Shoulder to shoulder with low-income people," Bullard says, "it actually feels much worse." There is "no safety net that is going to make it up," she reports. In sadness, she concludes, "I don't know how anybody raises a family and limits how much food each kid can eat." That might be "what you'd think you see in a third world country, but not in ours." For Bullard, "it is tough to witness, it gets harder and harder for even the staff to bear it, though we are blessed with longtime folks who have been in the food struggle for years."

THE SURPRISING CLIENTS

The people who use North Carolina food banks may surprise you. As Earline Middleton of the FBCENC explains, "They aren't who you think. They're not the person on the side of the road holding a sign. More likely, they are your neighbors." They're usually employed. They're almost always ashamed. They are people who "used to have good jobs, some who even volunteered at the pantry," she says. But now they are working at low-wage jobs and they need help. "We see the folks with the low-dollar jobs, folks barely getting by." They are "doing what they are supposed to do, they have always tried to do that, but they can't get the work and the wages they need to make ends meet."

Alan Briggs indicates that audiences he speaks to simply can't believe that nearly 2 million of their fellow state residents are hungry. "Where are they? I don't see them," they'll say. In reality, Briggs explains, "they are the people sitting next to you at church, or waiting on you at the restaurant, or taking care of your kids." They aren't obvious. They aren't lying out on the side of the road. They're not just old or young or black or white or emaciated. And a large number of them, Briggs reports, "are either kids or they are over sixty-five." (Though many nonclients object, he reminds me, that food banks don't require drug tests or impose work requirements.)

Clyde Fitzgerald adds, "North Carolina's hungry aren't the few standing out at the traffic stops; they are the people most of us work with, the people who wait on us, the family that lives across the way." They could as "easily be me or the people I care about." Most of the people Second Harvest serves are "embarrassed or, frankly, humiliated to come to us," says Fitzgerald. "They worry what their friends, their peers, would think." That is, he regrets, "especially true of kids here at the pantries and at school." Some stay away just to avoid the humiliation.

"In North Carolina," he continues, "hunger doesn't manifest itself like it does in Africa, with people falling to the ground and literally dying before your eyes." For many of Fitzgerald's neighbors, "that is the vision they have of hunger and they much prefer to keep it that way." They believe that there is no actual hunger here, since they don't see it. Fitzgerald says, "I always tell them, if you've got a half-hour, come on with me, get in the car, I'll show it to you." They invariably decline.

Alan Briggs insists that if people want a "typical face" for those who use North Carolina food banks, it would be a working mother with kids and a full-time job. Almost everyone the food banks serve wants to work. In Briggs's experience, the two most frequently asked questions by food bank clients are "Do you know anyone who is hiring?" and "Do you know where I can get safe, affordable child care?"

It can be easy to fall over the edge. Earline Middleton tells me of the man she served recently at a pantry who "goes to work and has a car." Not a great one, but still, he has a car. Then, though, he got a flat. It cost money he didn't plan to spend. "I don't have fifty bucks extra," he said. "I live right at the edge." So "I've had to cut back on food for both me and my son."

Middleton recalls a teacher in their food lines whose child had gotten seriously ill. She was already on a very tight budget because they don't get paid well. "We had insurance," the teacher explained to Middleton, "but it didn't pay for everything." So "we really got set back," she said. "I'm embarrassed, especially that if somebody from school might see me, but now, even though I'm still working full time in what is thought to be a decent job, I'm having to use the pantry," she said, near desperation.

Another client Middleton highlights was doing fine, working in the Research Triangle Park, but then "the tech stuff got shaky." She got laid off and indicated, "I can't get a job that pays anything like I was making." So now she works at a retail store rather than being unemployed, "but I can't make up what I lost, no matter how many hours I work, and I can't always pay for both food and rent."

Then there is the worried lady at the pantry in Wilson who, Middleton explains, "had been standing in line since 4:30 that morning." She said she was doing it for her handicapped daughter, who couldn't manage the long line herself. Middleton says the mom "gets there before dawn because she can't afford to run the risk of not getting food for her daughter." She'll come as "early as she has to, because you do what you have to do."

And then, Middleton reminds me, there are the thousands of seniors they see who live on fixed incomes. Folks barely getting by who know they are never going to have any more money than they have right now, she says. They haunt her. "We take care of a lady in her eighties at one of the pantries who will always say she's doing just fine, that she doesn't need any help," Middleton reports. But she will also say that she is worried about a couple of her friends. When a volunteer went to her house, Middleton indicates, she had no food in her refrigerator at all. Not a morsel. She admitted she hadn't had any meat or fish for months. Still, she didn't want to take anything from the pantry. She was "way too embarrassed."

Middleton adds that there are more and more college students using campus food pantries springing up across North Carolina. The Niner Food Pantry was launched in 2014 at UNC-Charlotte. Other pantries have opened at UNC-Chapel Hill, North Carolina State University, North Carolina Central, Meredith, Durham Tech, and Winston-Salem State. The Feeding America food bank system estimates that now, nationwide, 10 percent of its clients are students. Squeezed by rising tuition, increasing rents, diminished contributions from their economically strapped parents, and the fearful specter of poor employment opportunities, students frequently have to sacrifice meals.

Curt Kedley, a volunteer at the Good Shepherd Food Pantry in Bertie County, in northeast North Carolina, has been surprised not only at the explosion in demand at the agency he loves but also that so "many of them are former farm laborers who have little in the way of Social Security." It hits him deeply. "You see all these older people in line at the pantry," he notes. "They wait patiently, even the ones who can hardly walk," Kedley says. "My heart really goes out to them," he sighs. "It reminds me of photos of bread lines years ago, but it is here today."

Karen James, who is grateful to have been able to use Catholic Parish Outreach in Raleigh, especially when her food stamp allocation was delayed or unavailable, says, "Every month it can be a new juggling act, a new struggle," with two part-time jobs and three children to feed. "I've been in situations where I have to decide whether to pay my light bill or eat."[13]

Kay Stagner of Orange Congregations in Mission (in Hillsborough) describes most of her clients, echoing a line heard at many pantries, as being "one event away from having nothing." It might be a lost job, a work injury, a foreclosed house, a totaled car, or a sick kid or parent. In the last several years, "we've been helping more people who are better educated, people who are new to needing help." Stagner's organization now serves a "surprising number of men and women who used to donate to our agency before the economy fell apart for them." They now say, "I never thought I'd need this kind of help myself."

Alan Briggs echoes the trying cycle. He describes a family he met at Manna Food Bank who had taken care to introduce their young children to charitable obligation, bringing them along on their weekend volunteer stints at Manna for years. Then the father lost his job. The mother went to work, but at a much lower salary, as her husband tried to find new employment. Then she got cancer. She explained to Briggs that finally breaking down and asking people for help was the hardest thing she'd ever had to do in her life.

These are folks who don't fit the hunger stereotype. The studies show that they regularly make choices most of us never face—choices between food and rent, or food and electricity, or food and medicine, or food and child care, or food and transportation. Those who live with such uncertainty speak of challenges that multiply and compound. The realities for these citizens of North Carolina are difficult to square with the obvious plenty that surrounds us. "Food insecurity can't be predicted," Jill Bullard says. "It can't always be protected against, prepared for," she explains. The food pantry patrons also demonstrate that "you can't actually and accurately lay blame," she says. Though Bullard concedes that most of us "choose to blame the person in need because it is so much easier." Otherwise, we'd have to "accept responsibility for it ourselves."

KIDS AND HUNGER

Earline Middleton draws a powerful link between childhood hunger, eating, and dignity. "At the kid's cafés we run," she explains, "we also try to get the children healthy food." That isn't always possible at home, she says. But sitting down to eat with other kids and friends helps them make progress. Middleton recalls a young girl, who, for the first time, bit into a fresh pear. "It dripped down her cheek and she was sort of embarrassed," she said. It was clear to Middleton she had never seen a pear before. "Our goal is to give these kids the healthiest food we can under the most digni-fied circumstances possible," she notes. Food and eating play a large role in people's lives, Middleton insists. "Why can't poor people have that modest value, that simple dignity, as their own?" she asks.

Clyde Fitzgerald describes his own learning curve on child hunger. "When they were growing up, my kids and my grandkids got really ex-cited when it was a snow day," Fitzgerald says. They knew they "were going to have lots of fun when the blizzard came." We stocked up on food and milk, got out the snow gear, and looked forward to a having a big time. "It certainly never occurred to our kids that they might not be able to get enough to eat," he says.

But then "I started to see that the kids we work with get scared when they learn that it might be snowing tomorrow," Fitzgerald reports. "They get anxious and depressed," he explains. The reason is "they know that, for as long as school is closed, they aren't going to be able to eat," he says. It's hard to accept that you might be hungry for days.

Food pantry veterans put flesh on that claim. Many programs aimed at feeding children are tightly intertwined with school. In the winter of 2015, in most North Carolina communities, schools were closed for a week or longer, leaving hundreds of thousands of impoverished children, for days on end, without the meals they depend on. Because schools were still closed on Friday, weekend backpack programs were thwarted. After-school snack programs, then, were also delayed or eliminated due to troubling road conditions. Food bank volunteers were unable to make it to distribution centers to help in the delivery.

Families, additionally, struggled to pay for extra child care and for higher heating bills, and to put more food on the table during the storm. All the while, paychecks were often rendered even smaller by business closings. "We worry very intensely about kids not getting anything to eat over snow breaks," Kyle Abrams of Inter-Faith Food Shuttle explains. Not having enough to eat puts great strain not only on the children but on the entire family. As Sylvia Wiggins of Raleigh's Helping Hand Ministry reports, "When you are working with families, you don't want people to get frustrated." When they get frustrated, sometimes they turn on the children. Having something to eat can "calm the storm," literally and figuratively.

This also suggests, of course, why childhood hunger in the summer is such a daunting problem in North Carolina. Clyde Fitzgerald indicates that "people always assume that since we have these massive school lunch programs during the year, surely somebody is doing the same thing for kids in the summer when school is out." But generally that's not so, Fitzgerald says. There are "entire counties in our service area," Fitzgerald suggests, "with no summer food program for children whatsoever." And even in the larger counties, coverage is limited and sporadic.

When the broader public fails to grapple head-on with these realities, we tacitly accept hardship, knowing that the stress of growing up malnourished and poor is both concrete and tangible. Research demonstrates that poverty and malnutrition "can hurt a child's brain development even starting before birth." Such hurdles visit demonstrable changes in brain structure, resulting in measurably diminished brain surface in poorly nourished children compared with their peers. Cognitive skills in reading and memory decline accordingly.[14] As Jill Bullard puts it, "The damage can be done by six or seven. We have to work fast."

For Fitzgerald, the impact of hunger on children is the driving force of his work. "When kids aren't hungry, they learn better, they can focus better, their demeanor is better, their behavior is better," he says. A lot of classroom disruption "goes away when kids get something to eat," accordingly to Fitzgerald. The kids "deserve to be fed." They "deserve their food." They "need it physically, emotionally, mentally, spiritually." They can't get it on their own, and "we can't stand by and let them be sacrificed." His phrases are pronounced with no small emotion.

Earline Middleton speaks passionately about "the kids" she serves as well. Not having enough food, she says, is the physical price. But there is also the emotional side of it. So many of the children served are "too embarrassed at school to let anyone know they don't get enough to eat." It cuts into "their sense of self-worth, it crushes their hope of dignity," she reports.

Middleton has no doubt that we ignore these realties at our peril. A teacher sees a child struggling in class. "What do we do?" she asks. "We don't even know he's hungry." Then he starts to misbehave. Before we know it, he's out of school. Then, of course, he gets in trouble with the law. "And we act surprised," she says. We shouldn't be.

To Middleton, "it's just a simple matter of justice." Everybody should have basic food, especially kids. "No one should have to eat out of a garbage can," she explains. A kid "won't be able to learn if he's hungry. He'll get in trouble, when sometimes, what he needs is an apple, a piece of fruit," she says. If he can study and learn and get an education, "then there's the potential," she concludes. From a "justice perspective, I don't see why every kid in Raleigh can't have that much." We expect the same behavior and the same responsibility from all our kids, she says. "Why don't we at least make sure that they have the basics?" Surely, as a first principle, Middleton says, "we have to give all our children an equal chance."

ACCEPTING A SENSE OF SHARED OBLIGATION

Jill Bullard started Raleigh's Inter-Faith Food Shuttle from her porch twenty-five years ago, recovering food from grocery stores in the back of a station wagon. Now, bolstered by over 6,000 volunteers, the food shuttle recovers or grows over 7 million pounds of healthy food a year and serves about 65,000 people a month throughout the Raleigh-Durham area. Inventing new ways, as she puts it, to move "beyond the No. 10 can." They have developed a remarkable network of "person helping person helping person" with fresh food and sustainable agriculture. But even the optimistic Bullard now believes that "if we don't do something, we're on a fast train heading into a dark tunnel." Surely we are a "better people than that, surely we are a better state."

Clyde Fitzgerald is equally direct. Some traumas are unavoidable, but "hunger is a tragedy that doesn't have to happen." It occurs here only "because we choose to tolerate it." And it will keep happening in North Carolina "until we refuse to tolerate it." This is a "real crisis." A matter of "great and surpassing" urgency. "I don't see how people can ignore it," he emphasizes. It is "absurd and indefensible," in the supposed breadbasket of the world, that we let people starve.

There is clearly "enough food for everybody," Fitzgerald reminds us. It is just "getting it delivered and distributed to everyone in the best ways that we are not so good at." So his goal at Second Harvest is "to provide as much food and as much hope to people as humanly possible." That's "our aim, our simple mission," he says. It is "what we try to do, every day, day in and day out." They seek to provide food and hope "for as many of our unfortunate sisters and brothers as we possibly can—people who have far too little of each." A broad army of volunteers also tries to give their clients the tools and the sustenance needed to work through "the hard things, even beyond necessary sustenance, that always come with being poor."

Still, as both Fitzgerald and Bullard concede, there are naysayers.

Fitzgerald is a retired corporate executive. He says his former business colleagues often ask, "Don't you feel guilty about constantly enabling people who are too lazy to work by giving them food?" After a time, Fitzgerald says, the question can grow tiresome. "I'm not so naive as to think that there aren't some people at these pantries that take advantage," he acknowledges. But he also knows, firsthand, that the "numbers of those who abuse our generosity are very, very small." You come to understand the people you serve, he explains. "The vast majority of the people, the families, that we see, are working, they have jobs," Fitzgerald notes. But they are "working fewer hours, for decidedly lower pay, than they were getting before." They don't have health care, they're vulnerable at every turn, he explains. They do everything they can, but they just don't have enough money to make all the ends meet; that's the simple reality of it. So Fitzgerald works to help people understand that, to get past their misconceptions. "I also try to make people a little uncomfortable about their predispositions," he notes. Sometimes, he finds, they get the moral issue exactly backwards.

I ask Jill Bullard about the frequent claim from pundits and commentators that terms like "food insecurity" and "food hardship" are padded and meaningless—that we have little actual driving hunger in the United States, that these standards are invented to justify unneeded government programs. Bullard says that she "is speechless in the face of such stupidity." There are, she stresses, almost 120,000 children in her service area (greater Durham and parts of the Triangle) who receive either one or sometimes two meals a day at school. "If these kids didn't receive subsidies," Bullard says, "a very high percentage of them would get nothing to eat at all because their families can't provide it." If the school programs were eliminated, "we would have a hunger disaster like we've never imagined in this country." North Carolina "already pays a huge price for hunger, in our schools, in our hospitals, in our prisons," Bullard attests. The result, if we were to eliminate a system of assistance that is already too thin, "would be unimaginable," she believes. So when "folks quibble with definitions like 'food insecurity,' they miss the gigantic issue right before their eyes," she says. If we were to send those 120,000 children home without any access to food, "it would cause harm we can't imagine."

As for political and religious leaders who claim that the moral or spiritual high ground now demands a sort of "tough love"—refusing "to aid and abet" those living in hunger and poverty—Bullard, herself a minister, says she "waits for the thunderbolts." This "harshness" message is "such a misinterpretation of both the demands of justice and the demands of Christianity" that it takes her breath away. "Jesus chose to be among the poor," she reminds me. He "didn't seek out the wealthy and the prosperous." He would say to us now: "Go back and find the poor, like I did." That anyone can claim "our present harshness is consistent with being a Christian nation utterly baffles me," Bullard moans. Maybe they ought "to try reading the New Testament."

There is no one, simple thing we need to do to fight hunger, Bullard believes. But the strategy surely needs to be broader than the mere delivery of food parcels: "We have to see ourselves as part of a community. What I can do might be different than what you can do. But we are all called to do a part to 'honor the fabric.' If I could do anything, I'd have us learn to walk together. That's the difference between the Jill Bullard of today and the Jill Bullard of twenty-five years ago. The difference between charity and justice, that's where I'm trying to move. It's not just a question of food and hunger. You can't just give away bread. We have to move toward justice."

THE HUNGER SILENCE

The statistics and stories of hunger in North Carolina describe a sobering reality. More than one in five of the state's kids experiences food hardship, one of the highest rates in the nation. One of its major cities is often characterized as the hungriest in America. Other principal metropolitan areas fare poorly as well. The problem is particularly acute for children of color and for those five years old and younger. The sprawling First Congressional District, stretching across much of eastern North Carolina, sets the standard for hunger in the United States.

Alan Briggs frames the challenge plainly: "The gap between what food banks can provide and the depth of the hunger we face is gigantic, it is way too big, it can't possibly be bridged." He "asks parents to think, when they sit in line to drop their kids off at school, that one out of four of those innocent little kids going into the schoolhouse isn't getting enough to eat." And then he asks them to remember all the problems that hunger triggers: "harm to health, harm to cognitive ability, harm to learning, harm to the ability to concentrate."

Briggs continues:

> I lose sleep when I think of the rippling effects of not investing in people getting the food they need. For kids under six, there is the wound to their mental development. Then, by the third grade, they are falling behind and we wonder why. We act like we don't want to connect the dots. It is no wonder that these kids, as they grow up, usually can't fight [their] way out of the patterns of hardship and suffering. Then their food challenges affect their health and we end up paying for their health care in the most expensive way possible— at the emergency room.

But in fighting hunger, Briggs reports, "our hardest battle, actually, is one of awareness." To most Tar Heels, hunger "is out of sight and out of mind," he reports. And if people do find out about it, "the scale is so huge, a quarter of all our children, that most of the rest of us usually just turn away." Why isn't it a public issue, he wonders. "It is absolutely absent from our public discourse, from our political discussions," Briggs notes. Hunger is, surely, one of North Carolina's most intense and pervasive problems, but "it is not even the elephant in the room—we act as if there isn't even an elephant."

It is even more difficult, perhaps, to accept and to justify the long-standing and traditional willingness of North Carolina elected officials to simply ignore hunger. The state enjoys frequent and intensely fought electoral campaigns. They are, perhaps, more vigorously contested than those in many other locales. But neither Democrats nor Republicans in North Carolina speak much of hunger.

In 2012, the Reverend William J. Barber, president of the North Carolina National Association for the Advancement of Colored People (NAACP) and the state's leading civil rights activist, the Poverty Center I then led, and an array of colleagues conducted a multifaceted set of poverty tours across rural and urban North Carolina. As it concluded, we sent a brief documentary of the tours and letters, including the findings from the extensive town hall meetings and summit the tour triggered, to the gubernatorial candidates of both political parties asking them to disclose their plans for dealing with hunger and poverty in North Carolina. Despite the thousands of people involved in the tours and the surprisingly extensive publicity it received, neither candidate answered our queries. Receiving no replies, Reverend Barber and I then approached the local media figures assigned to moderate the upcoming gubernatorial debates and asked that they question the candidates on their proposals for combatting North Carolina's massive hunger and poverty challenges. No such questions were forthcoming. Nor had any major statewide candidate addressed our nation-leading hunger challenges in 2008 or 2010 or 2014 or in 2016.

I asked Alan Briggs if the silence surprised him. Sadly, it did not. He explained:

> I wish that I had the ability to change that. It is a great responsibility to speak with and for people who don't otherwise have a voice. It is hugely frustrating not to be able to transform the public's perception of the crushing problem we face in this state and the public's wildly inaccurate perception of the people we serve. The people who suffer from intense hunger in North Carolina don't have a platform. They aren't part of our mainstream conversation. Hunger isn't part of it. It is just left out. We might be willing to donate some cans or some money or a little bit of our time, at one of our churches, once or twice a year. And those things are really important to the work we do. But very few of us are willing, really, to even look hard at the significance of the problem we face. We're not willing to haul that gigantic iceberg out of the water to see just how big it is. To see what we're sailing toward. We remain unaware. It's like we prefer it that way. That's what keeps me up at night. The iceberg that's coming, that we don't even see.

4

INEQUALITY

IN HEALTH

If I woke up tomorrow and got an email telling me I qualified for some type of insurance, it would change my life. It would be such a godsend to me and my family. It is so disheartening now, because my kids don't want to lose their mother and they see I have to fight for every bit of medical care I get. I've got grandkids. I want to see them grow up.

—Tonya Hall, Hertford County, North Carolina

Tonya Hall, a fifty-five-year-old mother and grandmother, lives in Ahoskie, North Carolina. She hails from a family of sharecroppers. "It was instilled in me at a very young age, if you want to eat, you have to work," she says. Hall has worked full time her whole life, as a bookkeeper and a manager for a variety of retailers. But in 2011, she was forced to endure a six-hour fusion operation for scoliosis. Two metal rods and five plates were inserted in her back. Losing insurance coverage after the surgery, she had to forgo physical therapy treatments because she couldn't afford them.

Hall also has long had a broken plate in her mouth, inhibiting her ability to smile. As she says, "It's hard to have confidence in yourself when you have no teeth in the front of your mouth."

Hall's family has a worrisome history of cancer. In the past few years, she's had troubling symptoms in her GI tract, bowel, and intestines. But she now has no access to screenings because she doesn't have insurance and can't afford to pay for the procedures. She and most of her family are situated in North Carolina's large Medicaid coverage gap. Her kids' father was diagnosed with cancer in September 2015. He wasn't eligible for health care coverage until he was terminal. He passed away in February 2016. "I live in fear," she says. "My kids deal with the constant worry that they are going to lose their mother. I feel like I'm fighting for my life and the state of North Carolina could care less."

It is often said on the political stump that the United States is "the only major country on earth" that doesn't provide universal health care coverage.[1] It turns out that is essentially true. Almost all OECD nations—the general international marker of advanced, wealthy nations—assure their citizens universal coverage as a foundational human right. Only Mexico and the United States are outliers (although there is a good deal of dispute about whether Mexico's system is now universal and, perhaps un-surprisingly, whether Mexico is, in fact, an advanced, wealthy country). Even so, there is no doubt that Mexico comes much closer to univer-sal coverage for basic health services—consultations with doctors and specialists, tests, screenings, examinations, and surgical and therapeutic procedures—than the United States does. Of the thirty-five OECD coun-tries, the United States routinely places thirty-fifth in access to health care.[2]

That means, of course, that the United States does a worse job in as-suring health care for its citizens than the Scandinavian nations such as Sweden, Denmark, Norway, and Finland. And it fares poorly in compari-son with the western European democracies like Great Britain, France, Germany, Italy, Austria, Switzerland, Belgium, and Spain, as well as our New World colleagues Canada and Australia. But Japan, Turkey, Chile, Estonia, Hungary, and Latvia also put us to shame. The European Social Charter demands that health care systems "be accessible to the entire population as a basic human right." Among the wealthy, advanced na-tions, we stand alone in exclusion.

Within the United States, meaningful access to the health care sys-tem varies markedly among the individual states. In Massachusetts, only 2.5 percent of residents are uninsured, while almost 17 percent of Tex-ans have no health coverage.[3] The advent of the Affordable Care Act im-proved rates of health care coverage notably. From 2014 to 2015, forty-seven states saw significant reductions in the ranks of their uninsured. Some 20 million Americans reportedly gained health care coverage be-tween 2010 and 2016. And the uninsured rate nationally fell to just below 10 percent, likely for the first time in American history.[4]

In North Carolina, 10.4 percent of residents—some 1 million souls—have no health care coverage, by the latest figures.[5] This, too, reflects an encouraging improvement. In 2014, 13.1 percent (1,276,000) were un-insured, and in 2013, the rate was 15.6 percent (1,509,000). Over a third of uninsured adults in North Carolina are full-time workers.[6] For once, on health care coverage measures, children fare better than (nonsenior) adults, typically because of more generous federal support programs for children. The uninsured rate for kids in North Carolina dropped from 7.7 percent in 2010 to 4.5 percent in 2016.[7]

Still, North Carolina's health care coverage and health outcome statis-tics compare unfavorably with those of the nation as a whole. The state's uninsured rate is 2 percent higher than the national average. Its rankings in overall health, in number of family practice physicians, in infant mor-

Map 1. Health insurance coverage by county

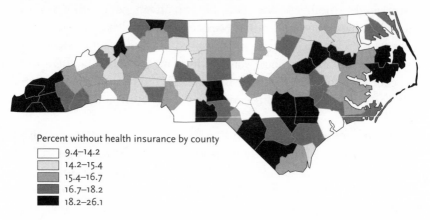

Percent without health insurance by county
- 9.4–14.2
- 14.2–15.4
- 15.4–16.7
- 16.7–18.2
- 18.2–26.1

Source: U.S. Census Bureau, 2010–2014 American Community Survey 5-Year Estimates. All maps made using QGIS.

tality, and in life expectancy are well below national norms, according to the United Health Foundation's annual studies.[8]

North Carolina is one of nineteen states, largely southern, that have refused to expand Medicaid under the provisions of the Affordable Care Act, though the federal government would pay at least 90 percent of the cost.[9] This has meant that 463,000 low-income Tar Heels who would otherwise receive coverage under the expansive federal program have been left without affordable access to the health care system.[10] Unsurprisingly, the uninsured rates in the nineteen states that have refused to expand Medicaid are notably higher than in the thirty-one states that have chosen to participate in the (generously funded) federal program. The Center on Budget and Policy Priorities has reported that states that have expanded Medicaid have an average of 6.5 percent of their population without health care coverage, while the average uninsured rate is 11.7 percent in states that have refused expansion.[11]

Careful studies have indicated that North Carolina's decision to reject Medicaid expansion is a costly one. Not only does the state forgo tens of billions of federal health care dollars, hundreds of millions of state and local dollars in tax revenue, tens of thousands of jobs, and hundreds of millions of savings for uncompensated hospital care, but, more directly, nearly a half-million low-income Tar Heels would receive needed health care coverage under expansion. As a result of rejecting expansion, huge numbers of poor residents are denied routine medications for treatable conditions such as diabetes, high blood pressure, and depression. They don't receive the tests and screenings—mammograms, colonoscopies, sonograms, and the like—essential to maintaining reasonable health. Accordingly, as many as 1,145 deaths annually occur prematurely, and many thousands more North Carolinians suffer needlessly, triggering soaring and disproportionate medical costs for emergency procedures.[12]

But it is not my purpose, at this point, to examine deeply North Carolina's recent legislative policy choices concerning the delivery of health care services to poor people. My goal here, rather, is to explore the alarming challenges faced by those denied effective health care coverage and services. To do that, I will try to move past the assembled data and economic frame to explore the actual, daily-lived-and-experienced impact of being denied health care coverage, and, in real terms, being ejected from the medical delivery system, on the well-being of low-income North Carolinians.

IN THE WORDS OF DOCTORS AND PATIENTS

Steve Luking is a family physician who has practiced medicine for over thirty years, almost all of it in Rockingham County, North Carolina. Dr. Luking and his brother, Scott, run a broad family practice serving about 6,000 patients. When we spoke, Steve Luking indicated his youngest patient was 3 days old; the oldest, 102 years. He often cares for four generations of a single family simultaneously. About 35 percent of Luking's practice is pediatrics. Most of the kids, thankfully, are covered by Medicaid. Many of their parents, though, are not. Uninsured adults make up about 10 percent of the people he sees. He says that in his decades working in Rockingham County, he has come to understand why nearly every industrialized country (except the United States) provides a basic level of health care for all of its citizens:

> For more than thirty years, I have watched my patients with no
> insurance pay a terrible price. I've seen women die of invasive breast
> cancer and cervical cancer when they couldn't afford mammograms
> and preventative checkups. I've hospitalized patients who stopped
> their medicines so they could pay other bills. I've spoken to the next
> of kin in funeral homes about symptoms regretfully ignored by those
> afraid of the cost of evaluation. You name just about any cancer
> or serious disease, and I can tell you about uninsured patients
> who delayed coming to see me, often with disastrous results. I've
> witnessed the slow death by invasive colon cancer in the patient who
> could not afford a colonoscopy, the diabetic who could not pay for

insulin and the resulting dialysis, the families who are left bankrupt and depressed after a serious illness, and on and on. Despite what people say, the emergency room doesn't provide the care these folks need. When was the last time someone received a pap smear or a screening colonoscopy in an emergency room?

Dr. Luking speaks of particular patients and their unyielding challenges:

I think of the middle-aged, caring man I saw recently in my office. He once had good insurance and a full-time job at a factory but had to quit his job and come home when his mother suffered a devastating illness. Otherwise, she would have been forced into a nursing home. I had placed him on several medicines for health issues. When I asked him if he had done his blood work, he started to cry. He told me he now had no insurance. The folks at social services had told him he wasn't earning enough to qualify for insurance support. He now works for minimum wage twenty-five hours per week and told me he has been skipping medicines in order to make ends meet.

Another patient I saw last month is a woman in her thirties. I diagnosed her with rheumatoid arthritis last year. She came back to see me because she could not afford visits to her specialist. She also had stopped her costly immunosuppressant medicines, yet these meds are her only hope to avoid the gnarled hands and deformed joints that will inevitably come her way. She, too, didn't qualify for insurance support at her low wage. She was advised at the government center that her only hope was to quit her job and go on permanent disability.

Just before we spoke (2016), Luking saw a child, one of his regular patients, who came in late in the day struggling with a variety of issues related to an ear infection. It was hard for Luking not to notice, though, that the child's mother seemed to be in even worse shape. She indicated, under his probing, that she, too, had been ill for several days. He asked if she had seen her doctor. The mother explained that she didn't have a physician. She was uninsured, though she had been working for over ten years for one of the county's largest businesses. For many years, she had been able to get only twenty-six hours a week, though she constantly requested more work. The same was true, she said, of most of her friends at the store. She had tried to get Medicaid but was told she didn't qualify, and she was unable to receive subsidies under the Affordable Care Act. So seeing a doctor seemed out of the question. Luking indicates that he sees patients in similar circumstances about a half-dozen times a week. Another comes to his office once a year, essentially to continue her limited medications. Though her family has a strong history of cancer, she, in her early fifties, has never had a mammogram or any other screening tests because she can't afford them. Luking worries that her effective exclusion from the medical system will eventually prove tragic for both her and her family.

Luking has come to have a particularized vision of the low-income community he is so frequently called upon to serve. There is, for Luking, little echo of the stereotypes that often mark our political discourse. His patients, more frequently, inspire and transform:

> Twenty years ago in the middle of the night after an emergency C-section, the obstetrician at Annie Penn Hospital (in Reidsville) handed me a newborn infant in need of resuscitation. I did my job, though I was taken aback by the swollen head twice the normal size of a healthy newborn. Since that night, I have seen that child as a patient hundreds of times in my office and at the hospital. Through dozens of hospitalizations, some of which I seriously thought might be his last, I have watched a pure kind of love emanating from his mother that defies my description. My patient cannot walk, or see, or talk. His feeding tube, brain shunt, and permanent tracheostomy, along with fifteen medications, sustain his bodily functions. But his mother sustains his soul.
>
> Always at his bedside, she has sacrificed her life to the loving attention of a severely compromised son. With the help of nurses, she has cared for him at home. I consider her a saint. Her husband works as a farm laborer; her life's work is a labor of selfless love. Together they earn less than the threshold for insurance coverage and would qualify for insurance coverage in most other states. She has skimped on her own health care. Her husband last year developed potentially ominous symptoms but declined a referral from the emergency room to a specialist because he already has outstanding medical bills.
>
> They aren't "takers" looking for a handout. These working poor are our cousins and our neighbors. They sit with us in the pews on Sunday; their children and grandchildren go to school with ours. Some have watched well-paying jobs fly to Mexico or China. Some,

through personal or family circumstances, earn meager wages. Some have employers who craftily maintain them under "temp" status or keep their hours worked under thirty per week to avoid insurance obligations. Some have reached their God-given potential. Who are we to pass judgment? The fact is that near-poverty has left them all uninsurable without some form of government assistance. Some in Rockingham County will surely die—if they haven't already—because of the decision to reject Medicaid.

Luking "works one day, one patient, at a time," trying to serve the people and community he has grown to deeply love. He became so distressed about the impact on his patients of North Carolina's decision to refuse Medicaid expansion that, two years ago, he wrote a powerful letter to his senator, majority leader Phil Berger, and then-governor Pat McCrory outlining the devastating effects he sees daily in his practice. The letter was eventually published in the Greensboro, Reidsville, and Eden newspapers. Neither leader replied.

Dr. Pradeep Arumugham is a heart specialist in Kinston, North Carolina. Lenoir County, where Kinston lies, is one of the state's and the nation's poorest. The doctor has had big-city options but prefers the quiet, friendlier life of eastern North Carolina. He has a thriving practice that selflessly includes a potent commitment to impoverished residents who are uninsured and yet can't pay the fare. They are, he explains, typically hardworking folks who struggle economically: waiters, maintenance workers, cooks, laborers, and retail employees. He also says that, as a heart doctor, he tries to see his poorest patients on a monthly basis because "they tend to be at greater risk of dying."

The failure to expand Medicaid, he reports, has had a devastating impact on his low-income, uninsured patients. The most wrenching of those consequences occurred last year when one of his patients, who made about $10,000 a year working in a local diner, faced severe dangers of heart failure from a troubling genetic abnormality. Arumugham had treated her initially in the emergency room at the Lenoir Memorial Hospital. He was able to stabilize her and send her home, but her heart remained very weak. She was in her early sixties. Her sister had died from the same malady. She needed a defibrillator, which for an uninsured patient could cost over $80,000. She couldn't get coverage on the open market because she didn't have enough money. She couldn't qualify for subsidies under the Affordable Care Act, astonishingly, because she was too poor; the program's cutoff was above her pay level. Arumugham saw her for several months, but he was unable to secure a defibrillator. As a result, the waitress died. "We could have saved her," he says. "I treated her for free and the medicines she needed weren't that expensive, but we couldn't get the device she needed." She would "be alive today if we had accepted the Medicaid expansion." That's the "simple fact."

Arumugham speaks of another patient, Shelton Trace, a truck driver, with serious heart disease. His heart function had dropped to about 35 percent of capacity, so it wasn't possible any longer for him to drive a truck professionally. He lost his job and his health insurance. He has attempted to get disability benefits, but as yet he has been unsuccessful. He cannot walk for more than a few minutes without becoming exhausted. He also needs a pacemaker, which, of course, he cannot afford. The trucker's son is autistic, so his wife can't work because she needs to care for him at home. Arumugham believes Trace's advanced problems could have been avoided with earlier, proper treatment. Now the doctor and the patient fear for his future—and that of his wife and son. And, of course, with Medicaid assistance, he could be fully treated.

James Drinn, sixty-four, worked for years repairing tractors. He had a heart attack in 2007 and eventually needed bypass surgery. Then he had a stroke in 2011. Drinn needs a specialist to receive catheterization, but that would cost thousands of dollars that he cannot afford. Thus his health and perhaps even his survival are threatened. In more than thirty other states, he would qualify for federally funded Medicaid. Janet Dees, fifty-three, the manager of a local bingo hall, makes less than $10,000 a year. She has asthma and has repeatedly been forced to go to the emergency room and sometimes, while there, has been placed on a ventilator. She spends many of her scarce dollars on inhalers and medicines. Medicaid expansion would notably relieve her plight. Arumugham knows that much of the political leadership in Raleigh is adamant in its opposition to expansion. He says, "I wish they would come to Kinston and meet my patients."

"Every day, every single day, I see the way we allow these people to suffer, just because they don't have money and we won't let them have insurance," he says. "I know people say, 'I'm against giving them money they don't deserve,' as if they were being handed some kind of generous disability check," the idealistic doctor reports. But that's not what is happening, he insists. "We're only saying, you are sick, or you are injured, and we are going to try to fix you," he notes. "Why is that seen as something radical or extraordinary, or as something a human being doesn't deserve?"

Evan Ashkin is a doctor of family medicine at the University of North Carolina Medical School. He serves patients at Prospect Hill Community Health Center in southern Caswell County (among other clinics), where a majority of the North Carolinians he sees are Spanish speaking and poor. Almost half are farmers (black, white, and Latino). A quarter are on Medicaid, 30 percent get Medicare, and 40 percent are uninsured. Ashkin notes that his patients don't fit the often proffered stereotype—lazy freeloaders looking to game the system and get a free handout. "That viewpoint is possible only if you have never worked with anyone in this patient population." He sees them every day, he explains. "I've never met a freeloader here." His patients are "simply people in excruciating circumstances, in intense distress arising from circumstances beyond their control." They are waiters, gardeners, farmhands, motel workers, dishwashers, day laborers, retail employees, housekeepers, and, ironically, home health care workers. They include families with young kids and part-time students trying to work and finish community college. Maybe policymakers ought to come down the road a few miles, he says, and get to know them.

"Poor folks pay a terrible cost for not having health care coverage—it takes a terrible human toll," Ashkin explains. When you can't get care, your health suffers markedly. "When your health is poor, you frequently become poorer, you are more likely to become or to stay unemployed, your family is more apt to suffer, there is more harm to kids and to their communities," he notes. And, of course, there is more harm to North Carolina itself. "Right now we are paying a terrible cost as a state by not expanding Medicaid and broadening health care coverage," he says. It is "morally indefensible."

Ashkin helps oversee a special clinical track at the medical school for young doctors who come to the university explicitly to learn to work in these distressed and endangered communities. "The students come here wanting to serve; we take them to these clinics so they can learn to do this kind of health care work, to make the kind of excruciating decisions (poverty) doctors have to make." They know what they are getting into, he says, "They are brave souls." They learn a sad, trying and unacceptable reality. "They have to be trained to deal with it," Ashkin notes.

Ashkin describes the choices that restricting health coverage triggers. A man comes in with chest pains, but he's uninsured. Do we give him the stress test we would offer if he could pay? The clinic can't afford to continually pay for expensive procedures. So maybe the patient gets the test, maybe not. What if the doctor guesses wrong and the patient has a heart attack? "We say we couldn't stand to have a two-tier health system or to have rationing," Ashkin notes. "But this is rationing, it's just rationing via 'the wallet biopsy,' the worst possible basis to allocate care." It is "gigantically immoral, the worst criterion." He tries to be ethical, Ashkin concedes, "but why should a doctor be making such decisions?" Why is a doctor exercising "this excruciating balance"?

One of Ashkin's patients is undocumented and has lived in Caswell County for seven years after fleeing violent abuse in Mexico. She was in significant distress early in a pregnancy—bleeding, badly in need of an ultrasound, presenting the serious possibility of an ectopic pregnancy. Because of constraints on public funding for her care, even if Medicaid is expanded, the clinic is hard pressed to provide a needed ultrasound. And if it does, the decision may work, economically, under existing regulations, to foreclose important scans late in the pregnancy, essential to protect both the mom and the baby. The baby, of course, will be a citizen, as is his sibling—suggesting how artificial noncitizen funding restrictions can be. "So I have to help the mother through this wrenching choice—a choice that no mother should ever be required to make," Ashkin says. "No one but a poor person would ever have to make such a choice; we want to avoid an early sonogram, but if we guess wrong, it might prove disastrous." Ashkin thinks of what he calls the "brother-sister test": "Would I think it tolerable that my sister had to make such a choice?" But we force this dilemma on a "hugely vulnerable population—pregnant women, uninsured, sometimes the parent of a citizen, who isn't one herself." He and his medical colleagues make decisions like that, he says, every day.

And because of the cabining restrictions (limitations on Medicaid expenditures), Ashkin says, large numbers of his patients roll in and out of Medicaid coverage. They get rehired and have a little money, so they lose coverage. Or they lose their job or they go bankrupt, so their Medicaid status changes. But a man who has asthma needs an inhaler, insurance or not. When he goes off Medicaid, he can no longer afford it. Or perhaps he needs blood tests or diabetes medicine or heart pills or high blood pressure medicine, but he can't get help because he is uninsured. Then, because he gets sicker, Ashkin notes, he perhaps loses his job. As a result, he goes back on Medicaid. Then he gets the inhaler or the insulin or the blood pressure medicine he needs, but "permanent damage has occurred" in the meantime. "I hear these stories every week," Ashkin says. They represent "an immensely destructive way to practice medicine," a way that is also "hugely inefficient—people get sicker, the family suffers, the community suffers, the tax base suffers." Every month Ashkin "sees patients who get much worse outcomes, and who later trigger much higher emergency room costs, because they move in and out of Medicaid." With expansion, he says, that wouldn't happen.

Another of Ashkin's uninsured patients, in his late forties, has multiple sclerosis. He couldn't qualify for Medicaid because he makes a little too much money. But he doesn't make nearly enough to be able to afford his medications, which will combat the disease effectively but are pricey. So he had to go off his medication for over a year while trying to get accepted into a charitable care program. If he gets accepted, he will have suffered "real and permanent damage in the interim," Ashkin says. Similarly, a young man Ashkin sees, out of prison for a year and a half, has diabetes. Ironically, of course, he had good health care while he was incarcerated. Having had no medical care since he got released, however, he developed advanced diabetic foot disease. Because he had no health insurance coverage, "when he finally came in to see us, he'd lost a tremendous amount of weight, was throwing up all the time, and, eventually, may require amputation." He had to be admitted to the UNC hospital system for dialysis and the installation of a feeding tube. The hospital, Ashkin reports, will eventually have to spend over $100,000, because it was impossible to spend a relative few dollars earlier. It is, sadly, "a very, very typical story." By Ashkin's lights, "it's a bizarre way to allocate health care.

"I believe that health care is a human right. I also believe that on a purely economic basis the argument to extend Medicaid is unassailable. Locally, regionally, statewide. We are doing ourselves a huge disservice. Ideology is overcoming rational, commonsense decision-making. And it is taking a hideous toll on some of the most vulnerable people in North Carolina."

Dr. Julius Mallette has been the chief medical officer at Kinston Community Health Center for seven years. He also has a private practice as an OB/GYN in Lenoir County. Mallette explains that community health centers in North Carolina work to fill the gap for people without health care coverage through either private insurance or Medicaid. The Kinston Community Health Center charges patients on an income-based sliding scale, capped at 125 percent of the federal poverty standard. A "lot of folks in Kinston," he says, can't meet the sliding scale, modest as it is. He estimates that about 10 percent of patients have to be turned away because they can't pay the fee.

But needing to see a specialist is a larger problem for the poor and uninsured than not being able to get in the door of the center in the first place:

> We have a great screening process, figuring out what patients need. But referrals to specialists, which are often critical, are problematic for our non-Medicaid patients. First, there may be large transportation costs from Kinston to East Carolina or to other larger medical centers. Many of our patients can't pay to get to the referral. Then, there is the specialist's fee. They typically demand several hundred dollars up front, so our patients accept a suggested referral but often do not actually go because they can't afford it without insurance. So they aren't able to get the specialized heart or obesity or diabetes or dermatology or dental treatment they need. We can tell them the treatment that would help them, but we can't secure it because the patients can't afford the programs or the specialists needed. If you are uninsured and obese, with the challenges which come from it, we can't get you into a program of treatment. And then, of course, the obesity ties into a lot of other chronic conditions. So, for a lot of our patients, if we can't get them into an insurance program, we can't fully treat them. Even with small referrals, like dermatology, 90 percent of our folks cannot afford the up-front fee, so they end up getting diseases in their bodily systems and, eventually, needing hospital care. Most of our self-pay (uninsured) patients know they can't actually use the referrals. Some folks in their fifties just sort of give up, knowing they won't actually have access to health care, so they don't think they are ever going to get well.

Then there are all the other services that the center has difficulty providing poor, uninsured patients. "Women need mammograms, but if our patients aren't insured, they can't get them." Blood pressure medicines "are very effective," Mallette notes, "but our patients can't afford them if they aren't insured." Even if some could get help with half the medicine costs or the screening charges, it would often be enough to make the difference, he says. So they go without essential medications, and too frequently, Mallette notes, "we see them later in the emergency room after they've had a stroke or a heart attack." Then, of course, the cost to the health care system will be $90,000 to $100,000. "It's a false economy," he sighs.

Diabetes medications, he notes, are expensive for uninsured patients. With insurance, patients might incur only a $5 co-pay. But without it, the "meds may cost $500." So they ask, "Do I pay my rent or do I pay for my diabetes medicine?" Then, he says, shaking his head, "we see them later in the intensive care unit, which costs everyone four or five thousand bucks, but it's all because they didn't get diabetes medicine in the first place." Yesterday, Mallette noted when we spoke, one of his patients finally cleared for traditional Medicaid. Last year, he says, she went to the emergency room six times, costing the system a whole lot more than it was supposedly saving by turning her away.

"It would be a huge benefit in Kinston," Mallette argues, if Medicaid were expanded. There is still a "big mindset here" that "I won't go to the hospital unless I'm at death's door." That costs everyone in the long course, he notes. "I practiced medicine in South Africa when I was younger and you really saw it there." Pregnant women would wait weeks or months to see a doctor, often leading to disaster. It means "you can't really have a civilized medical system," he says. "We are courting disaster and we are not living up to our ideals."

Running a rural community health center and thinking about almost 500,000 North Carolinians being excluded from Medicaid, Mallette is certain that "expansion would not be a financial burden in this community but would instead prove to be of tremendous fiscal benefit, as the federal tax dollars we already pay would return to support our rural and urban hospitals, create thousands of jobs that we need, and promote a healthier workforce and population." It would also help us, Mallette notes, to actually have the kind of health system we all say we believe in.

Dr. Charles van der Horst, an internationally renowned AIDS researcher and recently retired professor at the UNC School of Medicine, has volunteered for years at clinics in Raleigh and the Triangle to serve low-income, uninsured Tar Heels. The patients he sees there are largely young working poor: "those who build our houses, feed us, sew our clothes, teach our youngest children, serve our burgers, answer our phones, and take care of our elderly parents." Because they can't afford health insurance, he explains, his patients often have little to assist them in avoiding the ravages of life-threatening, chronic diseases.

When we met, van der Horst, like a scientist, brought along the numbers. Among the more than 400,000 North Carolinians in the Medicaid gap, two-thirds live in families where either they or another family member works. These working but poor families, van der Horst notes, are our neighbors. Almost 60,000 are construction workers, 56,000 work in food service, 46,000 are employed in retail, 43,000 are cleaning and maintenance laborers, 36,000 are textile and laundry workers, and 34,000 are bus and taxi drivers. Stunningly perhaps, 16,000 work in health care. For them, he explains, the evidence is clear:

> For people without insurance, or who have high deductibles, they go to the doctor much less often. We know that if people have insurance, they do see doctors and they enjoy an understandably greater peace of mind. For people who don't have insurance, they just don't go to a physician, or go only when they can't manage otherwise. But even young healthy people need to go to the doctor for preventative screenings—cholesterol, diabetes, blood pressure, mammograms, colonoscopies, or for vaccines, or smoking cessation treatments, etc. Diseases can often be prevented outright if the symptoms are caught in time. We have set good standards in place that decrease disease, and we've had a major impact on disease through preventative treatments.
>
> But that doesn't happen if people aren't screened. It is bad for those people and it's bad for all of us. If you are diagnosed with HIV and get on a treatment regime, you'll have a normal life expectancy. You'll work, you'll pay taxes. If you aren't screened and diagnosed, you'll have repeated hospitalizations, a reduced work life and life expectancy. Dialysis and kidney failure, for example, costs lots and lots of money to treat. Privately insured people end up paying more because hospitals have to jack up costs in order to cover the expenses of treating the uninsured.

To illustrate, van der Horst mentions a recent patient he'd been treating at a clinic. An older male, he came in with symptoms of liver disease. Eventually they learned his liver was riddled with cancer. He had also had esophageal cancer but lacked the means to seek treatment. "He died in a week," van der Horst said. If he had had health insurance, his life could have been saved; these were treatable conditions. Plus, he would have had a notably better quality of life as he struggled with his illness. "But people don't get care because they feel like they have no choices," he says.

Another patient, who worked for years for a local bank that consolidated and moved operations to Charlotte during the recession, lost her job because, given family obligations, she couldn't move to Charlotte. She looked unsuccessfully for decent substitute employment for many months. In the meantime, she became ill and started "letting things go," van der Horst explains. Her teeth were very bad, and since she worked in customer service, no one seemed willing to hire her—as she said, her "smile not being so good." Having lost employment and health care coverage, she had also run out of her blood pressure medicines. Effects on her hypertension were substantial. Van der Horst recalls that, as she explained her plight, she sobbed in his arms. He indicates that this pattern is not really uncommon. When he saw a half-dozen or so patients on an afternoon visit, one or two would likely burst into tears. In part, he thinks, they cried because someone was listening and trying to help, but mainly, he says, they were just beaten down by the crush of poverty. Having health care coverage, he notes, would pointedly improve the quality and optimism of their lives.

One young man van der Horst was seeing had worked for a number of years in a secure, full-time job, paying taxes, with health care coverage. He had severe hypertension that required treatment with four different medications, but these had, in turn, successfully controlled his high blood pressure. Then he developed a complication that affected his balance. He was adamant to keep working—"he's a good guy who works hard and enjoys working because he wants to contribute to society." With the new disability, though, he was unable to secure full-time work. In quick succession he had lost his job and his health insurance, and he had run out of his blood pressure medicine. His blood pressure soared, and he started to develop kidney damage. The doctor thought that, through the work of the volunteer clinic, they would likely be able to get his blood pressure back under control. But if that forecast proved wrong and he developed kidney failure, he would need dialysis, which would cost $75,000 a year or more. "For the want of four inexpensive medications," van der Horst indicates, "the health care system may be on the hook for hundreds of thousands."

Dr. van der Horst, sadly, could go on and on. The "decision to reject Medicaid expansion has a powerful, direct, and devastating impact on my patients, leading to avoidable costs, unnecessary deaths, and intolerable cruelty," he concludes.

KINSTON COMMUNITY HEALTH CENTER: PATIENTS AND STAFF

Daphne Betts-Hemby is the chief financial officer of the Kinston Community Health Center. She is quick to explain how much better the center would be able to serve its "particular population if we could get Medicaid expansion." The center operates on a generous, sliding-scale fee basis in its effort to serve uninsured, low-income patients. But "a lot of folks can't meet the co-pay and even more don't bother to come in because they don't think they'll be able to afford it." These are often the folks "who need health care coverage the most." They have chronic diseases; they "can't get their hypertension medicine until it's too late." It is "cheaper to get an oil change on a regular basis than to wait until you have to replace the engine," Betts-Hemby says. She knows that, to many observers, saying that a $50 or $100 co-pay is prohibitive, either to see them at the clinic or to take a referral to a specialist, seems absurd. But "$50 is a lot of money for some of our people; it's like asking for $10,000," she reports.

Other staff members ratify that conclusion. "Sometimes we can provide the diagnosis, but the uninsured can't afford the treatment, so they stop coming back," one explains. "Others give up because they think a doctor won't see them unless they are about to die and then it'll be too late," another adds. "The community need in Kinston is intense, and growing; the failure to expand Medicaid is, literally, killing our folks every day," she continues. Felicia Daniels, another staff member, says a lot of people "make too much money to meet our criteria, but not enough to pay for health care, so we're forced to leave people without the service they need." They will see a lady with a lump in her breast, but because there's no insurance, they can't order the mammogram. "Then she'll end up having to have her breast removed because she couldn't get health care coverage," Daniels notes.

Virginia Reed, a patient in her forties, explains: "I don't like to go to the emergency room; they only give you the least care they possibly can, so that they can turn you loose; they only consider the most desperate issues." And, she adds, "I can't miss work because then I won't get paid, so I have to decide whether my health or my family comes first—for me, it's always my family."

Brent Rogers, a center patient in his thirties, works full time in the construction industry, but his diabetes sometimes limits his work hours. "It takes every penny I bring in during the week to manage my household and have something to eat." As a result of neuropathy, he suffers from stabbing pains in his feet. The center doctors have referred him to a specialist in Greenville, but the doctor "wanted $195 before he would even take" an appointment. "I'm in the Medicaid gap and I don't have enough money to pay for a specialist," he says. It takes "all I've got to pay for housing and food and gas and heat, and health care ain't cheap." Even with diabetes, he says, "you've got to eat." Rogers lives in fear that the center won't be able to help with his neuropathy medication. "If they can't help, I'll end up being one of those people in the scooter at Walmart, and I want to work," he notes. "I've also had to put my dental problems on hold, because I can't afford to take care of my diabetes as it is—my teeth are in bad shape but it's been so long since I've seen a dentist, I'm scared to find out how bad things are," he says.

Charlie Train, a young woman from Kinston who is also a patient at the center, is diabetic as well. As a childless adult, she can't qualify for Medicaid, even though she makes less than the federal poverty standard. Her diabetes has led to a cascade of related health challenges. Still, she has worked almost her entire adult life at various retail and food service operations. Most of her employers haven't offered health benefits. Despite that, she managed to graduate from Pitt Community College with a focus in biotechnology, hoping to become a lab technician. But she's been unemployed for over a year and has difficulty standing on her feet for significant periods of time. She has developed severe carpal tunnel syndrome as well. Her pain, she reports, is constant. And she lives in fear that she won't be able to continue to afford the limited medications she now receives. When we asked her how often she thinks about her health care dilemmas, she answered, "every few hours—I'm just waiting for death to come and take me, but I wish I didn't have to be in such pain while I'm waiting."

SPENDING THE MOST, GETTING THE LEAST: THE HIGH COST OF INEQUALITY

Of all the forms of inequality, injustice in health care is the most shocking and inhumane.—Dr. Martin Luther King Jr. in a speech to the Medical Committee for Human Rights, 1966

When exploring the impact of poverty on health in North Carolina, we might assume that, as a society, Americans, and Tar Heels, are simply unwilling to spend as much on health care services, medications, technologies, therapies, and products as other nations and communities spend. But as is widely known, exactly the opposite is the case. The United States spends far more, per capita, on health care than any nation in the world. The Commonwealth Fund report, comparing health care spending and outcomes from the eleven high-income OECD nations—the United States, Canada, France, Great Britain, Germany, the Netherlands, Norway, Sweden, Switzerland, Australia and New Zealand—determined, yet again, that the United States spends much, much more than any of the other nations, per person, and reports far worse health outcomes.[13] "The amount we are spending in this country is not gaining us comparable health benefits," Dr. David Blumenthal explains. American per capita health care expenditures are at least 50 percent higher than those of the other wealthy countries, while we have the worst overall health rankings, infant mortality, life expectancy, and chronic disease rates.[14]

The Peter Peterson Foundation adds that "the United States per capita health care spending is more than twice the average of the developed OECD countries."[15] In 2013, the United States spent $8,713 per person, while the United Kingdom spent $3,235, France spent $4,124, Canada spent $4,351, and the OECD countries averaged $3,453. By 2015, the U.S. per capita rate had risen to $9,990, or over $3.2 trillion in total. This constituted 17.8 percent of the country's gross domestic product, about twice as high as other wealthy countries. Americans spend about $3,000 more per person on health care than the Swiss do, though the Swiss have income levels as high as our own.[16] In 2016, the U.S. per capita health expenditure rate was estimated to rise to $10,345,[17] and $3.35 trillion in total. Still, we have the lowest life expectancy among the advanced, wealthy nations (78.8 years, compared with 82.2 among the eleven wealthy countries),[18] the highest infant mortality rate (5.8 deaths per thousand, compared with 3.4),[19] and the highest rate of disease burden. And of course, we are the only OECD country that fails to provide universal health care coverage to its citizens. We spend the most and cover the fewest, by far.

But even the overall per capita spending rate, taken alone, fails to reveal the oddity of our health policy choices. The United States also spends more on health care than any other nation from government-imposed, taxpayer-based resources, as it leaves millions of its citizens outside the borders of the health care system. In 2013, the United States spent $5,960 per capita on health care from tax funds. Medicare, Medicaid, and the Veterans Administration, after all, constitute 48 percent of all American health care expenditures. This number, too, is the highest for any nation, including France, the United Kingdom, Canada, and Sweden, each of which has a strong system of universal coverage.[20] As Dr. Steffie Woolhandler has written, "We pay the world's highest health care taxes. But patients are still saddled with unaffordable premiums and deductibles."[21] Dr. David Himmelstein adds that Americans "already pay for national health insurance but [they] don't get it, [as] thirty-three million are left uninsured."[22] Comparisons with the other wealthy OECD countries also indicate that the U.S. spends much less, as a percentage of GDP, on social services—for housing, employment, disability, and hunger—than any of the other countries and is the only advanced nation that spends more on health care than it does on the provision of social services.[23]

The high cost of health care in the United States is, no doubt, caused by an array of factors. It is not the case, apparently, that Americans have a greater number of doctors or hospital visits or clinic visits; on these fronts the United States is well below the average for advanced wealthy nations. But we do spend a great deal more than other countries on technology, pharmaceuticals, and of course (insurance) administration.[24] It is also clear that we are the advanced world's outlier, spending much more than any country, achieving notably poorer outcomes, and leaving, by a huge measure, many more of our brothers and sisters out of the health care system, in the cold.

5

CHARLOTTE: CONCENTRATED POVERTY AND LOW-WAGE WORK

They don't want to help you when you're in crisis—child care, food stamps, and stuff. But they also don't want to pay you enough that you can get by without those things either. I think they do it on purpose, to leave you trapped. We're made to feel like we don't count. No matter how hard we work, we can't get ahead. Everything we get, everything our kids get, is the worst. I'm angry about it. We work as hard as the folks in the offices do, even harder. They get rich off of the work we do. I want to ask them, "Why don't you pay us a wage we might be able to live on? You make plenty of money to do that. Why don't you care whether the people who work for you can have a life if they work hard and do right by you?" You know you can't make food and rent and transportation and electricity and day care on eight or nine dollars an hour. I work hard. I do a good job and I'm responsible. But I've gone for years without a real raise. I want a life like other people do. I want a chance to get ahead. And maybe, just for a minute, to enjoy life a little. All you people talk about being so religious all the time. Where's the Christianity in this? What's decent about it? If you feel so responsible to your shareholders, why don't you feel any responsibility to the people who work for you? Why don't we matter? Why won't you pay us a wage we can live on?—Cynthia L., low-wage worker and volunteer, Crisis Assistance Ministry, Charlotte, North Carolina

North Carolinians typically think of poverty on a rural/urban axis. The state boasts, rightly, of booming, economically vibrant, expanding, often wealthy metropolitan centers. These urban lodestars exist in parallel, too often, with struggling, chronically and pervasively poor rural communities, mostly in the east and mountain west. The state's prospects and

59

attainments are divided. And in the urban powerhouses, economic prosperity reigns.

This traditional portrait is accurate, so far as it goes. North Carolina's "persistent poverty" counties are all primarily rural, located on the eastern coastal plain. Per capita income is markedly higher in urban counties. Poverty and unemployment rates, on average, are elevated in rural ones.

North Carolina's policy framework, understandably, reflects this divide. What the state's Department of Commerce designates as Tier One counties—the most economically distressed—frequently qualify for more generous subsidies and developmental incentives. The listed Tier One counties surprise few lifelong Tar Heels: Hoke, Scotland, Robeson, Lenoir, Halifax, Wilson, and others in the east, and Cherokee, Clay, and Swain in the west. Perhaps obviously, Mecklenburg, Wake, Durham, Guilford, and Forsyth—home to the state's largest cities—are not on the list. But as we know, broad categories can be deceiving.

A few years ago, Allen Serkin and Stephen Whitlow studied North Carolina's most highly distressed census tracts, drilling down to neighborhood levels.[1] They found that countywide averages mask deep pockets of poverty in otherwise prosperous metropolitan centers. Residents of distressed urban tracts, they concluded, often experience even higher levels of poverty, child poverty, and unemployment—and report lower median income and high school graduation rates—than their rural counterparts. Surprisingly, the poorest parts of North Carolina are actually to be found, they concluded, smack in the middle of Charlotte, Raleigh, Durham, Winston-Salem, and Greensboro. Poverty remains a crushing rural issue in the Tar Heel State. It is also a potent urban one.

Scholars at both the UNC Poverty Center and the Center on Urban and Regional Studies have since updated Serkin and Whitlow's work. The phenomenon continues and even increases. Statewide, concentrated poverty tracts tripled between 2000 and 2010. Two-thirds of the most heavily afflicted neighborhoods are now urban. And the intensity of their poverty rises.[2]

In Durham, for example, the child poverty rate in highly distressed census tracts rose from 48 to 56 percent over the last decade. Several individual tracts showed child poverty rates well over 80 percent.[3] Today, nine of the state's ten most intensely distressed census tracts are located in Charlotte, Winston-Salem, Greensboro, and Raleigh.[4] But nowhere is the contrast between urban prosperity and pocketed want demonstrated more glaringly than in what we call the Queen City, Charlotte, North Carolina.

CHARLOTTE

Charlotte is, on most fronts, an economic marvel. It enjoys one of the state's highest per capita personal income levels and likely its greatest accumulations of wealth. It is North Carolina's largest city. A massive financial and energy center, it is home to the Carolina Panthers, the NBA Hornets, NASCAR, the Billy Graham Library, strong colleges and universities, vast and imposing medical centers, a bevy of Fortune 500 companies, one of the country's busiest airports, and a congenial system of light rail. It is stocked with surprisingly impressive galleries and museums. The symphony is first rate. It places well on lists of America's best cities. It enjoys a deep sense of civic pride.[5]

Mecklenburg County, which Charlotte dominates, is home to 13 percent of all the private businesses in North Carolina and 16 percent of the state's private sector jobs. The gross regional product of the greater metro area (over $163 billion in 2016) is 31 percent of the equivalent North Carolina figure. Per capita personal income in Mecklenburg County is over $4,000 more than that of the state.

Job growth and relative wealth have attracted new residents to Charlotte at a powerful rate. It is one of the fastest-growing large cities in the country, and the number of people who call Charlotte home increased by 15 percent between 2010 and 2016, more than twice the statewide average. Charlotte is the seventeenth largest city in the United States by population. Mecklenburg County crossed the million-person mark in 2014 and contains more than 10 percent of North Carolina's total population. As the billboards that dot the highways of the South touting the city's wonders claim, "Charlotte's Got a Lot."[6]

But Charlotte also has a lot of folks experiencing intense economic hardship. A series of national studies has cast something of a pall on the city's traditionally recognized prowess as an engine of economic opportunity and attainment. A Brookings Institution study of economic inclusion, and then another exploring national trends in concentrated poverty, highlighted troublesome problems of economic polarization in the Queen City. An Urban Institute report on affordable housing brought more troublesome news. And most notably, as indicated in the opening chapter, Raj Chetty, in his economic mobility findings through his Equality of Opportunity Project, concluded that a child born poor in

Charlotte is less likely to be able to make marked improvement in his or her economic status than in any other large American city—fiftieth out of fifty. There is ample reason to worry, in other words, that North Carolina's wealthiest city is not providing either a prosperity or an opened door of opportunity that is broadly shared.[7]

A searching examination of available census and state and local economic and social data makes the case, more pointedly and more particularly, that deep fault lines appear below Charlotte's often-gleaming surface. Charlotte's economy does, to be sure, generate impressive wealth and income. But a tangled confluence of race, isolation, educational disparity, neighborhood disadvantage, weakened family structure, intense wage stratification, and other factors has relegated many residents to the economic sidelines. Racial disparities are particularly troubling since they appear in multiple, interlocking guises. Mushrooming levels of poverty, child poverty, concentrated poverty, racial segregation, income inequality, and labor force segmentation and increasing percentages of low-wage work threaten to entrench and intensify Charlotte's notable economic mobility challenges. A racialized, concentrating poverty has led to the creation of some of North Carolina's most intense pockets of economic distress in the state's most commercially vibrant and successful city. Inequality in educational opportunity, economic fortune, and housing access have followed. In the last decade, significant labor market fragmentation—with the disappearance of much middle-income employment—threatens to make highly disparate patterns of opportunity even more rigid and sustained.

The troubling vectors seem to merge. Mobility, inequality, segregation, and poverty cannot be easily or effectively separated. They are the joined cousins of economic injustice. In a city of clear and even sustained economic prowess, deprivation of such magnitude and intensity also presents a potent and haunting moral question. A worrisome polarization—the pulling apart of economic prospects and possibilities—thus plagues Charlotte's promise.

INCOME AND WEALTH DISPARITY

An examination of income trends and levels in Mecklenburg County over the last quarter-century suggests both the city's accomplishment and its challenge. Although household income in the county, at all levels, experienced significant gains between 1990 and 2000, those advances were lost in the succeeding decade. The bottom two quintiles, unfortu-

Graph 1. Percent change in mean household income by quintile, Mecklenburg County

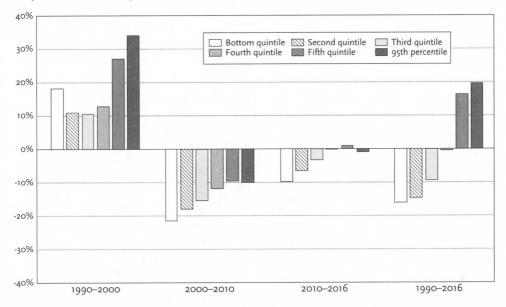

Note: All in 2016 dollars
Sources: U.S. Census Bureau, 1990 and 2000 Decennial Census; 2006–2010 and 2012–2016 American Community Survey

nately, suffered the steepest reductions, with the lowest quintile declining the most in 2000–2010 and 2010–2016.

But incomes of those at the top fared mightily. Families in the top quintile, especially in the top 5 percent, showed ample net gains between 1990 and 2016. They continue to outpace the remainder of the state by imposing margins. Charlotte has many more households at the upper end of the income spectrum than is typical of cities in North Carolina. Its median income is 15 percent higher than North Carolina's (23 percent for Mecklenburg County). Over a quarter of all households in Mecklenburg County earn more than $100,000 annually. Statewide, the percentage is 19. The 95/20 ratio (a measure of equality that divides the income of a household at the 95th percentile by the income of a household at the 20th) has steadily widened from 6.3 in 1990 to 9.2 by 2016, also exceeding that of the state at large.

These overarching measures also conceal very notable disparities by race and gender. Seventy percent of African American and Hispanic households have incomes less than $60,000 a year. Sixty percent of white

Graph 2. Percent of black households by income, Charlotte/Mecklenburg County

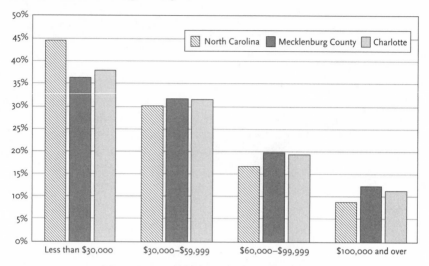

Legend: North Carolina | Mecklenburg County | Charlotte

Y-axis: 0% to 50%

X-axis categories: Less than $30,000 | $30,000–$59,999 | $60,000–$99,999 | $100,000 and over

Source: U.S. Census Bureau, 2012–2016 American Community Survey

households, on the other hand, enjoy incomes over the $60,000 threshold. At the median, income for white households ($77,297) in Mecklenburg County is almost twice as much as that for black ($40,775) and Hispanic households ($40,348). Earnings levels broken down by gender further highlight the distinctions. Of full-time, year-round workers in Mecklenburg County, white men enjoy the highest earnings. They bring in 34 percent more earnings than white women and far more than Hispanic and African American men. White women, on the other hand, report higher earnings than blacks and Hispanics of both genders. Men and women with similar educational attainment experience very different earnings at the median. The discrepancy broadens with additional schooling, but even at the high school dropout level, men make over 38 percent more than women. Men with a graduate or professional degree earn 80 percent more than similarly educated women.

Median household income also varies dramatically by household structure. The median household income for married couples in Charlotte is double or more than that of any other household type. And households headed by a single woman register a median income of just over $34,000, compared with over $90,000 for married-couple families.

Charlotte, therefore, enjoys median income levels decidedly higher than those of the state at large. It also has many more households earning

Graph 3. Percent of white households by income, Charlotte/Mecklenburg County

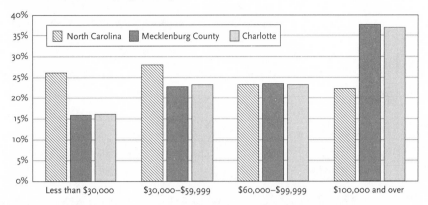

Source: U.S. Census Bureau, 2012–2016 American Community Survey

very high incomes than the remainder of North Carolina. Still, income disparities by race, sex, and family structure lead to massive chasms between the prospects and conditions found in varied Charlotte households and communities. The middle class, overall, also appears to be shrinking notably. Between 2000 and 2016, the share of middle-income households in the Charlotte area dipped from 51 percent to 39 percent, while the portion of adults in lower-income households rose from 23 percent to 36 percent.

POVERTY

Poverty, to no one's very great surprise, echoes income trends. In 2000, when median incomes were at their peak, poverty rates in Charlotte fell to about 10 percent, notably lower than statewide figures. As median household earnings dropped over the next decade, the city's poverty rate rose and now closely approximates that of the state.

As with income, poverty rates reflect an intense racial disparity. Black and Hispanic residents are three times more likely to be poor than whites. For kids, again, the numbers are troubling. Five percent of white children in Charlotte live in poverty, while 30 percent of black and 35 percent of Hispanic children are designated poor. Working-age African Americans (19 percent) and Hispanics (22 percent) are twice as apt to live in poverty as whites (9 percent). And for residents over sixty-five, 5 percent of whites, 16 percent of blacks, and 25 percent of Latinos are impoverished.

Graph 4. Poverty rate by age group, Charlotte/Mecklenburg County

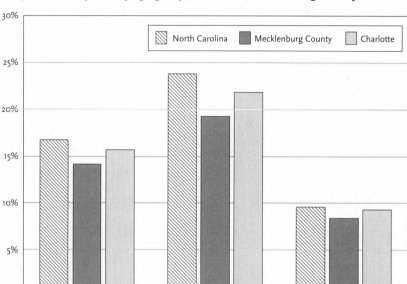

Source: U.S. Census Bureau, 2012–2016 American Community Survey

For women, the differentials often multiply. Although boys and girls under the age of eighteen experience poverty at similar rates, women between the ages of eighteen and sixty-four tend to be poorer than men, and the differential continues throughout the rest of life. Women who are single heads of households experience the greatest economic hardship. They are five times more likely, in Charlotte, to be poor than married couples are.

Despite its economic success generally, in other words, Charlotte is no longer immune from the deep poverty levels often seen in other parts of North Carolina. Its poverty rate is on par with the state's. About one in five blacks and one in four Hispanics are poor. Most worrisome, child poverty can be greatly elevated. Thirty percent of black kids and almost four out of ten Hispanic children live in wrenching hardship. Black and Hispanic poverty rates across the board are about three times as high as those of whites, and the poverty rates for black and Hispanic kids are about six times as high as those experienced by white children. The number of Charlotte residents, especially those of color, facing intense economic hardship is as disconcerting as it is surprising.

Graph 5. Poverty rate by race/ethnicity, Charlotte/Mecklenburg County

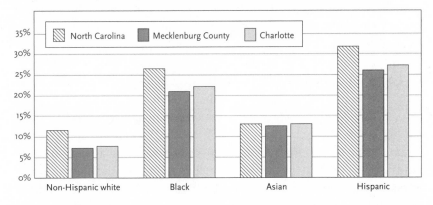

Source: U.S. Census Bureau, 2012–2016 American Community Survey

Graph 6. Child poverty rate by race/ethnicity, Charlotte/Mecklenburg County

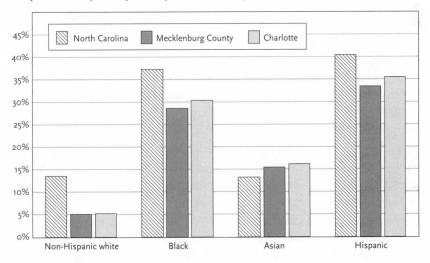

Source: U.S. Census Bureau, 2012–2016 American Community Survey

The next two sections, relying on federal census bureau data and federal and state labor and educational statistics, explore the depth of Charlotte's growing economic and racial polarization and its fragmenting workforce. They echo a much longer and more substantial report that research associate Heather Hunt and I wrote on economic hardship and concentrated poverty in Mecklenburg County in 2016.[8] The maps and charts, particularly, reflect Heather Hunt's skills.

CONCENTRATING RACIALIZED POVERTY

Rapidly rising and greatly disparate rates of poverty in Charlotte are immensely problematic. But growing concentrations of poverty—the clustering of poor people in very poor neighborhoods—may provide an even larger set of challenges. In intensely poor neighborhoods, impoverished residents must cope not only with challenges stemming from their own deprivations, but also with hardships arising from the tensions experienced by their neighbors. Unsafe neighborhoods, substandard housing, elevated crime levels, increased foreclosures, weakened schools, sparse transportation, diminished commercial activity and opportunity, environmental degradation, inadequate private and nonprofit infrastructure, isolation from community resources and services, and of course, diminished hope are often pervasive. As the Federal Reserve's national study of concentrated poverty put it: "There is a double burden imposed on poor families living in extremely poor communities."[9] Neighborhoods of concentrated poverty compound and intensify instances of individual poverty.

The last fifteen years have produced very marked increases in Charlotte neighborhoods in which more than 20 percent of residents are impoverished. In 2000, roughly 19 percent of Charlotte census tracts had over a fifth of residents living in poverty. Now almost 35 percent of tracts do. Tracts where over 40 percent of residents live in poverty have risen even more significantly (four such tracts in 2000, 17 by 2014). Fifteen years ago, 34 percent of poor people in Mecklenburg County lived in a high-poverty census tract. By 2014, 64 percent of poor people, and almost a third of all residents, regardless of income, lived in high-poverty areas.

The burgeoning concentrations of economic distress are also highly racialized. Of the 22 Charlotte census tracts, in 2000, that were over 70 percent black, 17 were high-poverty tracts. Of the 66 tracts that were over 70 percent white, none were high-poverty enclaves. Thirty percent of African Americans at all income levels lived in high-poverty neighborhoods, while only 3 percent of whites did. By 2014, 70 of the 79 high-poverty census tracts were majority minority. Sixteen of the 17 tracts that were 40 percent or more poor were at least 60 percent nonwhite, and many of these were almost entirely so. Only 2 predominantly black census tracts were not high poverty, and one of those was teetering on the brink with a poverty rate of 19.4 percent. As in 2000, none of the tracts that were 70 percent or more white were areas of concentrated poverty. By 2014, over half of Mecklenburg County's black residents lived in high-poverty census tracts. While the number of whites who resided in high-

Map 2. Poverty by census tract, Mecklenburg County, 2000

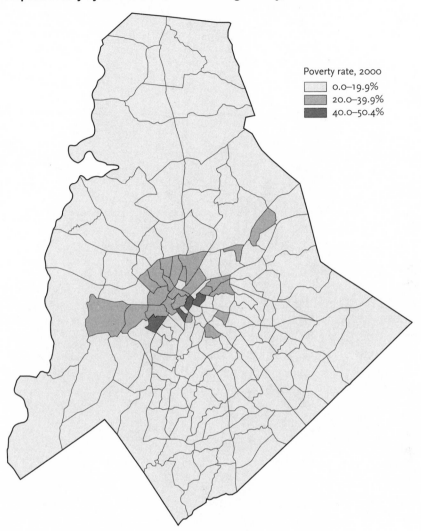

Poverty rate, 2000

- 0.0–19.9%
- 20.0–39.9%
- 40.0–50.4%

Source: U.S. Census Bureau, 2000 Census. All maps made using QGIS.

poverty tracts jumped 460 percent between 2000 and 2014, the proportion was still comparatively small (15 percent).

Accumulating patterns of poverty, skewed by race, are reflected in the public school enrollments as well. Over 60 percent of Charlotte schoolchildren attend schools where more than half of the students qualify for free and reduced lunch programs. Only 23 percent of white children attend such schools, while 77 percent of black and 80 percent of Hispanic

Map 3. Poverty by census tract, Mecklenburg County, 2014

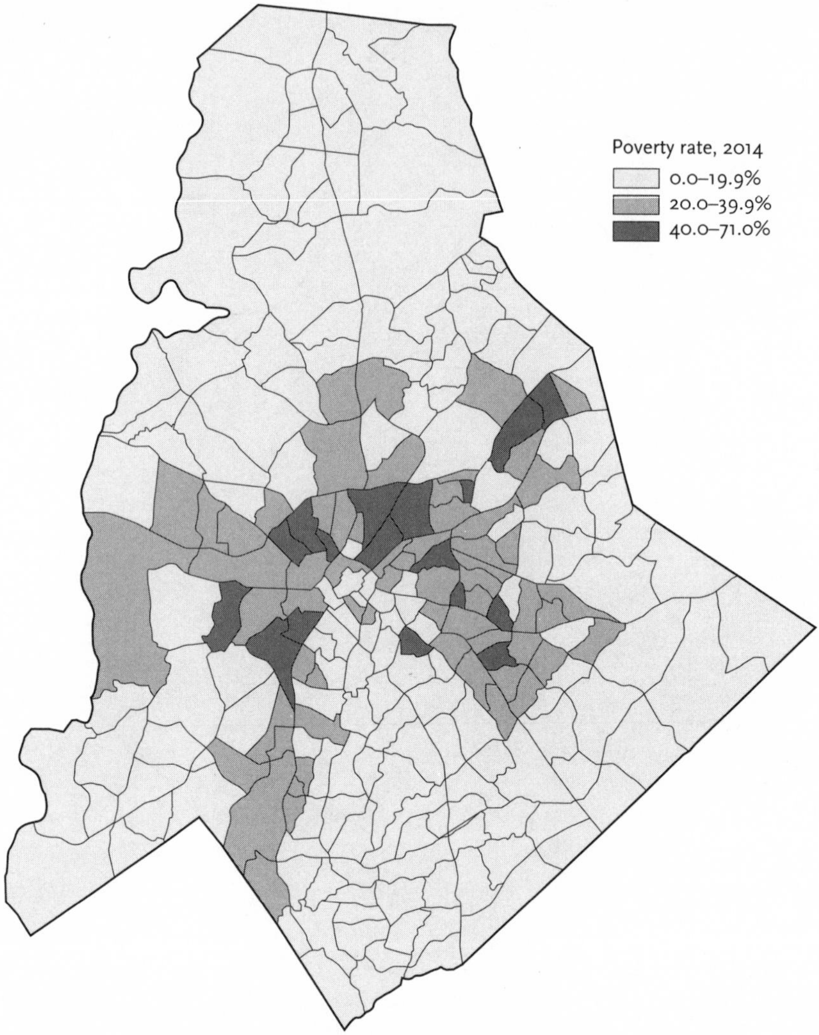

Poverty rate, 2014
- 0.0–19.9%
- 20.0–39.9%
- 40.0–71.0%

Source: U.S. Census Bureau, 2010–2014 American Community Survey 5-Year Estimates. All maps made using QGIS.

students do. Almost 89 percent of minority students attend majority-minority high schools. Many of these schools are almost entirely comprised of minority students. Ten of the twenty-six majority-minority high schools are over 90 percent minority students, and fifteen are over 80 percent.

If all schools in the Charlotte-Mecklenburg school district represented

Map 4. Percent black and Hispanic by census tract, Mecklenburg County, 2000

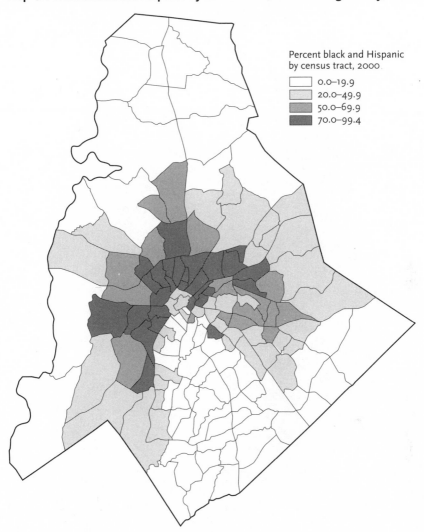

Percent black and Hispanic
by census tract, 2000

☐ 0.0–19.9
☐ 20.0–49.9
☐ 50.0–69.9
☐ 70.0–99.4

Source: U.S. Census Bureau, 2000 Decennial Census. All maps made using QGIS.

the racial makeup of the district, they would enroll about 70 percent minority students and 30 percent white students. Given segregated housing
patterns and the general use of neighborhood schools, most white students (61 percent) attend schools that are majority white and almost all
(87 percent) minority students go to schools that are majority nonwhite.
Nearly half of all minority students (49 percent) go to schools that have
more than 90 percent nonwhite students. Ten of the thirty-one high

Map 5. Percent black and Hispanic by census tract, Mecklenburg County, 2014

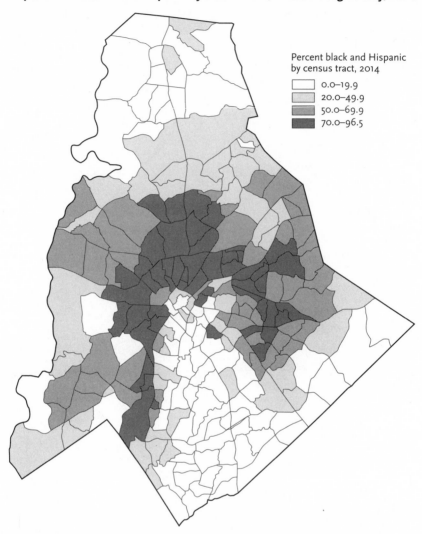

Percent black and Hispanic
by census tract, 2014

☐ 0.0–19.9
▨ 20.0–49.9
▨ 50.0–69.9
▨ 70.0–96.5

Source: U.S. Census Bureau, 2010–2014 American Community Survey 5-Year Estimates. All maps made using QGIS.

schools in the district are over 90 percent minority students. Fifteen of the high schools are over 80 percent students of color. And unsurprisingly, schools with very high percentages of minority students tend to have extraordinary numbers of poor students. Of the high schools reporting free and reduced-price lunch data, over half of students qualify in eleven of the twenty-one majority-nonwhite schools. None of the majority white high schools have free and reduced lunch participation rates of over 30 percent.

Almost everything we know about American education suggests that these high concentrations of poor, minority children in public schools bode poorly for these students' educational outcomes. A *New York Times* analysis looking at data from the Charlotte-Mecklenburg schools, among other things, found that white students were 2.3 grades ahead, while black and Hispanic students trailed by .9 and .6 grades, respectively. Under North Carolina's legislatively imposed school grading system, all of Charlotte's failing schools and 72 percent of its schools receiving a D have student poverty rates of 50 percent or higher. All schools receiving an A and 86 percent of the schools getting a B had student poverty rates of 50 percent or less. Students in impoverished and racially segregated schools tend to enjoy fewer resources and fewer highly qualified teachers and often have weaker frameworks of parent and volunteer involvement than their wealthier and whiter counterparts.[10]

Of course, concentrated poverty and racial segregation impose ample consequences beyond education. For example, the median home value in census tract 51, one of Charlotte's most economically distressed, where 3 percent of residents are white and 45 percent are poor, is $72,000. In tract 29.05, which is 93 percent white and 8 percent poor, the median home value is $870,500. The median home value, Charlotte-wide, for white owners ($224,600) is over $100,000 more than for blacks ($123,700) and over $90,000 more than the home value for Hispanics ($133,200). The housing market crash of 2007 made racial disparities worse. Between 2007 and 2014, the value of owner-occupied homes in Charlotte dropped 8 percent for whites, 14 percent for blacks, and 20 percent for Hispanics. The homeownership rate for black residents in Mecklenburg County dropped from 48 percent in 2000 to 43 percent in 2014. Forty-nine percent of Charlotte renters and 31 percent of homeowners are "cost-burdened," meaning they pay more than 30 percent of their income for housing. The Urban Institute estimates that the number of Charlotte rental units available for extremely low-income residents (making less than 30 percent of the area median income) has shrunk by half since 2000, even as the need doubled.

A University of North Carolina study of North Carolina's most economically distressed census tracts revealed that four of the state's ten most brutally disadvantaged tracts are located in Charlotte (see table 1).

Map 6. School "report card" grade and poverty rate by census tract

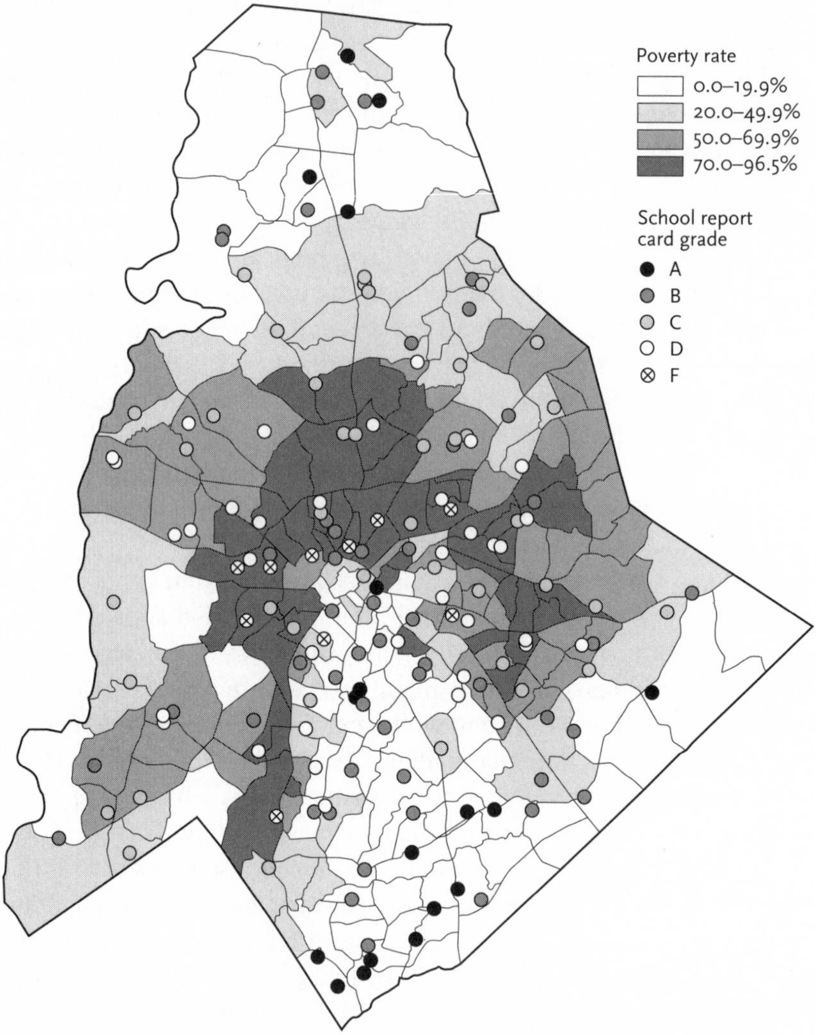

Poverty rate
☐ 0.0–19.9%
☐ 20.0–49.9%
☐ 50.0–69.9%
■ 70.0–96.5%

School report
card grade
● A
● B
○ C
○ D
⊗ F

Sources: NC Department of Public Instruction, NC School Report Cards; U.S. Census Bureau, 2010–2014 American Community Survey 5-Year Estimates. All maps made using QGIS.

THE ECONOMY, THE LABOR FORCE, AND LOW-WAGE WORK

Charlotte's economic hardship, disparity, and polarization are bolstered and entrenched by unfolding patterns of employment and compensation, the increasingly dominant impact of low-wage work. Economic expansion, to be sure, produces robust job creation and labor

Table 1. Economically distressed census tracts in North Carolina
(ranked by urban area and most distressed overall)

Urban tract rank	Overall tract rank	City	Census tract	Neighborhood
1	2	Charlotte	52	Lockwood
2	3	Charlotte	56.04	University City South and College Downs
3	4	High Point	139	Leonard Ave.
4	5	Winston-Salem	8.01	Waughtown and Columbia Heights
5	6	Charlotte	23	Grier Heights
6	8	Charlotte	39.03	Capitol Dr., Jackson Homes and Boulevard
7	9	Raleigh	509	Central Raleigh and South Park
8	10	Winston-Salem	5	Northeast Winston
9	11	Winston-Salem	7	East Winston
10	11	Greensboro	110	Cumberland

Source: William High and Todd Owen, "North Carolina's Distressed Urban Tracts," *Center for Urban and Regional Studies*, February 2014, https://curs.unc.edu/files/2014/02/NC-Distress -Update-final.pdf (12 February 2018)

force participation in the city. Still, racial disparities in rates of unemployment and compensation limit access to opportunity and mobility for much of the community. More universally, middle-income jobs lost over the last decade have been increasingly replaced by strongly stratified employment opportunities for all residents. A high percentage of newly created jobs pay very modest wages, and salaries in many expanding industries either have been stagnant or have actually declined over the past decade. The result is a polarized workforce with large numbers of residents living at or near poverty, with few available pathways for mobility and economic progress. Poverty and concentrated poverty, therefore, are often fostered and preserved by employment patterns of increasing stratification.

Charlotte's unemployment rate, unsurprisingly, spiked notably during the recession, peaking at almost 10 percent. By 2015, unemployment had dropped to a more traditional level, 4.4 percent, modestly better than that of the state. Still, unemployment remained at relatively elevated levels for black and Hispanic workers, roughly double that of white residents. The city's economy, however, has become notably more separated along high wage/low wage lines. Significant numbers of jobs have been created in industries employing educated, white-collar workers.

Graph 7. Employment by industry, Mecklenburg County

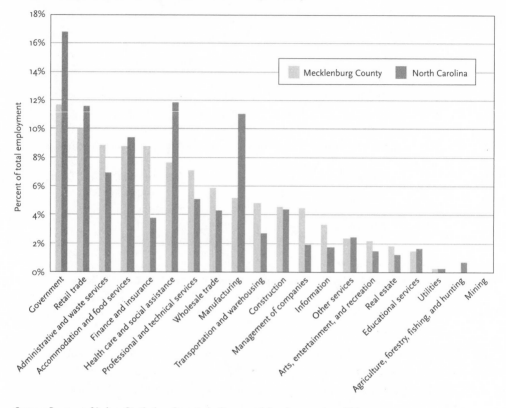

Source: Bureau of Labor Statistics, Quarterly Census of Employment and Wages

Employment in the finance, professional, and technical services and the management and information sectors has been both dominant and impressive. On the other hand, low-wage industries—retail, administrative services, and accommodations and food service—make up a growing share of the city's economy. These three low-wage industries now employ the largest number of workers in Mecklenburg County.

Nearly ninety percent of the jobs lost between 1994 and 2014 in Charlotte were in manufacturing. The great bulk of them provided middle-income wages, $45,000 to $60,000 annually. Many of the jobs that have replaced them, however, are either high- or low-earnings positions. Of the industries producing the largest number of jobs, 28 percent pay $117,000 or more, while 44 percent pay $38,000 or less. Only about a quarter have wages in the middle.

Every major occupational group with a median annual wage below

Table 2. Industries with largest employment gains, 1994–2014

NAICS code	Industry	Change in employment	Annual average pay
722	Food services and drinking places	24,664	$17,987
561	Administrative and support services	23,634	$37,559
522	Credit intermediation and related activities	17,160	$117,012
551	Management of companies and enterprises	16,207	$124,412
541	Professional and technical services	16,062	$82,673
621	Ambulatory health care services	13,612	$66,571
481	Air transportation	9,683	$66,024
624	Individual and family services	8,287	$26,944
523	Securities, commodity contracts, investments	7,410	$141,560
452	General merchandise stores	6,567	$31,621

Source: Bureau of Labor Statistics, Quarterly Census of Employment and Wages

Graph 8. Employment by occupation, Mecklenburg County

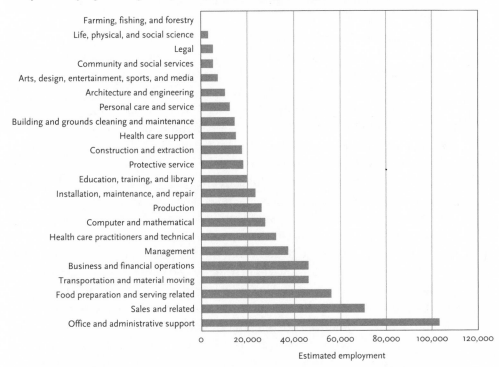

Source: NC Department of Commerce, Occupational Employment and Wages in North Carolina

$35,699 experienced flat or declining pay over the past decade. For example, while the median annual wage for managers increased 30 percent between 2004 and 2014 (from $88,634 to $114,828 in 2014 dollars), wages for food preparers and servers and health care support workers dropped 7 percent (from $20,131 to $18,750) and 14 percent (from $28,178 to $24,110), respectively.

Seven of the ten largest specific occupations in Mecklenburg County have a median annual wage less than $35,699. They account for 17 percent of employment in the county. Almost half of employment in Mecklenburg County is in occupations with a median annual wage of less than $35,699 annually. And seven of the ten occupations projected to have the greatest employment growth regionally between 2012 and 2022 are similarly low wage. As employment in predominantly low-wage occupations expands, the income gap between workers will intensify and Charlotte will become increasingly unequal.

A recent Brookings economic development study examined the country's 100 largest metropolitan areas on three essential measures—growth, prosperity, and inclusion—over the past decade. Charlotte ranked 18th on growth, 50th on prosperity, and 95th on inclusion.[11]

CRISIS ASSISTANCE MINISTRY

Despite the data and demographics, Charlotte's intense poverty remains invisible to most residents. A VISTA member working with some of the city's most economically distressed residents told me recently that, on a trip to a clinic, a local doctor had asked what she did for a living. When she reported working for the poverty-fighting program, he said, "That can't be, there's no poverty here. . . . I've lived in Charlotte all my life; if there was poverty, I'd have seen it."

The underinformed doctor would no doubt be surprised by the statistics described above. He would also be taken aback to arrive any weekday about 5:00 A.M. at the offices of Crisis Assistance Ministry, located on the edge of uptown Charlotte. There, in the shadow of the city's great banking towers, roughly 150 to 200 economically pressed residents line up daily, hoping to avoid the ravages of eviction and homelessness. Crisis Assistance Ministry was founded in 1975 by generous local churches that pool their overstretched charitable resources to meet the needs of low-income families in financial crisis in Mecklenburg County.

The ministry runs a massive distribution center for clothing and housewares and a furniture and appliance operation, providing essentials of life free of charge for people living in or near poverty. For over two decades, it has also operated as a central hub of Mecklenburg County and United Way emergency financial assistance efforts, relying on local, state, federal, and private funds to try to help stem the tide of privation. The ministry staffers have their work cut out for them. As Raquel Lynch explains, "We have thousands and thousands of people living in poverty here, but people think unless you look like the folks on television starving in Africa, you're not poor, and they're comfortable thinking that."

The stories of the impoverished, often exhausted and fearful Charlotte residents waiting in the long, snaking line outside the front doors of Crisis Assistance Ministry, hours before sunrise, remind us of the trage- dies and terrors of life at the edge: homes foreclosed, apartments bolted, increased and unaffordable rental rates, shuttered buildings, power sources shut off, kids in the cold and on the streets, lost jobs, reduced hours, ballooning health care bills, ruined marriages, families doubling up and still unable to make it. Those in line often speak of helplessness and desperation. Most of all, perhaps, they reveal a fear and a shame about what might happen next. What will it mean to my kids, my loved ones, the ones who depend on me, if we're evicted and can't go anywhere else? Most of the clients are well aware that a few blocks from Crisis As- sistance Ministry, desperate and defeated residents live in the woods and under the bridges near uptown Charlotte. Few can bear that prospect.

Thanks to a partnership with the marvelous staff of Crisis Assistance Ministry, my colleagues and I have had the honor of repeated and de- tailed conversations, conducted over a period of eighteen months, with a group of about a dozen clients and former clients of the program. Daniel Valdez and Raquel Lynch have organized and hosted a Circles of Care group, alumni of the ministry—folks who have struggled, and still struggle, at the edge of poverty in Charlotte's most challenging neigh- borhoods. The Circles of Care women—and this group was all female— know well the fear and anxiety of the Crisis Assistance Ministry morning line and all it entails.

All were employed; several had more than one job. They were in their thirties, forties, and fifties. They worked in varied low-wage pur- suits: home health care, medical records, behavioral health, and com- mercial, business, and food services. Several had experienced layoffs in the downsizing of the banking, housing, and other sectors, so they worried over unexpected future barriers and security. Each woman had struggled with burdensome mortgage or rental expenses and the costs of utilities, child care, transportation, and medical care. All were or had been single parents—frequently having experienced the hardship of trying and unsuccessful marriages—and spoke of the challenges of "hard to navigate family relationships." Most came from impoverished families themselves. They were, typically, intensely devoted to the welfare of their children and extended families, habituated to sacrificing for others. They know the meaning of hard work, concern for their neighbors and communities, gratitude for needed assistance, and an overarching and potent desire to give back and lend a hand to those experiencing even greater hardship. Our Circles conversations didn't sound much like chamber of commerce videos.

Poverty's causes and its cures, surely, are complex and variegated. But some things, they reported, are nonetheless fairly straightforward. Residents fighting to keep their families out of poverty utter a common, even repetitive refrain. They are usually too polite to phrase it this bluntly. But at heart their claim is consistent: low-wage work does not allow them to meet their most pressing needs—"it's the wages, stupid."

Everybody knows it's impossible to pay for food, rent, electricity, transportation, and health and child care on $7.00 or $8.00 or $9.00 an hour in Charlotte, they explain. That's true if you work overtime. It's true if you work two jobs, or even more. As Cynthia L. puts it: "I've gone for years and years without a raise. . . . Why don't they pay a wage a person might be able to live on? We work as hard as the people in the offices, even harder. Why don't you care whether the folks who work for you can have a life, if they work hard and do right by you? To live off that amount and pay for housing and everything, and then to have to go to the foods banks, and everywhere you can find to get help, it's a full-time job just staying alive."

Avril sums it up this way: "I'd gladly work twenty-four hours a day if they'd just pay me what I could live on." As Yolanda explains, "I guess I'm one of the working poor, but I'm not looking for a handout, just decent wages so I'm not living check to check" all the time. "I work full time and attend school part time and I ought to be able to make it on that," she says.

It can be difficult not to feel trapped. "They don't want to help you when you're in terrible trouble, helping you keep your house or pay electricity or take care of your kids," Melissa, another Crisis Assistance Ministry client and volunteer, notes. But they also "refuse to pay you a fair and decent wage so you don't have to have that kind of help." It "looks to me like they do it on purpose," Melissa says. The modest benefits available, she believes, actually subsidize employers who treat their workers as if their lives don't count. "We're made to feel like we don't matter no matter how hard we work." Leitha adds, "The people who run things are attached to this idea that you can't pay people a decent wage and still make enough of a profit." Melissa reports:

I don't mind hard work. I've done it all my life. But I also want to have a little bit of a life like other people do. I want the chance to advance. I want to be treated fair, to have a real chance. I'm tired of living mediocre, or less than mediocre, always left with the worst of everything. We're always the ones who get limited. Where we live, the schools our kids go to, they're always the very bottom of the barrel. We just want to enjoy life a little. That's never really possible. Plus, I'm getting too old to keep going like this. Pretty soon, I won't be able to keep up.

Cynthia L. echoes the challenge:

I want to grow. I want a chance to make some progress. And even if it's McDonald's, why can't people like me afford to just sit with their kids and buy a little something. I mean, just a little hamburger or something. I'm not talking about fancy lattes or floats or nothing like that. I think we deserve a wage that we have half a chance to live on. We want to help our families get ahead, we want to put back into our neighborhoods. God knows they need it. But none of us can afford to do that.

Melissa adds that "the company I work for is getting ready to lay off again." She escaped it last time, she says. But "I've got my doubts. . . . We had a meeting the other day about letting us know which of our jobs will be offshored to India." That's what "I'm stuck with." But, "look, I don't want anything given to me. . . . I want fair, livable wages where I can make ends meet for myself and I can help my family and the people I care about." "I don't want to be on the receiving end," she says. "I want to be on the giving end." Cynthia N. echoes the squeeze: "The people you work for act like their employees don't have actual lives." Where she works, they "just let ten people go and they didn't think about it for two minutes," she believes. "Just out the door—the bottom line is all that matters," she claims.

Cynthia N. explains that it can be even worse when the work isn't steady: "Sometimes I'm desperate just looking for a job. That means a lot of times I have to work as a temp because I can't get a regular job, and they treat temps real poorly. The work is not steady, the hours aren't dependable, so your family can't count on it. And, of course, when you're a temp you only do the things that nobody else there wants to do. It can be pretty miserable."

Leitha got caught in the downsizing of the financial services industry, where she worked for eighteen years. Now she does home and commercial health care services that are backbreaking. But "I'm stuck," she says; "there's no use crying about it, it's a lot more dog eat dog in the health care trenches." Bosses look, every day, "only at the bottom line, the dollars." The people "I care for, though, they have no one else." So there's a mismatch between her approach to work and that of her bosses. "It is the only check I can get," she says, "so I put up with it." Life pulls some "big turns on you." She continues:

> The pay is dreadful in home health care, even though it's so important for the people who need it. I keep working extra hard, trying to get higher wages, or a promotion, but there's nowhere to go in this work. Sometimes my salary even goes down, like when I had to shift to [another employer] when my last place had some trouble. I worked there for more than five years. . . . I know what I mean to the people I care for, though that's not what the people I work for think. But it's God's work caring for people who are in tough shape, folks who don't have anybody to help them. God put me here for a reason. I live just like a whole lot of people I know, just sort of at the edge. But I bring smiles to the faces of the folks I take care of. I guess I have to try to get by on those smiles. I just wish I could pay the rent and the electric bill easier while I'm doing it.

Trying to Keep You Down

Rebecca, who often works more than one job, explains that "if you get any benefits, you have to report every cent you make." And if you "go one dime over the limit, you can't qualify for food stamps or child care, even though you still can't pay your bills," she says. "It almost seems like they are trying to keep you down in that place." Cynthia N. adds, "They pray that you make that one cent above the cutoff, so they can take you off any benefits."

Leitha feels the same frustration: "The message is you have to quit your job if you want to get some help." Women have to "take care of the house, the family, the children, and we are the working poor," she says. "You're looking at them, around this table." Just because you made a little bit over, "you don't qualify for anything at all," she emphasizes. "But how are you going to get further, if you're not working?" she asks. "I've done whatever I could to stay in my house, working two jobs to pay the mortgage, but why does that mean I have to lose any help?"

Yolanda, who has two young sons, works full time, and goes to community college part time, explains: "I was told under the new rules passed by the legislature my income was $100 too high, so I couldn't get any more help with child care." That meant her expenses would go up by hundreds of dollars a month. "I've had to quit jobs before to keep my child care, and my kids are all that matters to me, . . . but I wouldn't let them make me quit this time," she says. In theory, child care help is supposed to be available, "but there's a huge waiting list and no money."

It is common to feel trapped in another sense as well. Rebecca and Leitha indicate that "sometimes we've had to give up our independence because we didn't have enough money to stay by ourselves." Cynthia nods her head:

> I'm living with my daughter now. She moved down here and lives
> in my house. We sort of had to do that because I didn't have enough
> money to make the rent and the bills. So, I had to give up my
> freedom, my independence, since I didn't have enough money to get
> by. I'd rather not do it, but I had no choice. Sometimes you have to
> give up your freedom to be able to just have a place to live. Most of
> my life I have worked low-paying jobs, and I know that if it were not
> for my family, I'd be living in poverty. It hurts my heart that my kids
> have to help me; I think I ought to be helping them. But things didn't
> work out that way and you've got to take the balls that life throws at
> you. You don't set out to be this way, you don't want to be divorced,
> you don't want to be unable to pay your bills. But you've got to have
> the courage to face what comes and not give up.

Tough Communities

Other challenges of Charlotte's burgeoning concentrated poverty are reflected powerfully in the lives of Crisis Assistance Ministry clients. Yolanda explains that in her neighborhood, "we have a lot of young men and they have no outlet, so they are hurting each other." And "no one values them," she says. There is nothing for them to do, no jobs, no community centers. "If my son goes out with the kids he sees, he's getting in trouble," she explains. There are "no programs for the teenagers, no day care for the little ones. . . . There is no transportation where you can hop on a city bus to get somewhere. . . . You have to have a vehicle or else be prepared to walk a mile to a bus stop."

Cynthia adds: "There used to be different programs where kids could participate and feel a sense of accomplishment, get your energy out. . . . But we don't have those anymore. . . . They decided to close the library; now the kids just get in fights." Rebecca agrees: "There is nothing but bad stuff for them to do when they get twelve or thirteen; there are summer camps, but no one I know can afford them." There ought to be "changes in our neighborhoods," she says; "kids learn from what they see and what surrounds them." And more worrisome, she adds that "when young white boys misbehave, they're just being boys, but young black boys are regarded as thugs." In Melissa's experience, "a lot of crimes happen here because kids came up in a family that couldn't give them the things they wanted and needed."

Katie is more blunt. "My community is terrible; there are a lot of men who work hard, but they like to get drunk a lot," she says. "I don't leave my children outside because they are very drunk and they like to pee in the streets, it's not safe." Sometimes, she notes, "I call the police, but that causes bad feelings and can make things worse." As a result, "I can't let my kids play in the yard or be out of doors without me," she says. Cynthia adds, emphasizing the point, "The church I go to is in Grier Heights and it's a very, very rough neighborhood." There are "a lot of drugs and a lot of shootings," she notes. "They have 'loaves and fishes' programs at the church on weekends and sometimes the people coming in beat each other up over food," she says. It seems like "every week or so somebody is killed," she reports; "we always have flowers on Sundays, left over from all the funerals. . . . You feel like a prisoner when you can't afford to go somewhere else."

Resilience

But if the communities where the Circles of Care heroes live are tough, the women are tougher. Their resilience and courage and selflessness can astound. Yolanda's entire life is, quite literally, committed to the welfare of her two boys. "For me, independence is just about being able to take care of my kids, to be there for them"—that is all that matters. "I worry about my kids all the time, that's the only thing I ever think about," she sighs. "But, I also know my own worth," she adds. "When I got no raise in over five years, I said I wasn't going to put up with it. . . . I had to step out in faith and confidence and not be scared, and I did it," she smiles.

Melissa concedes that she's been through a lot. She had to divorce a husband who struggled with addiction. "I realized I had become an enabler," she says. The changes "were tough and lousy and scary." But, she is certain, "they made me stronger in the long run." All that change, all the struggle made her more independent. "Now, my son has a job he likes and my daughter is about to get her associate degree," she proudly reports. "I have also learned a lot, I found my voice, I got out of my shell," she notes, looking around the table to her Circles friends. "The truth is, as a people, this is what we've always been through, all our lives," she announces. "It is what our families went through before, always a fight, always stress, always struggling to get by," she concludes. "We don't give up."

Rebecca frets that she's single, that she has only one income. "That makes it twice as hard to get by, to just pay my bills month to month," she says. "But I'm still able to be the kind of person I want to be, if I see someone in trouble, I try to help them," she says in a matter-of-fact way. "Even if it comes back on me, even if it costs me, that's just the way I am; it's the way things were where I grew up," she says. "I believe in it," she beams, "I still do."

Leitha recognizes that the stress can be enormous. But she's staying. "I have a very modest house, and I have my daughter and my little grand-daughter," she indicates. "I'm the matriarch. They need me. I can teach them what's important. Respect. Culture. Honesty. Simplicity. Faith. You are only as good as your word. You don't find too much of that these days. But I can make sure they see it, they know how to live it. That's what I'm put here for."

Cynthia L. is committed to living her life with dignity and purpose. "I see the challenges around me," she admits. But they are to be faced, not ignored. "You know these people who say they don't know about the poverty in this city, how can that be?" she wonders. "It's impossible not to see it," she says. "On my way into downtown for work, I see it every day," she reports. "There's somebody sleeping on every bench, how do you not know about it?" she asks. "You don't want to know," she says, answering her own question. "People living in a park, people waking up outside," they are all over, she notes. "They move the homeless out of downtown of course. . . . They want to keep saying Charlotte's a great place to live," she says. "Just be careful not to cross the train tracks," she laughs. "Don't tell me you don't know, it's pure denial." But Cynthia says, "I won't live that way."

And faith, for most of the Circles women, is never far removed from their resilience. Avril is adamant that "I would have lost my mind if I didn't know God was on my side, I trust in the Lord." Melissa broadens the claim: "I learned to trust the things I couldn't see because I couldn't depend on what I could see."

Most of the low-income Charlotte residents who met with us are not after a big government or charitable program designed to provide more housing or welfare or health care. They want wages they can live on in exchange for a difficult and demanding day's work. They say they don't want to be passed over because of their race or their sex or as a result of their bosses' expectations and shortcomings. They explain that they want a fair shot. They want a chance to advance and make economic progress. They want livable wages that recognize that if a person works hard, is responsible, and makes a contribution, she shouldn't have to be destitute. She shouldn't have to worry that she'll lose her housing or not be able to feed her kids. "If we would get a decent salary," Cynthia L. says, "we wouldn't need to be thinking about food stamps or rent subsidies, we could make it on our own. . . . That's what we're after."

6

GOLDSBORO: ISOLATION AND MARGINALIZATION IN EASTERN NORTH CAROLINA

The greatest issues in Goldsboro are poverty and segregation. Our kids miss out on a lot of the possibilities of life. They miss out on relationships with all sorts of different kinds of people, with different backgrounds. There are a lot of people I know in town who will never come further than Ashe Street. For any purpose, at any time. So our students can be constrained by that. We work hard against it. It's harder for a lot of our kids to get a full view of the world. I was able to go to UNC and I loved it. But for these kids, it'll be harder to get that chance. I worry that they'll see just what they see now. That they'll just be relegated. Young girls sometimes think they'll just have a baby so they can set up their own family. I miss seeing black and white people walking around together. Even blacks in the county feel separate from blacks in the city here.—Danielle Baptiste, Dillard Academy, Goldsboro, North Carolina

It is amazing what we do to poor people here. We marginalize and punish people for being poor. Goldsboro has layers and layers of poverty. That means multiplying layers of problems. The poor in this county, chronically, have never been given a real chance. A good system would try to reach all of them. Poor families start to think they don't deserve any better. That this is just what their lives are meant to be.—Shirley Edwards, 72, civil rights and community activist, Goldsboro, North Carolina

Goldsboro is a long way from Charlotte, in almost every conceivable way. Located over 200 miles east of the Queen City, its population of approximately 36,000 has grown relatively little over the past twenty-five years, and has even lost numbers since 2000. While in Charlotte policymakers struggle to link impoverished communities with the economic forces that drive dominant sectors of an urban powerhouse, in Goldsboro vibrant commercial streams, even in favored neighborhoods, can be hard to come by. Though Charlotte is among the nation's fastest-growing and wealthiest metropolitan areas, Goldsboro is regularly identified as one of the country's poorest and most economically polarized cities. It is part of North Carolina's eastern plain, the state's poorest region, where chronic, persistent poverty and racial isolation plague economic and social progress.

In 2015, the *Wall Street Journal* listed Goldsboro as the fifth poorest city in America.[1] Professor Raj Chetty's mobility studies found that the greater Goldsboro area had more intense mobility challenges than 95 percent of all the counties in the United States.[2] Kids born poor in Goldsboro are all but certain to stay that way. Perhaps most telling, the Pew Charitable Trust concluded in 2016 that Goldsboro had experienced a drop in median household income of a stunning 26 percent over the last decade—the second steepest fall in the country.[3] Another Pew study, of the nation's shrinking middle class, found that the share of adults in Goldsboro who are middle income fell from 60 percent in 2000 to 48 percent in 2014, the greatest decrease experienced by any metropolitan area in the entire country.[4] The share of adults in low-income households also rose from 27 percent in 2000 to 41 percent in 2014.[5] It's hard to imagine a starker economic verdict.

Poverty rates are explosive, especially for African Americans and their children. The city also suffers from great racial disparities in income, employment, and wealth. Pockets of very deep, concentrated poverty mark much of urban Goldsboro. School segregation is intense. Economic distress pervades much of the city. In many neighborhoods, opportunity, safety, and hope can be difficult to find. The city shares challenges too commonly seen across much of eastern North Carolina.

In earlier eras, Goldsboro played a more significant role in North Carolina's economic and political development. Originally known as Waynesborough, the town grew quickly in the 1840s after the Wilmington and Weldon railroad was completed. By the onset of the Civil War, it had become a vital rail junction of the South and a major trading center for the large, slavery-dependent cotton plantations in the region. When the war concluded, African Americans participated significantly in both state and federal "fusion" politics, helping elect four black congressmen from the famed Second Congressional District, until violent state and private forces drove black North Carolinians from the polity at the turn of the century.

The Goldsboro community grew notably from 1910 to 1920, especially after the conclusion of World War I. Agriculture production, though, slowed dramatically during the Great Depression. The Seymour Johnson Air Force Base was constructed in southeast Goldsboro during World War II, bringing historic numbers of jobs and triggering an economic expansion not before seen in the region. Even today, Seymour Johnson is Goldsboro's largest employer, sustaining an almost $300 million annual payroll. Beyond the Air Force, principal large employers include the local school district, the North Carolina Department of Health and Human Services, Wayne Memorial Hospital, a large state-run psychiatric hospital facility, and Walmart. In the early 1990s, *Money* magazine recognized Goldsboro as a Top Ten City in the United States.[6]

During the first half of the twentieth century, the white and black populations of Goldsboro grew at similar and roughly proportionate rates. A majority of residents were white, and from 1910 to 1960, the black population ranged from 41 to 46 percent. The 1960 census revealed that 58 percent of Goldsboro residents were employed, up from 55 percent in 1955 and representing a modestly higher rate than North Carolina statewide or the United States as a whole—likely due to the sanguine impact of employment opportunities connected to the Air Force base.

Public school integration controversies and backlash apparently led to white flight from the city (Goldsboro) to the county (Wayne) in the mid-1960s. By 1970, 49 percent of Goldsboro residents were African American (up 8 percent from the last census), and the white population had dropped by 18.2 percent. New family dwelling construction declined pointedly in Goldsboro as it increased substantially in the county. Many white families withdrew their children from the Goldsboro public schools, either opting for relatively recently opened local private schools or moving to a separate public school district in the county. White student enrollment in the Goldsboro school district dropped precipitously. From 1964 to 1973, the white student population in city public schools dropped from 54 to 41 percent, while the black student count rose from 46 to 59 percent districtwide. An overall decline in Goldsboro city school enrollment also led to a marked loss of teachers and resources.

Continuing enrollment, desegregation, and funding tensions led the North Carolina General Assembly, in 1991, to allow a merger of the Goldsboro and Wayne County school systems. In 2009, the North Carolina NAACP sued the merged school system alleging that discriminatory attendance zones placed a strong majority of poor, black students in highly segregated institutions, denying equal educational opportunity. According to state Department of Public Instruction data for the 2015–16 school year, the student body of Goldsboro High School was more than 88 percent black and less than 2 percent white. More than 90 percent of all students there qualified for the free and reduced-price school lunch program. Patterns of school segregation accompany, and perhaps intensify, housing and residential polarizations. Concentrations of poor and minority households, especially in some city center census tracts, reveal an array of intensely distressed neighborhoods in Goldsboro, some of which are almost entirely African American. They present remarkable rates of poverty, child poverty, and unemployment.

Despite these robust challenges, or perhaps because of them, Goldsboro is also home to a remarkable cadre of selfless and indefatigable community activists, educators, and social services providers who make it difficult to despair for the city's fortunes. Driven frequently by religious commitment and seemingly unconquerable sentiments of brotherhood, they bolster and sustain even hugely challenged communities. It can be hard to digest the full measure of their strength, endurance, and benevolence. They are often outpaced only by the wrenching and expansive hardship endured by the clients, colleagues, sisters, and brothers they seek to sustain.

DEMOGRAPHICS, INCOME, AND POVERTY

Goldsboro and surrounding Wayne County are, in population makeup, racially inverse. Goldsboro is 55 percent black, while Wayne County is 55 percent white. The white population in Goldsboro fell below 50 percent in 1990 and now stands at about 36 percent. It has been falling every year for decades. Wayne County's black population has remained relatively constant, on a percentage basis (33 to 31 percent), since 1980. The black populations in both the city and the county are substantially higher than the respective figures for North Carolina statewide.

Residents of Wayne County and Goldsboro are less likely to have a college degree than North Carolinians generally. Only 17 percent of residents older than twenty-five living in Wayne County have a bachelor's degree, while 28 percent of Tar Heels statewide graduated from a college or university. A notably higher percentage of Wayne County residents over twenty-five years old have not graduated from high school

Graph 9. Percent of population by race, Goldsboro/Wayne County

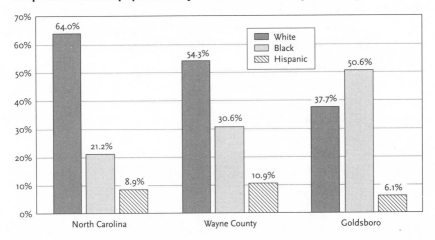

Source: U.S. Census Bureau, 2012–2016 American Community Survey

Graph 10. Population by race, Goldsboro, 1980–2016

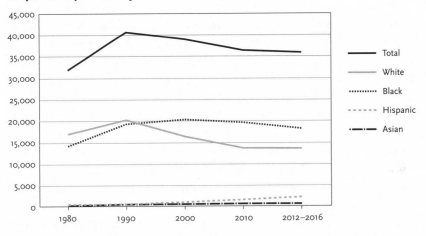

Sources: U.S. Census Bureau, 1980, 1990, 2000, and 2010 Decennial Census;
2012–2016 American Community Survey

or received an equivalency diploma than is true in the rest of the state.[7] Whites have higher levels of education than African Americans in both the city and the county, while only 6 percent of Hispanics, more numerous in Wayne County, have college degrees. The four-year cohort high school graduation rate is about 85 percent, without dramatic racial disparity—though students with limited English proficiency tend to graduate at significantly diminished levels.

Graph 11. Percent of residents with bachelor's degree or higher, Goldsboro/Wayne County

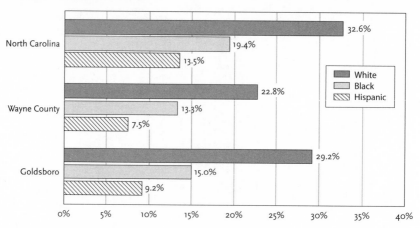

North Carolina
- White: 32.6%
- Black: 19.4%
- Hispanic: 13.5%

Wayne County
- White: 22.8%
- Black: 13.3%
- Hispanic: 7.5%

Goldsboro
- White: 29.2%
- Black: 15.0%
- Hispanic: 9.2%

Legend: White, Black, Hispanic

Source: U.S. Census Bureau, 2012–2016 American Community Survey

Median household income in both the city and the county is markedly lower than in the rest of North Carolina. While the state's median figure is almost $47,000 annually, in Wayne County it is a little over $41,000, and in Goldsboro proper, the median household income is a scant $35,086. Almost 40 percent of Goldsboro households earn less than $25,000 a year. Another 30 percent make between $25,000 and $50,000. In Wayne County, 12 percent of all households have incomes of less than $10,000 per year. Statewide, the figure is 8 percent.[8]

By race, income is even more differentiated. Whites make noticeably more, per household, than African Americans and Hispanics in both the city and the county. In Wayne County, for example, white families make about $50,000 at the median, while black households earn about $32,000 and Hispanics report roughly $27,000. The unemployment rate for African Americans in Goldsboro (23.4 percent) is almost twice that of whites (13.2 percent). For all racial groups, in the city and the county, median income figures have risen relatively little since 1980. All household income quintiles have lost ground over the past fourteen years. As in the rest of North Carolina, median income varies dramatically according to household type. Married-couple households typically make more than twice the annual income of other types of households.

Unsurprisingly, given what I've already said, poverty is high in Goldsboro and is rising. At its low point in 2000, the city's poverty rate was just below 20 percent—much higher than the state or national rates of

Graph 12. Median household income, Goldsboro/Wayne County, 1980–2016

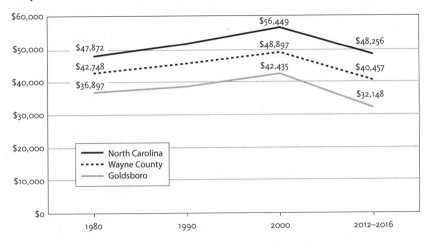

Note: All in 2016 dollars
Sources: U.S. Census Bureau, 1980, 1990, and 2000 Decennial Census; 2012–2016 American Community Survey

impoverishment. By 2014, it had risen to almost 26 percent. The Wayne County rate was 22.5 percent, also much higher than the statewide figure of 17.6 percent and the national rate of 14.5 percent. Almost half of Goldsboro residents live on incomes under 200 percent of the federal poverty standard, which is frequently used as a low-income standard. Over 10 percent of Goldsboro residents live in extreme poverty (less than 50 percent of the federal poverty level) on incomes of under $12,200 a year for a family of four. Higher percentages of Wayne County residents are uninsured than is true for North Carolina, and greater percentages are eligible for Medicaid.

Poverty in Goldsboro, as has now become almost expected, varies markedly by race. Fifteen percent of white residents are impoverished, while 33.2 percent of blacks are poor. The numbers are, as is typical, worse for kids, with almost 40 percent of all Goldsboro children living in poverty. Black kids are three times as likely to be poor as white ones. A statewide 2015 study ranked Wayne County among the most challenging, of North Carolina's 100 counties, for child poverty and well-being.[9] A UNC School of Government report a year earlier found that one in four children in Wayne County lived in a food-insecure home. More than 25 percent of Goldsboro households received food stamp/SNAP assistance in 2015.

Goldsboro, unfortunately, is also home to some of North Carolina's most highly concentrated poor communities. A study conducted in 2015—

Graph 13. Poverty rate, Goldsboro/Wayne County, 1970–2016

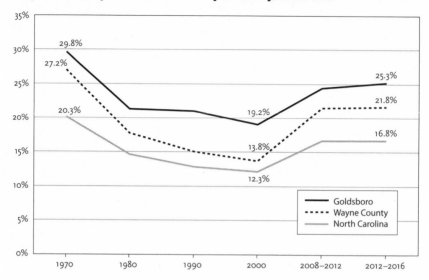

Sources: U.S. Census Bureau, 1970, 1980, 1990, and 2000 Decennial Census; 2008–2012 and 2012–2016 American Community Survey

Graph 14. Percent of poverty, Goldsboro/Wayne County

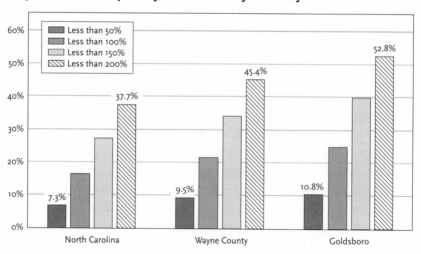

Source: U.S. Census Bureau, 2012–2016 American Community Survey

Graph 15. Poverty rate by age group, Goldsboro/Wayne County

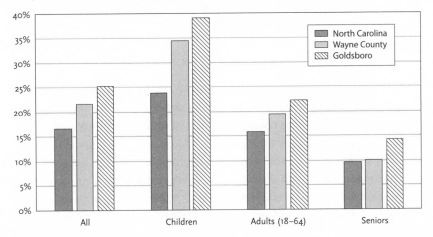

Source: U.S. Census Bureau, 2012–2016 American Community Survey

using measures of income, poverty, and unemployment—identified the state's most severely economically distressed census tracts. Three of the ten most disadvantaged are located in Goldsboro: tracts 15, 18, and 20, as identified by the U.S. Census Bureau. The statistics drawn from these neighborhoods are bleak.

Census tract 18, in central and west Goldsboro, encompassing downtown and adjoining areas, bound by US 117, East Ash Street, and Lionel Street, is almost 80 percent African American. Forty-two percent of all tract 18 residents live in poverty—28 percent of whites and 46.5 percent of blacks. Twenty-seven percent of all households have an income of less than $10,000 annually, and 52 percent of children live below the poverty threshold. Thirty-eight percent of residents are unemployed.

Tract 20, in west Goldsboro, bounded by US 581 and also including an array of center city neighborhoods, is 77 percent African American. Thirty-five percent of all tract residents are poor—a third of whites and 38 percent of blacks. Forty-six percent of kids are impoverished. Tract 15, located just south of tract 20, is similar. Eighty-five percent of residents are black. Thirty-five percent of all residents are poor—13 percent of whites and 37 percent of blacks. Almost 50 percent of kids are poor. Nineteen percent of all households earn less than $10,000 a year. The Equality of Opportunity Project identified five factors that correlate strongly with reduced economic and social mobility: residential segregation, income inequality, inferior primary schools, reduced social capital, and diminished family stability.[10] By such measures, the study determined, "Wayne County is very bad for income mobility for children in poor families. . . . It is better than only about 5 percent of counties (nationwide)."[11]

POVERTY, ISOLATION, AND CRUSHING HARDSHIP

Even for people in Goldsboro, even for those who would probably otherwise care about the issue, unless you see a child actually starving, or you see a homeless person, or unless something like that is actually occurring in your family, then poverty is not really a problem in your eyes. In an affluent country like the United States, poverty is hidden. You have to be willing to seek it out, to go and try to understand it. And if you don't do that, or if you come to poverty, like a lot of people do, with a judgmental attitude, you won't see it. You won't really grasp it. I've tried to see it and to understand it and to do what I could do to ease it.—Shirley Edwards

An array of the challenges of concentrated poverty are reflected in our interviews with low-income residents of Goldsboro and those who seek to serve them.

Doricia Benton is the director of the Community Soup Kitchen of Goldsboro, which serves about 50,000 meals (at lunch) a year. The kitchen has been helping to feed and serve impoverished community members for almost four decades. A good-humored core of volunteers from local churches, businesses, civic organizations, and as often occurs in Goldsboro, the Seymour Johnson Air Force Base, sustains the kitchen's efforts. Benton explains: "Most people in Goldsboro don't see the hardship that our clients endure, they just get slapped around by life." The shelter, she indicates, "is the safest place in Wayne County for most of them." Generally, they need more than a hot meal. "Most folks turn away from them, but that doesn't mean the problems go away. . . . It can be hard to find hope and opportunity," she explains. A lot of the "kids in this community only really get whatever food they receive at school," Benton reports.

Myra Johnson is grateful for the support Benton and her staff provide. Johnson has three kids ranging in age from four to seventeen, receives some social security disability support, and lives, as a lot of Goldsboro low-income folks say, "in the projects." Housing is very limited, she reports. So are food stamps. She typically works long hours at minimum-wage jobs, "but the kids miss their momma, and our housing area is very dangerous; they don't have playgrounds or parks," she says. A seven-month-old boy was shot some time ago; "it was on the news." Johnson's boyfriend and her son saw the killing. "So my kids can't go outside," she

Map 7. Concentrated poverty census tracts

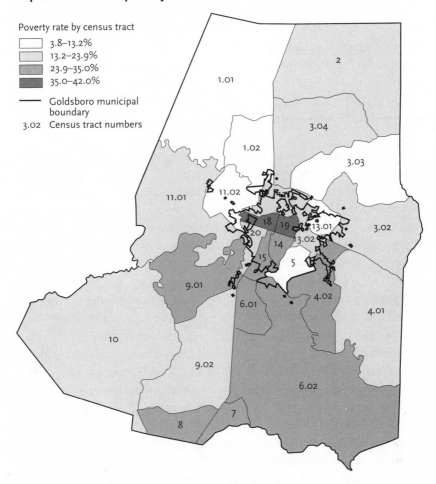

Poverty rate by census tract
- 3.8–13.2%
- 13.2–23.9%
- 23.9–35.0%
- 35.0–42.0%

— Goldsboro municipal boundary

3.02 Census tract numbers

Source: U.S. Census Bureau, 2012–2016 American Community Survey 5-Year Estimates. All maps made using QGIS.

says. "Cops don't come in here unless they have groups of three or four," she indicates. "And we're also the only white people out here, so my kids get targeted, here and at school," she sighs. Transportation to school is also a problem. "There's a school bus, of course, but it only comes up Slocumb Street and it is too dangerous for my kids to walk to Slocumb to get the bus," she says.

Johnson had a good job with a big solar farm company in nearby Pikeville for many years, but the project had to shut down. Unable to find a comparable job, she lost her house, and she and her kids lived in a camper for a couple of years, with their dog. "Now the place where we have to live is dangerous and insect-infected," she says; "my smallest one gets a lot of bites." They also have to sleep on air mattresses. It's especially hard for the kids because they've known better. And, Johnson reports, "my fear rubs off on my kids." There are gun shots sometimes. "I yell at them to get down," she indicates. "We need more housing that is safe and affordable," she notes emotionally. "Not that long ago, I had a good job and a house. Now I feel hopeless and I wake up dreading every single day."

Trish Bartlett, forty-eight, who also relies on the Community Soup Kitchen, echoes Johnson's worries over safety. "There were a lot of issues where I used to live relating to drugs and alcohol," she explains. "The summertime is the worst because Goldsboro doesn't offer programs for teens like it used to, there's less summer recreation." South Slocumb Street is terrible, she reports: "On a Sunday afternoon recently a teen-age boy was shot to death; everybody, including the kids, are scared to go out in the streets." Born and raised in Goldsboro, Bartlett lost her job two years ago and has had a difficult time since then obtaining work and housing. She is now homeless, without work or health insurance. There are few shelter resources available for women, she reports.

One doubts that anyone has worked longer, in more diverse capacities, to address the challenges of poverty in Goldsboro and eastern North Carolina than Shirley Edwards. Now a retired mental health administrator and principal driver of an earlier, innovative Crossroads of Understanding program, she has played strong leadership roles on the governing and operational boards of W.A.G.E.S. (Goldsboro's principal community action agency), the Salvation Army, the Wayne County Public Library, and a number of other service agencies. Edwards describes the expanding forces of local concentrated poverty this way:

> We have about ten big public housing facilities in Wayne County. The poor who live there are separated off, segregated out. That breeds discontent and disconnection. Crime multiplies there because everyone around you is facing difficulty and desperation. Their lack of meaningful alternatives keeps them from being able to escape or even think that they can or that they ought to be able to escape. The lack of real opportunity leads to lousy housing, lousy circumstance, despair, and an inability to escape—because they can't get a good enough job to get out. Most of the crime in Goldsboro happens in these communities. There is a lot of violence, a lot of abuse, a

lot of child sexual abuse, a lot of teenage pregnancy. And when you see that happen for four or five generations, it comes to seem insurmountable. But it's not. Though most folks find it easier to sit in their comfy seats and blame the poor in Goldsboro for being poor.

Esther Robinson is a full-time teaching assistant at a local grammar school and lives in the West Harris housing authority with her six youngest kids. To her great credit, her three oldest children are either in college or have graduated and are working, so they no longer live with her and the younger children. Robinson is divorced. She was married for fifteen years to a military husband who had risen to an E-6 classification by the time the marriage ended. Robinson had, herself, run a child care facility for many years as they lived at various posts around the country. Life changed dramatically, including the loss of various military support programs, with an unanticipated divorce.

Now she is something she never expected to be: a single parent. With six kids, she needs an apartment with at least four bedrooms. All she can afford, therefore, is the housing authority. "All the affordable housing here is terrible and dangerous," she indicates. When her husband left, "our kids didn't understand why they couldn't go to McDonald's or anywhere else anymore." At West Harris "there are gunshots all the time, day and night," she reports. Ambulances and the police are "out there all the time, they were there at ten o'clock this morning," she said on one of the days we spoke. Robinson wishes she had a backyard where the children could play safely, but that's not possible. One of the many good things about where she works and a couple of her children go to school is that "the school bus pulls right up to our front door. . . . The regular public school bus only goes down to the corner of the road and that's too dangerous" for kids to use. "My day starts at 6:00 A.M. in the school, where I teach the babies, as I have since 2004, and its safe for my own children to come later."

Denise Thomas lives a couple of blocks over, in the same complex. She delivers newspapers and has three kids, one of whom, her youngest, is hydrocephalic. She explains that she "can't be with the kids every second, but it's not safe to let them go outside—especially when all the hoodlums are out." There is a ditch with water in back of the house, but it has water moccasins, so the kids can't go there either. Thomas's rent is based on her income. If she makes more money, her "rent goes up, so there's not much incentive," she says. She wishes she could get out, having been there for over five years. "It's miserable," she explains. But she has to live near her parents, and West Harris is the only place she can afford in Goldsboro. "I'm trying to avoid having to move back home with my parents," she indicates. "It's hard to be a single mom, particularly with a little one who has special needs," she says, "and to still work and have the energy it takes for the kids." But you do what you have to do. "There are days I just sit there and cry, but I keep going because I have to. I may cry a little, but I pull on my big girl pants and keep going," Thomas says. She works hard to keep a regular schedule and assure some stability in her home. "We may live in the projects," she says, "but we don't have to act like it."

The Reverend Adeen George and her colleagues at HGDC Community Crisis Center serve the Webbtown community, where over 20 percent of African Americans live in extreme poverty and child poverty rates soar above 50 percent. She reports that there are "hundreds and hundreds of homeless here," and it can be hard for the center to meet the needs of those even in the immediate vicinity. "We feed 300 souls a week at the soup kitchen, we take folks to the doctor, help them with clothes," she reports. But in this neighborhood, the danger is intense: "We've had more people shot this year." The center has "food programs and programs for young boys, trying to give them things to do; one boy came to our program and two days later he was shot, just here down the street," she says, close to tears. Still, Reverend George won't consider leaving. "I'm determined to focus my life on the command, from the 25th chapter of Matthew, to feed the hungry, clothe the naked, and house the homeless. . . . Nobody's going to run me out," she makes clear.

Hilda Hicks, after a distinguished career as a federal administrator and former chairperson of the merged Goldsboro–Wayne County school board, founded the Dillard Academy on West Elm in Goldsboro. She emphasizes that, with the poor kids they serve, it is crucial to reach the children in the circumstances they actually and presently experience. All the schools in town want the top 5 percent, she says. "I want the ones no one else wants." Hicks learned quickly that it was necessary to provide door-to-door transportation for the students to the school. Our kids "get on the bus sometimes after witnessing a murder or a knifing or a rape," she comments; "it has a huge impact on them." Sometimes they cry and don't want to go home. "I fear in my heart, some days, when they leave," she says.

> It can be too dangerous to walk home or even to walk two blocks from a bus stop. We provide bus service to the door because we see

the dangers. We sometimes change the route or even get the police involved when it's really bad. Unemployment is really high here. Underemployment too. Our kids are exposed to a much greater level of violence, a much greater level of hunger, a much higher level of abuse than the kids across town. Our children have to be somewhat schizophrenic—they have to develop a playground personality, a home personality, a neighborhood personality, and a school personality. It's harder to learn if you spend the weekend hearing gunshots.

Danielle Baptiste graduated from Goldsboro High School, UNC–Chapel Hill, and the widely lauded North Carolina Teaching Fellow programs and then served six years in the U.S. Air Force, separating as a captain. Now she is operations director at Dillard Academy. She sees at close hand the challenges faced by children living in intense concentrated poverty. (Her son is a fourth-grader at Dillard.)

I take kids home with me sometimes. My son goes here and he expects it. It's a little like bringing a friend home, but, of course, it's really more than that. Sometimes the boys just need to come over to relax and sleep and not be terrified. One little boy came over a few weeks ago and said he loved being able to relax there and not be scared all the time. He really wished his mom could come stay too, it made him scared for her staying there alone. At one point, his mom called and asked him to come home because she was too frightened to stay by herself. My son knows that a lot of these little boys have a much different life than he does. It bothers him quite a bit. He's always giving away the money his father and I give him, even though it can be scary in our neighborhood too, we live on the cusp of the 'hood.

She laughs and says, "I can't get pizza delivered to my house."

On one of the days I was in Goldsboro interviewing Baptiste, after we'd finished our discussions at the school, she said,

After you left I had some students from school spend the night at my house with my son. The four-year-old brother of one of my son's friends came by and said he wanted to stay with the big boys. I told him it was fine and I talked to his mom. But after he'd been at my house for about a half-hour he said he needed to go home. I asked him if the big boys were being mean to him. He said, no, they were fine, but he needed to go home because "my mom doesn't like to be home alone because they would be shooting out where we live." I guess I looked upset because his older brother nodded at me and said, "Yeah they are shooting a lot more out there now." I called his mom and she came and picked him up. The next day I found out a teenage boy had been shot down the street from their house that night. It was the third shooting in inner-city Goldsboro that week.

I see first-graders, second-graders, walking in the streets, in tough, tough neighborhoods at 10 at night, alone. I'll pick them up sometimes and ask what's going on. They get no chance to be kids.

We did a program recently with a group of former gang guys— they were doing some work in the community, tattooed up, but serving hot dogs and cokes for the kids, trying to help the community out. We asked the local paper to come do a story and one reporter came. But he asked me if we could send some of our kids back up toward the school, back to the main road, because he was too scared to go into the neighborhood where the kids live.

We had a good team in the local soccer league. When we started winning, people began demanding ID and addresses for the kids, like we were cheating. These kids are almost completely cut off from the broader world. Even people I talk to in Goldsboro say to me, "Are you really going over to that side of town? Only troubled kids go to that school."

MEETING THEM WHERE THEY ARE

Shirley Edwards knows well the challenges faced by children in Goldsboro's neighborhoods and housing areas with the greatest concentrations of poverty—the dangers, the stresses, the perils, the hunger and hardship. Some have "little real family support to give them the encouragement and assistance they need." We know, she says, that a lot of our kids are in a different position. "It isn't that they can't learn, or don't want to learn; in a real way, they never got the opportunity," she says. "They don't have parents who will read to them, they don't have safe places to study, they don't have books, much less computers in their homes, and they don't have enough to eat," she indicates. All told, it can become almost impossible to prosper. A lot of teachers across the school system "resent that they have to teach these kids, instead of just the top ones." They complain that "they are left with the problem kids," Edwards says.

Dr. Thomas Smith is a behavioral specialist at Dillard Academy with a doctorate in human resource development and a thirty-five-year career in the Air Force, much of it as a command chief master sergeant. He explains that you "have to meet poor, often-threatened children where they are, otherwise you are just presenting another barrier." He says he chooses to work in these tough communities because "I believe in doing as much as humanly possible for the students who need us the very most." Their teachers "have to look at the whole array of difficulties these children face," he explains, "and they have to convince the kids that getting an education is more important to them than all the barriers they see every day." It's a tough assignment, Smith notes. "We attempt to teach them how to survive, and thrive, in their own trying circumstance," he says. Smith, who is a trauma specialist, sees it as an example of Maslow's hierarchy of needs in operation—first make sure they have safety, belonging, nutrition, clothing, support, he says. "Then maybe they'll be ready to learn something," he suggests. But you have to look at the whole child. It doesn't work "to ignore the fact that a student has had to walk past the victim of a shooting to get back to school," he emphasizes.

Teachers are replete with stories. I'll limit myself, for illustration, to one more. Danielle Baptiste indicated that not long before classes ended in June 2016, a teacher came by to ask her if it would be permissible to braid one of her third-grade student's hair. The teacher said the young girl "seemed like she was falling apart." She had asked if it was possible to get some snacks to take home to her little sister. She had been there for several years and never made a request like that. So it seemed odd. Baptiste asked if the little girl would like to talk to the counselor, but the teacher said the student really did not want anybody to know what she was going through.

It turned out, Baptiste indicated, that the girl's mother had lost her job and now the family was homeless. The mom was working at a hotel, and they could sometimes stay in a room there. But the student was worried people would find out, and she got nervous when the bus driver would drop her off after school. The school's bus monitor eventually went in to check on her. The girls had no food. The school's staff called the mom, and she came in to meet with their support folks. She explained the whole story, including the fact that they had been evicted and had no fixed place to live.

Dillard helped her with social services and extra food, Baptiste indicated. But the mother was adamant to support the five girls, come what may, and she was determined never to let them be split up. The school helped them get stabilized, but the teachers feared for what would occur in the upcoming summer months. Baptiste reported that it was "not as uncommon a situation with a lot of our parents as I wish it was." And she wonders what would happen to kids like this wonderful little girl if her teachers weren't able to pay close attention and, on occasion, intervene.

THE CENTRALITY OF EFFECTIVE EDUCATION FOR ALL

It may be that the loss and marginalization—the "relegation"—of a significant, if often troubled or jeopardized, segment of the community is the core of Goldsboro's economic and social challenge. Looking broadly and over the arc of time, that is how Shirley Edwards sees it: "Until education is offered to every child exactly as if he was our own," she explains, "we are going to be plagued with poverty, crime, poor health, hunger, and homelessness." She continues:

> The largest ongoing cause of entrenched poverty in Wayne County, I'm certain, is the lack of a quality education being offered and meaningfully directed to every child. The impact is layered here year after year and generation after generation. Schoolhouses have had their doors open, but there was no real quality education for every student offered. It has meant that the poor in this county have never been offered the real chance that they deserve. A decent education system just doesn't say "some of these kids are problems or they are having difficulties so I won't deal with them, I'll just teach the rest." A good system tries to reach every one of them. I've been in the schools a lot, for many, many years. The truth is we lose perhaps 25 percent of them. We expect to lose them and it doesn't matter to us. And then they act out, and create problems, and then they have kids of their own and we end up doing the same thing over and over again. By the age of eighteen a lot of them are expelled, or gone, or checked out completely. And then we just blame them. The teachers blame them, the principals blame them. It's been happening in Goldsboro for generations. And the absence of a high-quality education for all is linked to every single aspect of what we think of as poverty here—jobs, housing, health, crime, alienation, violence.

As it stands now, too often, Edwards believes, "we have a perception in the schools and in the community at large that you can do anything you want to poor people because they can't fight back, they can't do anything to stop it."

Edwards's conclusions are echoed by another longtime Goldsboro public servant and advocate for the poor, Pat Yates, fifty-two, director of Literacy Connections of Wayne County. Yates's life has been committed to Goldsboro's "second chance" students. "There is every reason for this place to be better off than it is, given its resources—the river, the Air Force, the train," she says. Yates's theory, moved to the language of her own discipline, is that "the underlying cause of the wrenching problems of Wayne County is low literacy." For "literacy," unsurprisingly, Yates adopts a bolder, more encompassing definition: "the ability to function effectively in the world."

> In the old days, in Goldsboro, real literacy wasn't really necessary to get a decent job. Good, family-sustaining jobs weren't dependent on those sorts of skills. But that's all changed. Now Seymour Johnson Air Force Base is not only the largest aggregate employer in the county, but all the workers that serve the base, and, then, all the federal, state, and city and county employers, and the sixty-eight manufacturing companies in the area—all these jobs require analysis, language, and technical skills. But one in ten adults in Wayne County is completely illiterate; one in four reads below the third-grade level; almost 60 percent read below a high school level. This creates a sense among many low-income residents that they're "stuck in Goldsboro"—while the children of many of the more affluent locals end up leaving eastern North Carolina. We end up exporting a lot of folks who could probably make things better. And the county has been comfortable keeping people in their boundaries, leaving them illiterate and disempowered. There is a strong sense of isolation, one person, one group, from the other. . . . I've got mine, that's the end of the issue for me. The people of influence and resources often prefer not to talk about it; they don't really want other people to talk about it either.

STORIES OF RESILIENCE

If an examination of some of the challenges of isolating, concentrated poverty in Goldsboro reveals intense hardship and indignity, it also illuminates inspiring examples of resilience, courage, and selflessness. No cascade of tragedy or torrent of disadvantage seems capable of diminishing the determination and resolve of Esther Robinson, whose eyes, smile, and bearing reveal, perhaps, more strength, soul, and depth than any I've ever witnessed. No wound or torment of "the projects" seems capable of forcing Denise Thomas to succumb to the desperation that regularly surrounds her. Myra Johnson's fears for her kids are real, but they are ultimately surpassed by her attachment to her family and its future, which remains the stoutest feature of her life. Trish Bartlett continues to fight despite past failures and shortcomings and despite barriers of circumstance and social predisposition, because, she notes, she's not a quitter and believes she and her daughter can fashion an enhanced and more comfortable and ennobling life.

In a sense, the selflessness of those who struggle against odds and against ease and societal acclaim and self-benefit to "lighten and enrich the lives of their fellows" is even more difficult to fully digest and encapsulate. Adeen George and her broad circle of allies-in-service at the HGDC Community Crisis Center have dedicated their lives to the often-struggling and jeopardized Webbtown community for nearly four decades. As Sylvia Barnes of the Wayne County NAACP puts it: "Everything they do at the Center is done in love." Reverend George gave up her "day job and retirement plan, to work the toughest streets of Goldsboro decades ago." Her husband thought she had lost her mind. Instead, she had determined to take seriously, and literally, the New Testament commands of service to the impoverished and rejected. Hundreds report that Reverend George and the crisis center staff have actually, not figuratively, saved their lives. "I'm seventy-seven," she says. "I had a stroke in 2005, I know I'm going to die over here." But at the crisis center they feed, still, over 300 broken souls a week. Her motto is from the Psalms: "They that sow in tears shall reap in joy." Reverend George doesn't get discouraged, having "already cried all [her] tears."

Doricia Benton, who runs the Community Soup Kitchen, pushes back against hardship that many find hard to endure. Inspiring hundreds of volunteers to serve thousands of their sisters and brothers, she says that for her, it is simple. "We make it too complicated really, I think we're all meant to help each other," she says. If you have the "goods and the food and the resources, why not share them?" she asks. "The gifts don't belong to me," she says, "I hold them in trust." So she gives the hard-pressed a card with her personal phone number. They ring her up at all hours, usually needing more than just a hot meal. Besides, "food shouldn't be seen as an incentive or a punishment," she explains. "It ought to be a blessing." As one of those Benton serves told us: "She believes in us even when we don't believe in ourselves. There were many days when we wished we were dead, but Ms. Benton's prayers brought us through. She seen something in us we didn't see in ourselves. She seen the best in us. Looking back, we are truly grateful that God placed her in our lives. The seeds [she] planted came up like wildflowers. She is our Good Shepherd. She gives us hope."

The remarkable Pat Yates, of Wayne County's Literacy Connections, has spent a life dedicated to the literally separated and marginalized—those unable to read or to read in English. Yates's pupils include home-grown residents who have struggled for years or decades with functional illiteracy. She also reaches out particularly for her "international folks," often from burgeoning Haitian or Latino or Chinese communities in the county. As a newly reading sixty-two-year-old former school janitor originally from Wausau, North Carolina, explained to me: "There are no teachers in this world like Ms. Pat. . . . Without her Goldsboro is not good for a lot of people like us." Yates struggles against the complacency she often sees in the broader community. The broken families, the intense poverty, the pregnancies, the isolation of those unable to take advantage of the possibilities readily available to others. "These are Wayne County's nasty little secret," Yates says. There are over 500 churches in Wayne County, she reminds me. "Imagine what could happen if each one of those churches adopted just one of these struggling families," she chides. "We need to hold each other accountable," she argues; "we all have a debt of responsibility." Jesus said the poor will always be with us, Yates reports, "but he didn't say we ought to take out the boot and push them down."

Dillard Academy's Danielle Baptiste explains: "When I was in the Air Force, I felt like I was doing a lot to serve my country, but it was nothing like the service I'm doing here." When she sees "the light come on in these kids eyes, it moves [her] soul." Baptiste grew up just across the road from Dillard's tough surroundings. "When I'm able to help one of these troubled kids, who may be homeless or traumatized, it gives my life meaning," she explains. It wears her out sometimes, she concedes, but not often. "I enjoy it and am inspired by it, my husband is great, when it's tough we have a date night," she says. It bothers their son sometimes to see the life many of his classmates have, but he's generous too. Having teachers who care "is especially important for our population, the kids know immediately who really cares about them, the parents do too," she says. They have to believe you care about their kids like they do—"they can see right through you," she reports.

And then there is Shirley Edwards, who spends "all her time, as [she has] for so many years, working on things to help the poor." She concedes her charge is "to try to assure these little girls and boys get the chance they deserve." It would be a lot easier, Edwards recognizes, "to sit on my comfortable couch and blame the poor for their shortcomings, like most folks I know do." But if we could fully educate a lot of these kids, she says, we could save them. Children want to learn. They want to do better, to be better. "Some may be slower to get there," she says, "but it's in all of us as human beings." Edwards is, in many ways, the beating heart of a Goldsboro civic community that is potently stressed but demonstrably resilient. I give her the last word:

I get beaten on the head about all of this every single day. But I keep coming. I like everybody. I love many. We could defeat poverty here in Wayne County. It's possible. Schools sometimes have to do what parents aren't able to do. In some ways the folks around here who are educated and doing well end up perpetuating the poverty—by the way they treat poor people, at the church, at the county and city governments. These are people who ought to know better.

This work has cost me, to be honest. I gave up everything to do my work at Crossroads. I was married then. My husband used to say, "Don't bring those AIDS people into my house or let them ride in my car." We disagreed. He said, "Don't bring those little hoodlums into my house." We got a divorce. It cost me a marriage. My daughters were raised without a father. I had to drop out of my doctoral program.

But I was inspired by my grandfather. He was a white man who loved poor people. His family had some resources. He called me "baby." He put me up in his tractor seat and we'd drive out to people's places on Friday to bring them food. He'd give me a bag of candy and we'd go around. He was kind to everyone. He never looked down his nose at anyone. He was my hero his whole life. I followed him around. I've seen preachers curse and shoot at each other—he'd talk things over with them and help work things out. He never faltered. He died at 105.

When he was dying he said, "I hear the singing in my head, the most beautiful music I ever heard." Then he passed away. I've always tried to emulate him. He had tragedies. Some of his kids died. He told me, "Baby, the hardest thing that can happen to you is to see your kids die." No matter how bad things get, I think of him and I go on with the work.

I have no deep sense that the church will do anything. But the church is in me. It is habitual. I believe in God, Christ strengthens me. I know we can do these things. I'm a walking, living miracle. I grew up in worship. Prince Charles has nothing to compare with it. That all meant I had to work hard to give back. Otherwise I would have turned into an arrogant little girl. And I couldn't have that.

7

WILKES COUNTY AND MOUNTAIN POVERTY

Mountain poverty is rural and isolated. It is invisible to a lot of the community. We all have our routines. I used to volunteer for Samaritan's kitchen. I'd be shocked when we take meals to people's houses. I was stunned at the neighborhoods we would see. It was like a tour of distress. People would have blankets over the windows, things like I'd never seen, though I've lived here almost my whole life. I was surprised there was such intense poverty three or four miles from my house. But I never went up those roads otherwise.—Tim Murphy, SAFE education coordinator, former high school counselor, Wilkes County, North Carolina

Wilkes County is a great place that has experienced a sort of slow motion disaster the last couple decades.—Bob Taylor, Hospitality House, Boone, North Carolina, shelter serving Wilkes County

Wilkes County echoes little of either Goldsboro or Charlotte. Nestled into the eastern slope of the Blue Ridge Mountains, the county spreads across more than 750 square miles. Its elevation ranges from about 900 feet in the east to over 4,000 feet in the west. Stone Mountain State Park is one of the most popular in North Carolina. The Brushy Mountains track the county's southern border, and the Yadkin River cuts through its central core. The massive Kerr Scott Lake is the largest body of water in the county and has, since its opening in the early 1960s, become a recreational mecca. Wilkes County also serves as host to the internationally renowned music festival Merlefest, held annually at Wilkes Community College and drawing on the locale's ties to bluegrass music and Doc Watson, the festival's founder.

Wilkes County is home to about 69,000 residents. Wilkesboro is the county seat and North Wilkesboro is the county's largest city, though the population of each remains less than 5,000. The county lies eighty miles north of Charlotte and forty-five miles west of Winston-Salem. It is a half-hour drive from Boone, which shares some of Wilkes's beauty and has experienced notably greater economic development because of its university (Appalachian State) and its draw as a tourist attraction.

Wilkes County's racial makeup is distinct from that of most of North

Carolina. Almost 90 percent of county residents are white, fewer than 5 percent are black, and it has a small but growing Hispanic population. Wilkes is a sprawling rural county, in temper, culture, and topography. Its history, expanse, geography, traditions, isolation, and mountain character make it a singular North Carolina community. They likely add to its economic challenges and perhaps lift its prospects, as well.

From the 1930s until the 1990s, Wilkes could boast a surprising array of successful and accomplished industries. Textile, furniture, and mirror factories supported a significant economic base that could readily provide jobs to support middle-income lifestyles for workers without a college or, sometimes, even a high school degree. Lowe's Home Improvement was founded in Wilkes in 1946, making the county home, as well, to much corporate and management-level employment. The Northwestern Bank, one of the state's largest until it was merged with First Union in 1986, was launched and headquartered in the county. The Carolina Mirror Company, founded in the 1930s, was for many years the largest mirror factory in America. Drawing perhaps on some of the county's moonshine traditions, the first NASCAR race took place in Wilkes County. Racing superstar Junior Johnson hailed from the county, and the famed North Wilkesboro Speedway became a potent source of economic thunder by the 1950s. Holly Farms, also located in Wilkesboro, was for decades one of the largest poultry producers in the southeastern United States. In 1989, it was purchased by Tyson Foods, which remains Wilkes County's largest employer.

North Carolina experienced more manufacturing job losses after the adoption of the North American Free Trade Agreement (NAFTA) in 1994 than almost any state.[1] The burden was often felt most potently in industry-dependent communities like Wilkes County. Textile and furniture companies were dramatically affected. Very high percentages of such jobs moved overseas. By the mid-1990s, the Carolina Mirror Company had faltered, resulting in an additional major loss of jobs. In 1996, the North Wilkesboro Speedway closed and the county stopped hosting NASCAR races. Then, in 2003, for a complex and, to many local residents, confusing set of reasons, Lowe's moved its corporate headquarters to Mooresville, North Carolina, a Charlotte suburb—though some significant management functions remain in Wilkesboro. The quick succession of these changes led to what seemed like a seismic shift in the county, shrinking its economic base to a fraction of what it had long been. Between 2000 and 2015, the number of Wilkes County residents employed in manufacturing dropped a staggering 53 percent. A leader we interviewed likened the rapid commercial losses to a "natural disaster without FEMA to assist in picking up the pieces."

The results of these changes have been challenging. Unemployment rates, unsurprisingly, soared in response to major plant closures and recession. In 2010, a breathtaking 15 percent of residents were unemployed. National studies noted Wilkes County's extraordinary losses, since 2000, in median household income, pegging them among the most imposing in the country. About a fifth of county residents now live in poverty. Large numbers of Wilkes County children are poor. Housing, for many residents, has become unaffordable. Drug addiction and dependency have risen to alarming and much-noted levels, again drawing national headlines. Perhaps predictably, large numbers of young, promising residents now choose to leave the county in favor of brighter economic prospects elsewhere. One indication of the flight is that though Wilkes County's high school graduation rate is now above the statewide average, only half as many county residents hold a bachelor's degree as in the state at large—even as North Carolina itself compares poorly in degree-attainment national rankings. Significant numbers of college-educated or college-bound locals leave the county, not to return. The population of Wilkes County is also now, on average, notably older than that of the rest of North Carolina. There are far more residents over fifty than between the ages of twenty and forty.[2]

Michael Cooper, a young lawyer and civic leader who grew up in North Wilkesboro, put it like this: "A lot of folks' prospects got shattered when the old-line industries pulled out of here; they've been on the losing end for a long time and feel like they've had the shit kicked out of them." Many residents believe that they live on the ruins of an earlier, brighter era. They still "grieve over the community they used to be," Cooper says. So there can be "a sort of crisis of spirit." The county, he continues, "is the kind of place where people exist in small, tight-knit communities—there is a church on every corner and folks stick to their own." The mountain heritage has instilled, deeply, a do-it-yourself attitude that can serve as both blessing and challenge, providing a potent source of strength and resilience against tough fortune but also frequently presenting barriers to public or community-based efforts to address economic struggle.

WILKES'S DISTINCTIVE DEMOGRAPHICS

Wilkes County departs from much of North Carolina in significant ways demographically. Unlike most urban centers, its growth is stagnant. Its total population is not dramatically greater than it was in 1980.

The North Carolina Office of State Budget and Management estimates that Wilkes's population reached its peak in 2015 and will essentially remain at current levels for the next two decades. As indicated, Wilkes is also overwhelmingly non-Hispanic white at 88 percent, while 4 percent is black, and 6 percent is Hispanic. North Carolina is 21 percent African American and 9 percent Hispanic statewide.[3]

Wilkes County also has, as I suggested, a far higher percentage of adult residents who have, at most, a high school diploma than the rest of the state. Fifty-one percent of county adults have a high school education at most, compared with 38.5 percent in North Carolina generally. Starkly, only 15 percent of Wilkes County residents over twenty-five have a college degree. The state rate (30 percent) is double that. A substantially higher percentage of women in Wilkes (52 percent) have some form of postsecondary degree or college experience than men (46 percent).

EDUCATIONAL ATTAINMENT

Income and earnings in Wilkes County are low, and often very low, compared with those in the state. Residents face both a shrunken economy and, ultimately, one that is markedly less generous than that of their Tar Heel counterparts. Median household income in Wilkes has historically been lower than state averages. But in the last fifteen years, household income has fallen at a noticeably steeper rate in Wilkes than across North Carolina, so the gap has significantly widened. The Pew Charitable Trust's Stateline initiative reported in 2015 that since 2000, Wilkes County's median household income dropped 30.4 percent, compared with 12.8 percent for the state. The Wilkes County figure was said to be one of the very highest county income losses in the nation.[4]

The most recent Census Bureau estimates, happily, suggest that Wilkes County's income may be on the rise. The 2015 one-year estimate, released in September 2016, found a potent leap to $40,919, which is above the previous year's $30,743 marker. This may foreshadow a welcome upswing, finally beginning to put behind recession and unemployment-driven damages. But smaller communities are also disproportionately affected by modest changes, so it will take several years to see if the optimistic trend holds. Still, at present, 38 percent of all households in the county have an income of less than $30,000, and only 10 percent of households have incomes of $100,000 or more, compared with 20 percent statewide. At every educational level, state median earnings are greater than the county's. Those with graduate or professional degrees

Graph 16. Level of education, Wilkes County

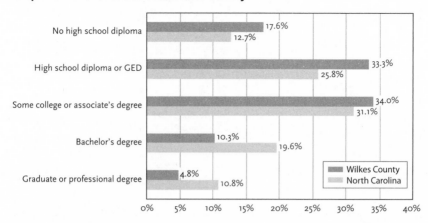

Source: U.S. Census Bureau, 2012–2016 American Community Survey

Graph 17. Median household income, Wilkes County, 1969–2016

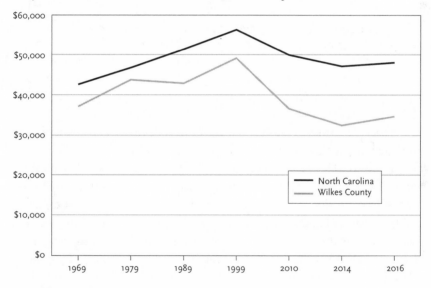

Note: All in 2016 dollars
Sources: U.S. Census Bureau, 1970, 1980, 1990, and 2000 Decennial Census;
2006–2010, 2010–2014, and 2012–2016 American Community Survey

Graph 18. Poverty rate by decade, Wilkes County, 1970–2016

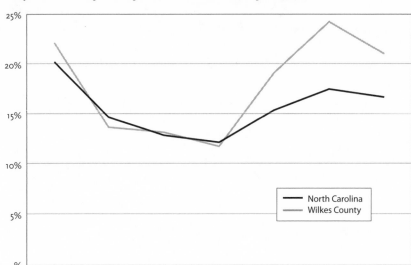

Sources: U.S. Census Bureau, 1970, 1980, 1990, and 2000 Decennial Census; 2006–2010, 2010–2014, and 2012–2016 American Community Survey

in Wilkes earn $18,000 less at the median than their state counterparts—a 31 percent pay reduction. Wilkes is unable to reward attainment in higher education to the same extent as the rest of the state.

Poverty, of course, echoes income. One-fifth of Wilkes residents, in total, live below the federal poverty threshold. Almost a third of all children are poor. The rate is even higher for black and Hispanic kids. The county's poverty rate is demonstrably higher than North Carolina's rate for children, adults, seniors, women, and men. It wasn't always so. During the 1980s and 1990s, the state and county poverty rates were roughly equivalent. In the mid-2000s, Wilkes County's poverty rate began to climb rapidly. By 2014, the county rate exceeded the state's by almost seven percentage points.

Five percent of full-time, year-round workers in Wilkes County live in poverty (North Carolina's rate is 3.5 percent). Twenty-seven percent of part-time or part-year workers are impoverished (compared with 23 percent in North Carolina). Almost half of the population (47 percent) of Wilkes County earns less than 200 percent of the federal poverty standard, a rough measure of the working poor.

Housing in Wilkes County is typically older than that of the state. The county and state have about the same proportion of houses constructed

Graph 19. Age-adjusted drug poisoning deaths per 100,000, by county

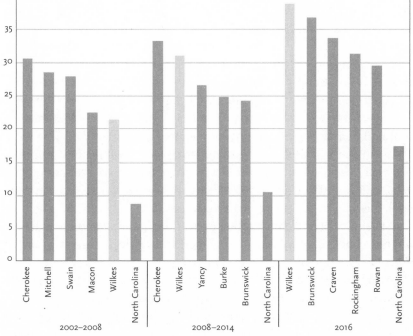

Source: Centers for Disease Control and Prevention

before 1950, but 44 percent of North Carolina's housing was built after 1990. In Wilkes the figure is 31 percent. Thus a significant portion of the county's housing stock is entering its fourth or fifth decade. Wilkes also has a much higher share of mobile homes (27 percent) than the state (13 percent). And in some census tracts, the mobile home rate climbs to over a third of all housing units. About 51 percent of renters in Wilkes pay more that 30 percent of their income for housing. While the number of affordable units has increased since 2000, it has barely kept pace with the expansion in the number of extremely low-income households (making 30 percent or less of area median income), which has almost tripled during that period.[5]

Wilkes is also one of the state's largest counties by size. It contains no major cities. People and services are widely dispersed. Public transportation is limited and fares can be prohibitive. So access to an automobile is imperative in order to commute to work and to conduct routine business. But in the sprawling county, a larger percentage of residents lack access to a vehicle than is true for the rest of the state. Thirty-three percent of households have one vehicle at most, compared with 39 percent for the state, and 7 percent in the county have no vehicle at all. Roughly 29 percent of Wilkes County residents travel more than thirty minutes to get to work. Over half actually work outside the county. Twenty-two percent of low-income workers commute more than fifty miles to work.

Predictably for a rural, manufacturing-based economy, disability rates in Wilkes County are high, 18 percent compared with 14 percent for the state. Fortunately, crime rates are lower in Wilkes than in the state at large and have declined in the last four years. In 2011, Wilkes had an index crime rate of 3,480 per 100,000 people. It declined to 1,861 in 2016. Drug poisoning death rates, though, have placed Wilkes among the top five counties for the state in the last two consecutive six-year periods. In 2016, Wilkes suffered 39 drug deaths per 100,000 residents (adjusted for age), the highest county figure in North Carolina.

Wilkes County's demographic, educational, and economic patterns often play out roughly in the lived experiences of local residents, young and old. Structures and barriers of hardship, hunger, illness, deprivation, stagnation, narrowed opportunity, threatened unemployment, abuse, addiction, diminished hope, and desperation harrow at close hand. De-termined acts of resilience, courage, obligation, commitment, gener-osity, and idealism instruct powerfully as well. As ever, they describe in brighter and more vivid tones than statistics can usually muster. Samples are only that, of course. But they illustrate, in ways that numbers fail to reveal, the nature of economic challenge in Wilkes County.

WAYNE HARRIS

Tina Krause is the executive director of Hospitality House in Boone, North Carolina. Her agency serves seven counties, including Wilkes, pro-viding food, shelter, counseling, and therapy to clients facing poverty, personal crises, and homelessness. Krause also lives in Wilkesboro, where she previously helped lead the local United Way offices. To Krause, Wayne Harris represents both the character and the hardship repeatedly found in Wilkes County.

"Wayne is a quiet and humble man," she says, "not that different than most folks here." Over the course of several years, he slowly moved closer and closer to homelessness "due to life circumstances that any of us or our neighbors might face," she says; "he is a good man who has had a great struggle." After years of labor growing up and working on a farm in Wilkes County and doing a long stint at Tyson, Harris experienced severe and continuous lower back pain and worrisome blood clotting in his legs

that made it tough for him to walk, let alone work full time. Homelessness, Krause notes, can look markedly different when you stare it in the
face. Harris explained:

> I love working. I've worked all my life, since I was a little boy. But
> after a while I was in so much pain, I couldn't handle it anymore.
> I didn't have the strength to keep going or to do the job like I wanted
> to do. I just prayed that the Good Lord would keep me going. That
> He would show me a way.
>
> I didn't have no insurance to take care of myself, so I just kept
> on going. Then I couldn't work no more. It broke my heart. To be
> honest, it was embarrassing. As a man, I'm supposed to take care of
> my family. I'm supposed to be the provider, go to work and take care
> of my own. I always done that. And I was trying to be strong because
> I believe in the Bible. But after a while, the worry really works on
> you. I kept praying and asking the Lord to let me get better so I could
> take care of my son and my three grandchildren.
>
> [After he lost his housing], it was deep down in the fall and I slept
> outside under a bridge for a while. I was very disappointed in myself
> and it was hard to understand how it got that bad. But I guess it's a
> part of life we have to go through sometimes. There were times I was
> really scared. I just kept praying and holding on to my faith. It was all
> I had.
>
> I wasn't looking for no charity. I just wanted to get my health
> better and find a home. Then I could start to help others again.[6]

Harris's path wasn't unfamiliar to Krause. Many of the wounded folks
served at Hospitality House struggle greatly with problems of addiction
or mental illness. On the first visit I made to the facility, an immensely
distressed client was threatening suicide in the parking lot. On the day
of my second interview, another long-term, struggling, vulnerable client
had ended his life. Krause wears her heart and her courage and her un-
ending patience on her sleeve. But she also explains that many clients,
particularly from Wilkes, don't have addiction issues or mental health
problems; they have just seen the bottom fall out. When Wayne Harris
walked through the door, Krause says, you could tell he was in crisis. "Our
first job was to get him the health care he needed," she says, then they
could deal with his challenges of income, savings, work, and housing.
Eventually, Harris got an operation and the necessary treatment for his
blood clots. The Hospitality House staff also helped him apply for disability payments. Unsurprisingly, he feels like they saved his life. "Hos-

pitality House gave me a miracle," he once told the local newspaper. "They're like my family, I finally made it home," he said.[7] For Krause, though, too many others slip between the cracks. "This is a low-income county," she explains, "with all that entails." In too many instances, that includes domestic violence, struggles with addiction, family dysfunction, closed doors to treatment, closed doors to opportunity, and closed doors to hope. As she puts it, "A lot of folks, in the community I love, have a lot of things to unpack." Still, Krause, like Harris, can't bear the thought of leaving. "I have a heart for Wilkes County and for where they are," she says. They are, "by God, Wilkes County." They "take care of their own." As best they can.

Gina Nixon has not had to endure the terrors of homelessness. But like thousands in Wilkes County, she has repeatedly struggled to support and care for her kids and extended family while facing an array of health and economic difficulties that would swamp most of us. Fear and poverty haunt her daily life.

Nixon, fifty-three, grew up in Hickory and moved to Wilkes County in 1990. Her first husband had passed away at a young age, and she felt obliged to help care for his parents, who lived in Wilkes. When Nixon's daughter was eleven, she was diagnosed with type 1 diabetes. A couple of years later, when Nixon applied for work at Tyson, she learned that she was diabetic as well. Nonetheless, she worked for years on the main line at the chicken plant—though, she explains, the work was "nasty."

Last October, Nixon had a heart attack. Though she hadn't experienced any chest pain, she had a hard time getting her breath and lost all her energy. By the time she got to the hospital, her hand had gone numb. But she got there in time to be treated and managed a slow recovery.

Since then, Nixon has worked in home health care. She is paid $8.35 an hour and her hours are capped at thirty, so she doesn't receive health benefits. Her second husband now works out of Elkin as a truck driver. He pulls a twelve-hour shift, seven days on and seven days off. He is paid a little more, per hour, than she is. They own a single-wide trailer that they can park on her husband's parents' lot. Their children are grown and live in Wilkes as well. Nixon's daughter also works in home health care. On bad days at work, Nixon has a hard time breathing since her heart attack. She gets limited health care through a local community health center. She can't pay for the course of rehabilitation they have prescribed.

Food stamps help but are not enough to cover their grocery bills. "I need to eat right to manage my diabetes," she says. "I start to feel sick if I don't get enough to eat." She and her husband "buy a lot of Banquet

TV dinners, we eat what we can afford to buy." Junk food costs less, she says. "We eat potatoes and pasta and hamburger helper, I don't get a lot of vegetables, but they take what we get on the EBT card," she reports.

"If our car gets tore up, like it does sometimes, I just cry," she admitted. "My husband lost his job for a few months a couple of years ago and we really, really struggled." Sometimes there was nowhere to turn when the food stamps ran out. Back then, she says, "we were so broke we couldn't even afford to pay attention."

Nixon's biggest worry, now, is her heart. She is able to see a general practitioner twice a year, and the health center helps with her insulin. She buys strips to monitor her diabetes at Walmart, where she can afford them. "I live in fear because of my heart, both my mom and dad died of heart attacks," she says. Her home health care work can be stressful physically, but she can't afford not to work. She can't really pay for her medications as it is. Last year, combined, Nixon and her husband made less than $20,000, though they hope to fare better this year as a result of his job. She appreciates that her daughter and son can take advantage of the sliding-scale payments for their family's health care. "But it needs to be lower," she thinks, "a lot of times they can't afford it." Housing and transportation "eat people alive here." My kids "have to drive all over the county," she says. Both Nixon and her daughter "have to pay our own gas" for the home health care work. And the hours logged driving across the county to get to a patient's house "doesn't count toward your hours."

"I do my best not to feel stressed," she says. "I trust in the Lord." Nixon has been a committed member of Harvest Time Christian Ministry for over twenty years. Her kids went to school there, and her husband has, on occasion, worked for the ministry part time. When they've had a "real hard time of it, the Church has helped us out," she explains. "But I feel like I should retire to avoid getting a heart attack," she admits. "I feel that way, but I just can't afford to do it."

POVERTY AND DOMESTIC VIOLENCE

Tina Krause indicates that the Hospitality House's internal research reveals that over 80 percent of the men served by the shelter and over 90 percent of the women they seek to assist, no matter what the immediate cause of their homelessness might be, struggle principally to cope with a major trauma or set of traumatic events. For the women, it is frequently spousal or sexual abuse. For the men, it is often child abuse. Janice Trine is not a resident at Hospitality House, principally because she inherited a somewhat ancient mobile home from her father. But her experiences demonstrate the pattern.

Trine is fifty. At present, she says, "I'm just pulling at strings." The only assistance she receives is food stamps. She was much distressed to report that, last month, she had to ask her daughter for $25 to help with her medicine. She tries hard not to burden her daughter. "I can't see well enough to read a lot of things now, like the numbers on the telephone; reading glasses aren't strong enough," she says. "I owe the hospital over $50,000 that I just don't have the money to pay, but I keep getting small strokes and seizures," she says. Trine has no health insurance, no Medicaid, no job, no disability. "I'm stuck, really stuck," she sighs.

Trine worked as a cashier at Bojangles in Wilkes County for over a decade. "Ms. Bojangles" is what everybody called her. Then she had a stroke at home one night. Several follow-on seizures came quickly thereafter. As a result, she had to quit working. "I'd been employed full time since I was sixteen," she says. She owns a 1987 trailer house and a 1978 pickup truck. She tries to keep them both up, but it is a challenge. She pays $150 a month for lot rental, $120 for power, $42 for the telephone, and $40 for car insurance. "That's hard to manage with no job," she notes. She keeps getting turned down for disability benefits. She gets some health care through the Foothills Free Clinic. The folks there are wonderful, she reports. Like family. She cleans the facility and takes height and weight measurements at the clinic on a regular basis as a volunteer because she's grateful for their care.

Trine was a victim of intense domestic abuse. Her husband assaulted her for decades. He returned to find her after he was released from prison seven years ago. He held her captive in her house for over four hours, inflicting vicious beatings. She reports that he "thrashed her very nearly" to death. "I had a restraining order but it didn't matter, the deputies were no help," she says. "I was married to him for more than twenty years and he abused both me and my daughters the whole time." She doesn't have a restraining order anymore and thinks they are useless. "I won't go back to the magistrate," she emphasizes; "I had enough of that business." But she says she does now have a gun. "I won't be beat no more. I live in fear every single day of my life. I can't come out on my front porch. But I won't be beat no more. Not ever."

The stress has had its impact. "I can't deal with the public anymore, though I did it every day for many years." Counseling helps a little, she says. But she also forgets people and says sometimes that "makes her feel like a fool," she admits. Still, she believes you just keep on trying, you keep going. "But now I'm so low down I can't really do for myself," she says. Trine has been living in her trailer for almost twenty years. She got married and had her first child at sixteen. She earned her GED in 2007. She goes to the Foothills Free Clinic once a month, and her care-givers help with her medicines. "I'd like to have enough money to pay my bills, and what I owe. I don't want a fine house or nice clothes. But a lot of times I can't come up with the $30 I need for my medicine. Then I just have to endure the pain until I throw up. I'm fifty years old now. Only eight years of my life have been free of abuse. One of my friends told me, 'You were born into your stress.' I guess that's right. I still get the night terrors anytime I hear the gravel flying from a car coming up the road. I don't know how to handle it."

"NO ROAD UP"

Tricia Shaw is a thirty-three-year-old single mother who lives in North Wilkesboro. She has two children, a twelve-year-old-son and a daughter who is two. "Double trouble" as she puts it. Great kids. Shaw graduated from high school in Wilkes County. Her father lived there and her mother resided in Virginia Beach. So Shaw grew up in both places. She has an array of medically related credits from Wilkes Community College and hopes to get a university degree.

Shaw explains that her parents lived in poverty, so she hasn't received any economic support from them. She began work at Trellis Farms in Wilkesboro in her early twenties as a temporary employee. Earlier, she had frequently put in long hours at fast food restaurants to make sure her son never went hungry. She might go without meals, she said, but not her son. Never. At Trellis, Moore quickly became full time, and now, for eight years, she has been a line supervisor in the boning room. It's a decent job and she is well treated, valued as an employee. She explains that "it pays the bills," even if there is no room to spare. Her son attends an after-school program and "skills camp" run through her church. He likes it. Her daughter attends a good day care program at Lincoln Heights School. A public voucher program helps her pay the fare. Shaw has health care, as do her kids, though her job does not include retirement benefits. She has a doctor her children can see regularly at Wilkes Pediatric. She has, for several years, been part of the Wilkes Circle of Care program, receiving advice and support and mentorship from committed volunteer Circles members. Circles is a big help in navigating life in Wilkes County, she says. "You can get help here, there is quite a bit of assistance here in the county and there are a lot of good-hearted folks, but you've got to know where to dig," she notes.[8]

Shaw is, basically, in "a good spot," she says. She and her kids live in a subsidized apartment in the Riverview Housing facility in Wilkesboro. Her rent is an affordable $135 a month, but when she works overtime or gets a raise, her rent goes up, so it doesn't seem to lift her prospects. "I frequently work six days a week," she reports, but "don't really get any more money by doing it because I lose it in rent." Her electricity bill is high, or "ridiculous," as she puts it, often more than $350 a month, "though I keep it cold," she says. They have three bedrooms, fortunately, but the building is very old. The "heating hasn't been replaced in forever and it feels like the wind is blowing inside." Still, it is a decent place to live. And it is also racially diverse, so she and her kids feel safe and included there, and it's not dangerous. Both of her kids "grow like weeds," she says. A twelve-year-old boy always needs something. In middle school, "every day it's something new." Kids are expensive.

"It is hard being a single parent," she says. There isn't enough for her son to do, and he is getting to an age where that is more worrisome. But Shaw's biggest concern is that there seems to be no road up. Her job is okay, but it offers no career path upward. No matter how hard she works or how well she does, there is no promotion possible. And there is no retirement program she can rely on. She has a car, a 2008. It has 60,000 miles, and when something goes wrong, it throws everything off. And she doesn't have enough money for any kind of new one.

What she really wishes is that she could go to college. Then she would have a future, rather than just skimming by. But her job, since it's hands-on supervisory, does not include any possibility of part-time work. "So, I am afraid that, if I tried to go to school, I wouldn't be able to take care of my kids," she notes. "I barely make ends meet now," she says. There are some chances you just can't afford to take.

She concedes that life can sometimes be challenging for a black family in Wilkes County. Her son has had some unreasonable problems at school, things that perhaps wouldn't happen in other parts of the state and shouldn't happen in Wilkesboro either. And at work, people are constantly telling her, given her supervisory role, that they are "shocked she has made it this far." She thinks the "Hispanics probably get it worse." Still, there are generous folks in Wilkes, too. And the churches try to help. But even if you have a stable job, a job that basically pays the bills, it is possible to feel trapped, unable to work your way out of the bottom rung.

And diminished opportunity can crush even if you are not facing home-lessness and starvation. "People need to be able to work toward a better circumstance," she explains.

THE IMPACT AND CHALLENGE OF
POVERTY IN WILKES COUNTY

Those who work in Wilkes County's broad charitable and social ser-vices community echo repeating themes.

Heather Murphy and her colleagues at the Health Foundation play a potent role in broad-based community efforts to improve the health and well-being of the residents of Wilkes County. The foundation itself has become a rare and effective vehicle for organization, coordination, and engagement, defining health care meaningfully and pervasively as something more than mere visits to the doctor's office. Murphy seems obsessed with the reality that "a child born today in Wilkes County is likely to live four and a half years less than a child born in North Caro-lina's healthiest county." Fortunately, she makes sure that lots of others become obsessed with that stark reality as well.

Murphy emphasizes, of course, poverty's central link to the "social determinants of health." She begins, as do many, with its frequent invisi-bility. "My family and I live in a middle-class neighborhood," she says. Last year, the dog got loose for a while. As she and her young son walked a mile down the road, her son saw a classmate at the edge of the road. "Why is he standing on the porch of that old shack?" he asked. "And yet my church, like lots of others, takes their youth group to Haiti," she notes. "It is a lot easier to explain to your kids why such wrenching hardship happens in Haiti than why it happens here." Gary Newman, who later took us through abandoned buildings where squatters live and up steep, almost impassable roads that serve to shield similar shelters from view, echoed Murphy's point: "I know the folks in my church would have no idea that this is here, you go to the lake or the club or the football game in Charlotte, there's no reason to drive up into these hills."

Heather Murphy has taken health outreach explorations beyond the usual parameters. "We've gone out to find those with the lived experi-ence of poverty," she says. Murphy spoke movingly of her conversations with Robert Jones, a man in his late thirties. He explained that his most important goal was to make sure his son didn't have the same life he had. "I don't want my child to grow up to be like me," he said. "I've had a tough time." He said he can't even work at McDonald's anymore. He gets too nervous being around people. He is ashamed that he cannot support his family. Murphy soon learned that Jones had suffered two heart attacks and had trouble getting his breath. His medical traumas were related to earlier dental problems he had experienced. He had no teeth and had developed infections in his gums. Stomach illness then developed.

"I noticed he was always tapping his two fingers," Murphy said. Three fingers were missing. Jones had worked for years at a sawmill, always in pain because of his teeth. One day the pain was so bad he took extra pills to make it stop. He then had an accident, and three fingers were cut off. "His life had been crushed," Murphy said, "because he couldn't get dental care." Like Jones, she is adamant to assure his son doesn't face a similar fate.

Shellie Bowlin is the program director of SAFE Spot, a child protection and advocacy center in Wilkes County. Poverty and economic hardship press hard on SAFE's clients. The link to unemployment and to wages is direct. "A family is doing okay, but then he loses his job," she says. Stress rises. The couple "get pissed at each other." He hits her. Then he goes to jail. So she is left in an even tougher spot. In the meantime, the agency budget gets cut and private donations taper off because there are fewer resources. "The economy can be the biggest cause of the ills we exist for and have to combat, but then the economy also makes it harder for us to provide the services we need." Wilkes has a lot of community pride, Bowlin reminds me. And people don't like to acknowledge problems of poverty and abuse. But the truth is, she explains, "we have to focus harder on our poverty problems in Wilkes County or we won't be able to deal with child abuse."

Fred Brason is the executive director of Project Lazarus in Moravian Falls. Brason works at the focal point of the county's much-noted addiction challenges. "This is a remarkable community," he says. Very prideful. "We all know hardship, we all know each other, we're entrepreneurial, we always have been," he says. For some, the present illicit commodities are not that different than earlier moonshine. "Moonshine, marijuana, medicine—they're just different commodities," he indicates. You can't separate the county's designation, nationally, for income loss from its parallel rankings for addiction. "There's no use pointing fingers," Brason says. "We have a real problem and we can either make it better or we can make it worse." Brason is dogged to make it better. "I spend a lot of time back in the hollers, and we've always been pretty insular," he notes. But being insular didn't matter as much when "daddy could go to work in textiles without finishing high school," he says. "We're independent, we like to do it our way, but now there's a bigger cost for that."

A lot of folks Brason knows used to log. "What do you do when that gets displaced?" he asks. The county is also "so spread out, there's no core here, no transportation, no great business to bring in," he explains. "Even the kids often think there's no future for them here, so the only coping method is escape," he says; "if I get $20 for food it's gone in a day, better to spend it on meth." That's why meaningful treatment work has to be about relationship, he says. No outside warriors here, for Brason; "you have to meet people where they are."

John Triplett has run Wilkes Ministry of Hope, sponsored by the Brushy Mountain Baptist Association, for nine years. The almost entirely volunteer-based faith ministry has served over 7,000 Wilkes County families—mostly with food but also with vouchers for rent and power and gasoline. Triplett also makes sure the agency can help with emergency transportation. The ministry typically sees about forty families a day at a generously donated facility on Elkin Highway in North Wilkesboro. Local churches of an array of denominations are heavily involved. The ministry relies on at least twenty-five volunteers a week, with responsibilities rotating among church memberships. Much of the food distributed comes from Second Harvest Food Bank in Winston-Salem, but nearly half is produced in local food drives. Hope Ministry also runs a toy store that is famous across the county, allowing impoverished parents to buy Christmas presents for their kids, paying about ten cents on the dollar. Last Christmas, it served over 5,000 children. The morning of our visit, before the ministry opened, a desperate family was waiting in the parking lot when Triplett arrived. They explained that their two daughters had not eaten in a day. Triplett opened early and brought them a box of food in the parking lot, giving them instructions to come back in the late afternoon after the kids had been to school. "We mean to be a place of warmth and safety and friendship," he said. Then people will come back.

Triplett has seen much. "Wilkes County was hit real hard about ten years ago; we're still reeling from it," he says. But he thinks people have had to "get used to it, to not having as much as they used to." Everybody is included in that, he says, his family too. The county just needs higher-paying jobs for people who haven't gone to college. "Wilkes has Tyson, but that's almost it, we still have some Lowe's jobs, but most of them require a bachelor's degree or at least community college," he says. There's no magic to it, he argues, Wilkes needs more jobs that meet people where they actually are. "We need to concentrate more on the people who come in here," he says, "the working poor." "My grandmother worked in a furniture factory from the time she was fourteen until she was seventy," he laments. It was a good job. "It wasn't going to make you rich, but it paid decent wages," he says. "Now that factory is gone," he sighs, "and so are all the rest."

Bob Taylor from Hospitality House says, "Wilkes County is a great place that has experienced sort of a slow-motion disaster the last couple decades." It is rocked by a lack of decent-paying jobs, a lack of affordable housing, forty- and fifty-year-old trailers, and thousands of folks hanging on by a thread. Transportation and day care that working people can afford are great challenges, he says. Maggie McCann from Crisis Ministry at St. Paul's in Wilkesboro sees the same focus. All the churches could tell you, she says, of so many people who can't afford their utilities and rent. A lot of times they are hardworking people who have just gotten "thrown off"—by a doctor bill or a car falling apart. Most of the residents she sees "just don't have enough to get by," she says. They are usually "still positive about improving their lives, but some are beaten down, depressed about their lives," McCann says. Even with a supposed economic recovery, it "seems like things have gotten worse," she says; "we're a lot busier at Crisis Ministry." St. Paul's "tries hard, but it can't do enough."

Denise Monaghan, a beloved "miracle worker" at the Wilkes County Health Department, worries that even their best efforts can't always meet people's most basic needs. "We make them move through so many hoops—do this here, and then go across the county to get that, come back in three days for this—sometimes they even have to go to Boone to get help, and we also make them work," she notes. Sometimes it isn't really possible to do it all. "We're splintered and spread out," she says. And "truth is, even a lot of our county workers are on food stamps themselves, just a few days away from poverty in their own lives," she reminds me. This is the "most beautiful place in the world," she says. "But we don't have the infrastructure to deal with people's challenges." Tim Murphy of SAFE adds, "This is a great community, lots and lots of people want to help, but they're all moving in different directions; we're like 300 mules in a field with none hitched up."

Tina Krause, Hospitality House's director, relates the challenges of the county not only to her clients but to her family as well. "My middle son was accepted to four universities, but, like almost all his friends, he chose to stay in Wilkes County at first," she explains. "Putting it as elegantly as possible, it is important for our kids here to see themselves as capable of doing something beyond Wilkes County." A lot of them may have to leave, but "if enough leave, maybe a lot more will come back." If families and teachers don't see them as capable of it, "they won't stretch them," she says.

"My son was at community college and working two minimum-wage jobs, forty-seven hours a week," Krause says. "It was heartbreaking to pack him up and send him across the state to thrive, but now I see his self-esteem soaring, his excitement is contagious," she says. She still wishes "he was here to cut my wood and walk the dog and lift my heart, but he needed to go." "I think he'll come back," she says, "but he needed to challenge himself."

On the other hand, Krause described a tiny event the day her son left Wilkes County:

> I left for the shelter before he'd finished packing up. On the way to work it occurred to me he'd likely need some money for gas and I hadn't left him any. I didn't have time to drive back home, so I turned into the gas station I knew he'd pull into before he left. They didn't know him, but I said, "My son will be coming by and he'll have a mattress on top of his car. When he gets here, will you go out and give him twenty bucks worth of gas?" "Sure," they said. I never wondered or hesitated for a moment. This is Wilkes County.

Michael Cooper is a young lawyer and author immensely tied to his native Wilkes County. At perhaps some financial sacrifice, he was determined to move back home. The hardship he sees pervading much of the county makes him lose sleep. His determination to help his hometown and overcome the challenges, though, is more than a match for his apprehension. Cooper steps back a shade, looking broadly. "What is happening here was always going to happen," he says. "In Appalachian areas, people have traditionally been less well educated, or at least less well formally educated," he notes. "But that didn't always hurt as much as it does now," he concedes. Then NAFTA came along, as well as globalization and other trade deals. And the jobs that could be had that pay a good wage and don't require higher education flew away. "It is true here in Wilkes, it is true in a lot of places—Hickory, Sparta—it is what is happening all over southern Appalachia," he points out. Lowe's and the speedway may have made it worse, but "it was coming, regardless." That means "this is our opportunity to help lead the way," he says. "I think, if we're serious, we also know that there is no savior who is going to come in and rescue us; there is not going to be another Lowe's or a Google or a bunch more Tysons," Cooper adds. "The next economy is going to come from the locals," he thinks. Some young folks are making progress in interesting ways. They don't get headlines like a plant closure. "Inviting folks in won't do it," he says, "we've got to do it for ourselves. . . . We need to increase local democracy and engagement and community commitment." And "I don't mean getting involved with the city council," he says, "I mean believing in, investing in, creating, and paying back this great community."

8

IMMIGRANTS AND DREAMERS: UNDOCUMENTED STUDENTS AND HIGHER EDUCATION IN NORTH CAROLINA

My high school guidance counselor asked me, "Ricsy, do you have a social security number, are you an illegal?" She used those words. It was at that moment it hit me what it meant to be an "illegal" in this country. I said, "What's a social security number?" She said that's what lets you get financial aid. "I don't have one," I said. I was lucky, later, to get two scholarships that didn't require a social. There are hardly any of those. My sister still can't go to college at all because she doesn't have a social security number and she has to pay out-of-state tuition, which is very expensive. A social is a number that doesn't define anyone. It doesn't show what you can do, what you're capable of, what you've worked hard to get. It sure doesn't define me, it doesn't determine what I'm able to accomplish.
—Ricsy Sanchez, undocumented North Carolinian, associate degree, Davidson County Community College

Marco Cervantes is now in his early twenties. His family came to the United States from a tiny town in Mexico when he was a baby. He has lived in or near Carrboro, North Carolina, since he was two. Marco has five siblings. His youngest brother was born at UNC Hospital in Chapel Hill, so he is an American citizen. Marco and the rest of his family are undocumented, though Marco had, at the time of our conversations, enjoyed some protections under the program known as Deferred Action for Childhood Arrivals (DACA).

Cervantes went to pre-kindergarten in Carrboro and then elementary and middle schools in Chapel Hill. His family moved frequently, from apartment to apartment, though always staying in Orange County. Through middle school, Cervantes says, he "felt like a normal, regular kid." Like most of the young guys he knew, he "had a lot of friends."

In his grade school days, he played soccer and football. Eventually, though, he was drawn more powerfully to boxing. He was pretty good at it, learning largely through an on-campus youth program at UNC. It took lots of energy and attention and strength. He had full doses of each.

Still, Cervantes, to his surprise, liked science and mathematics even more than boxing. "I knew even when I was real young that I wanted to be an engineer," he says. "I always loved to build things." And as with boxing, he was good at what he liked. Math and science came readily. One of his teachers asked him to join the AVID program—Advancement Via Individual Determination. AVID is a school-supported national effort aimed at "closing the achievement gap by preparing all students for college readiness."

"Since I did well in math," Cervantes explains, "I was put in the advanced-level classes with the better students." He was the only Hispanic in the select class. That eventually became true for most of his classes. "It motivated me to do my best," he says. Things worked pretty well. He had a few bumps in the road, like other students, but "I made good grades and my parents were always really supportive."

Cervantes's freshman year at Chapel Hill High School was more of the same. He had a broadening circle of friends, many of whom were non-Hispanic. He participated increasingly heavily in AVID. Like the others in the preparatory program, he began to obsess about going to college.

But sophomore year, when he tried to sign up for driver's education like all his friends were doing, he learned, for the first time, that his parents were undocumented. When he couldn't apply for a driver's license, everyone else knew as well. "Since I was the only one who couldn't drive, I sort of stopped getting invited places," he says. He wasn't sure if it was intentional or just kids now going in different directions. But whichever it was, for a sixteen-year-old, "it was heartbreaking."

The next fall the gap grew wider. Everyone around him talked relentlessly about college. It was, after all, Chapel Hill. Even students who had never taken high school seriously or worked anywhere close to as hard as he had or made grades anything like his As were making university plans. Cervantes's school counselor explained, though, that because Cervantes was undocumented, if he went to college, he would be forced to pay out-of-state tuition rates and he would be deemed ineligible for financial aid. For Cervantes and his family, of course, no matter how hard they worked, paying out-of-state tuition without financial aid was impossible.

And the nonresident business seemed odd to him. He had lived in North Carolina essentially all his life, but he was to be treated as a nonresident. His youngest brother could qualify for resident rates because he had been born in Chapel Hill and was, therefore, a citizen. A new kid he'd met who had moved to Chapel Hill from Virginia only a couple of months earlier could qualify as a resident, but Cervantes, despite having lived in North Carolina for over sixteen years, was excluded. And he would stay excluded even if he lived in North Carolina for eighty years. "The place where I had lived my whole life, and had given everything, and where I'd tried to be a good kid doing what you're supposed to do, sort of said it wanted to kick me out, like I was a bad person," he says. It didn't seem possible to him.

He had also lost most of his friends from the advanced classes. A lot of the kids he'd hung out with since he had learned he was undocumented had already given up on school, knowing they were not going to be allowed to go to college anyway. So what difference did it make? "You might as well get a job doing construction or landscaping or something," they'd say. "You might as well get started. What's the use of fooling around with classes that won't do you any good?" they'd ask.

Marco Cervantes, though, is both stubborn and optimistic. Unwilling to give up on his dream of becoming an engineer, he applied to both Elon University and North Carolina A&T. He was quickly accepted to both. Elon's tuition, he soon learned, was prohibitively expensive. At A&T, he was told that unless he could produce documentation of his citizenship, he would be required to pay nonresident rates, which were then more than $30,000 a year for room and board. So Cervantes began bussing tables at Elmo's Diner in Carrboro as his friends went off to college.

Still, he didn't accept his circumstances passively. Late in high school, he joined Immigrant Youth Forum, seeking to change the hand he had been dealt. "At first we mainly just supported each other," he says. But eventually they started speaking out and coming out for themselves and their friends.

One of the things they realized quickly was that a lot of people in North Carolina expected them to be ashamed of themselves and their families. But to Cervantes that was never a possibility. His parents were the strongest, most selfless, most courageous people he had ever known. No exaggeration. His parents, he knew, were heroes, not scoundrels or criminals. "They had sacrificed everything for my brothers and sisters and me, literally everything," he explains. "I loved them, of course, but I admired them greatly too," he says. "I still do, every day."

When Cervantes began speaking out, usually, along with his friends, in front of the post office on Franklin Street in Chapel Hill, he it found it very scary (unlike, say, a boxing match). Larger rallies in Raleigh and then Charlotte were worse. And, at least until he received deferred action from the federal government, there was a broader fear. Being detained and deported would be beyond devastating. As far as he knew, he'd never even been to Mexico (or at least not since he was a baby). He'd long wanted to meet his grandparents, but it was too risky to travel there, so he'd never seen them. He also worried, of course, about his parents. They had told him they approved of his activism, but they couldn't help but worry. Neither could he.

Cervantes was soon forced to learn other unpleasantries as well. He joined the North Carolina Dream Team, a group of young Hispanics like himself who couldn't go to college because the state insists on treating them like strangers, charging them tuition rates as if they had grown up on the slopes of Switzerland. At the time, about a dozen states had passed Dream Acts, allowing students who had lived most of their lives in the state and, typically, had graduated from the state's high schools to pay in-state tuition rates. The North Carolina dreamers tried to lobby local lawmakers to follow suit so that students like Cervantes would be treated the same as everyone else they knew. To that end, in 2012, he attended his first committee meeting at the General Assembly in Raleigh. He was still seventeen.

The committee hearing was an eye-opener. Cervantes told me that witnesses repeatedly castigated Latino immigrants. He hadn't heard people talk about his community like that before. Cervantes didn't speak, feeling too inexperienced. Nonetheless, as the hearing ended, a group of anti-immigration activists approached him. He recounts that they spewed, in various malice-riven phrases, "Get out, can't you see we don't want you and your type here? Go back home. Now." He tells me, "I got scared. I thought they were going to attack us. They acted like they were going to throw us all out physically. They were extremely hateful and threatening. I hadn't spoken. I was just sitting there. I couldn't understand what they were so mad about. They were the ones who had been saying nasty things that weren't true. I thought older people would at least have had some manners."

Since that hearing, Cervantes has had a good deal of experience with demonstrations and speeches and protests. He says he has chosen not to be frightened by folks like those in the committee room. He is also, despite a cascade of challenges, anxious to help those who have had an even tougher time. "So many people I know," he says, "have gotten in trouble because they don't have any future." He wants to work with "kids who are heading for trouble, before they get there," he says. But still, he hasn't been able to go to college. He works hard, often for long hours, but not at wages that would allow him to save anything like the tab required for UNC's nonresident tuition rates. He still wants to be an engineer. He's more than smart enough to pull it off. The K–12 system has even invested specially in him (through the AVID program) to assure that's so. But he can't go to school because of a decision his parents made over two decades ago.

UNDOCUMENTED STUDENTS IN NORTH CAROLINA

Each year more than 2,500 North Carolina high school seniors are undocumented.[1] As a result of policies adopted by the state, all but a relative handful are effectively denied access to higher education. A few years ago, a study found that there were only 27 undocumented students in the entire sixteen-campus University of North Carolina system, as the state's overall undocumented population neared 400,000. Over 46 percent of North Carolina noncitizen children fail to graduate from high school. Only 13.5 percent of North Carolina Latinos, documented or not, have a college degree. The university system's UNC Tomorrow report, in 2007, noted that, given the state's "increasing reliance on Hispanics and minorities to fuel future economic growth, limiting access to affordable higher education for the growing Hispanic population raises serious concerns about our state's ability to remain competitive in the years ahead."[2] More importantly, when the exclusion works to deny meaningful opportunity and equal dignity to young women and men who had no role in the decision to emigrate; who frequently come from families in which younger siblings are, by virtue of having been born a year or two later, citizens; who have, against all odds, mastered the state's middle schools and high schools and labored mightily in search of the American dream; and who are then culled from their friends and schoolmates and marked as a subclass to provide low-cost labor but not to enjoy the economic and humane prospects of North Carolina life and development, denying income and needed resources and creativity to the commonwealth, the "personal" injustice rises to tragic proportions.

Over three decades ago, the U.S. Supreme Court ruled, in the landmark *Plyler v. Doe* case, that regardless of immigration status, all children have a right to public, K–12 education.[3] An attempt by the state of Texas to exclude undocumented children from the public schools was ruled unconstitutional. "Aliens, even though in the country unlawfully, are still 'persons' protected by the Fourteenth Amendment," the justices determined. Texas's attempted denial of education, Justice William Brennan wrote, "raises the specter of a permanent caste of undocumented resident aliens, encouraged by some to remain here as a source of cheap labor, but nevertheless denied the benefits that our society makes available to citizens and lawful residents. The existence of such an underclass presents most difficult problems for a Nation that prides itself on adherence to principles of equality under law."

But *Plyler*'s principle was never extended to public higher education. As a result, states have been deemed free to set their own standards and practices in dealing with the access of undocumented students to colleges and universities.

In North Carolina, until 2004, in both the UNC system and public community colleges, campuses were free to set their own policies concerning immigration status. All state universities and about two-thirds of community colleges allowed undocumented students to be admitted. If no proof of legal North Carolina residency could be proffered, however, students were required to pay markedly more expensive out-of-state tuition rates. Beyond that, nondocumented students were typically barred from public-sourced loans and financial aid, such as Pell grants and other forms of educational assistance.[4] So the door, theoretically opened by the admission ruling, was, in actuality, closed.

An array of states proved more generous. Beginning in 2001, states such as California and Texas with large Latino populations decided to allow many long-term undocumented students to attend public colleges and universities at resident tuition rates. As of 2017, about twenty states, in total, welcomed a variety of undocumented but long-term residents under an array of "Dream" acts. A federal statute providing some similar protections has been introduced repeatedly in the U.S. Congress since 2001. It has never passed.[5]

In 2005, seeking to make higher education more attainable for immigrants in North Carolina, a number of state legislators introduced House Bill 1183. The proposed bill would have allowed undocumented immigrants to pay in-state tuition rates at public universities if they met various academic and residential requirements and applied for legal immigration status. The bill became decidedly controversial, particularly on the talk-radio circuits, and eventually died. University and community college officials vacillated on the applicable standards in subsequent years until, in 2009, the State Board of Community Colleges decided to, again, allow the admission of nondocumented students, though, as in the university context, they would be forced to pay nonresident rates— often 300 percent of the resident tuition standards. When President Barack Obama announced the DACA program, some states understandably took the position that DACA students should be recognized as residents for tuition purposes. The attorney general of North Carolina, however, closed the door to such undocumented student appeals in 2014. As a result, undocumented North Carolina students, even if they have lived almost the entirety of their lives in the state, are effectively excluded from public community colleges, colleges, and universities.[6]

My colleague Hannah Gill has shown that the exclusion of undocumented students from even the possibilities of advanced education frequently works marked harm by the time they are midway through high school. At best, too frequently "they drop out and find a job; at worst they engage in destructive behavior, lose self-confidence, and remain strongly isolated from mainstream society." It's like (quoting one student) "I could get a job tomorrow at Golden Corral, get some money, like most people say they are going to do, and buy a car." But then they are stuck in that track—in a society and in an age where education is the central linchpin to economic prosperity—when they "wanted to work to have a future."[7] North Carolina has nearly 900,000 Hispanic residents, about 9 percent of its population. The median annual income for Hispanics over age sixteen, though, is a mere $19,000, and the child poverty rate is a soaring 41 percent.[8] Excluding undocumented students from higher education makes those figures even worse. It does nothing to improve them.

Undocumented North Carolinians I interviewed described the dynamic powerfully: High school friends parting company because a student is without a social security card and driver's license. Graduations that were anything but celebrations. Hopeful teenagers thrown into unexpected and daunting depression. Teenagers skipping school and getting into trouble because they are made to realize they have no prospects. Friends "making wrong decisions" because they learn they're not going to be given a fair chance. Young people who had eagerly swallowed what they thought to be the American dream—with its claimed reward, despite the circumstance of birth, for effort and sacrifice—learning, brutally, that doors might be closed to them. Folks who had done everything they were asked to do but then felt the deck had been reshuffled, the deal withdrawn. Dread of a life robbed of opportunity and prospect in favor of one of fear and perpetual exclusion. Hostility from a broader world mocking the strength, resilience, and selflessness experienced in their own families. Reading of or hearing about suicides of young peers after they learned of the actual impacts that flow from being undocumented. Intrusions that Marco Cervantes found "heartbreaking" and almost unspeakably unjust. Stresses that, for many, became insurmountable.

Perhaps the most widely known undocumented student in North Carolina is Emilio Vicente. He received a rare private scholarship covering out-of-state tuition and costs, allowing him to attend and graduate from UNC–Chapel Hill. Vicente courageously came out, while on campus, as undocumented and, later, as gay. He became a noted student and immigration rights leader, declaring with others, "I am undocumented and I'm not afraid." Vicente narrowly lost an election to become student body president in 2014. The race received national attention. Frank Bruni of the *New York Times*, noting Vicente's still-jeopardized immigration and discriminatory tuition status, wrote movingly: "If we, as a country, aren't prepared to open our arms and our workplaces to strivers like Emilio, who could so easily have sunk into self-pity and had to summon a grace and grit that many of us could never manage, then we're not just callous. We're self-defeating. We're stupid."[9]

But even with the exceedingly rare full-scholarship assistance, Vicente's path reflected the cruelties and challenges of other undocumented young women and men. He arrived in the United States from Guatemala when he was six years old, seeing his father for the first time. He recalled his mother taking him under barbed wire into Arizona. Speaking a Mayan dialect in Siler City, he started school unable to understand either English or Spanish, an outsider in both communities. His mother and father worked long, tough hours in a chicken processing plant. They went to community college at night to learn English. They would show him blistered and bloodied hands, explaining that they wanted better for him. They demanded that he study hard. He complied, and excelled.

Then his father suffered a debilitating work accident when Vicente was fifteen. He required medical attention that he couldn't obtain here, so Vicente's father, mother, and sister were forced to return to Guatemala. Vicente elected to stay in Siler City with his older brother and eventually won the scholarship that would take him to Chapel Hill. He hasn't been able to see his parents for over ten years; the immigration risks are too high. He fears this his father will die before he sees him again. "Like every other undocumented person," he says, "I never turn my phone off." He lives in constant fear that something will happen to one of his family members either here or in violence-plagued Guatemala. "It could happen any moment, I feel it right now," he explains as we meet.

Still, Vicente speaks as one who is aware of his good fortune. "I'm just the lucky dreamer who actually got to graduate from college," he says. Most don't. There is only "a tiny percent of us" in higher education. "I'm different only because I got the scholarship," he says. But education ought to be a human right, he argues. "There is no drawback to having a well-educated population." He worries, like some other dreamers, that their struggles and against-the-odds accomplishments will be used to contrast them with thousands of other undocumented North Carolina students, equally deserving, if less well known, and all worthy of the educational opportunities open to other Tar Heel students.

A "dreamer" narrative, especially a high-academic-achieving narrative, can't be used to suggest that other undocumented students— perhaps technically less accomplished or who, like millions of other American teenagers, have made predictable mistakes and errors of judgment—deserve less than the fullest opportunities of higher education. Thus those who are already deeply marginalized are further penalized. All dreamers have their stories. None, surely, are perfect. In no other arena of American life would a surpassing perfection be demanded in order for someone to be allowed a meaningful chance. Vicente thinks of a high-achieving trap through the lens of his remarkable parents. "My parents never had the opportunity to do what I did," he explains, "because they were working fifty or sixty hours a week, year in and year out, to create a better life for me and my brothers and sisters." His parents, Vicente notes, "are the original dreamers."

Ricsy Sanchez lives in Thomasville, North Carolina, but she wasn't born there. She's originally from Honduras. She came to the United States without documentation at age eleven. Her mother and father had been working in North Carolina since she was three. She remembers being thrilled, not to move to the United States, but to join her parents.

Sanchez can recall a lot of the trip. "I crossed three frontiers to come here," she says. The first was from Honduras to Guatemala. The second was from Guatemala to Mexico. The third was from Mexico, at Rio Bravo, into the United States. "It was the last one that is always described as being illegal," she notes. But what it meant for her was getting to see her mother. "She had come to the United States when I was only three; I had really only looked at her in pictures." She had always wondered why her mother had left her. "One day she called and said, hey Ricsy, you and your sister are going to come here now." It was scary and thrilling.

Part of the trip was in a canoe. "I was scared because I couldn't swim and they said there were crocodiles," she remembers. The boat was crowded. There were thirty-two people in it. And she was just a kid. At one point she fell in and someone pulled her out—a "guardian angel," she believes.

"When we went through Mexico, we had to walk through tall grass," she reports. It was cold and they slept on the ground. "I got a whole lot of ticks on me and my sister had to pick them off; I still have scars from all the ticks.," she says. When she takes a shower, even now, she "always looks at the scars from all the ticks and remembers where I came from, I remember who I am," she insists.

The worst part was crossing the Rio Bravo. Sanchez had to be separated from her sister because the people in charge said it was best not to go through like a family. They crossed the river holding on to an inner tube. She slipped off and was terrified she'd drown. But again, someone pulled her back up. She said she lost her flip-flops in the water. "So that's how I arrived, barefoot." And it didn't look like it had in the magazines. No skyscrapers, no Statue of Liberty. Just a lot of dust and sand and some searchlights they were trying to hide from. "Then red and blue lights came after us, caught us, and took us to the detention center," she said. She didn't know what would happen then.

"They asked me about my sister, because we look a lot alike," she said. She told the immigration officers that wasn't her sister. "Later I apologized to my little sister for betraying her," Sanchez said. Her sister just kept looking down, confused and wounded.

Days passed. She was in a children's shelter, which at least didn't seem dangerous. But she was alone. Then someone came through the entryway. "I saw the lady, I thought, is that her, the lady from the pictures?" Sanchez recalls. She ran to her mother. "I felt something I'd never experienced before, a mother's love," she says. She had to learn to know her mother and her father, to learn to love them. "I didn't make the decision to come here," she says. "My mother decided it for me, but I'm so happy that she did. . . . I've never regretted her decision."

School was hard at first. She didn't understand English. Plus, the education system seemed different than she was used to. But she worked hard and caught on. She took AP (advanced placement) classes and she was selected for the National Honor Society. "For a long time, until late in high school, being undocumented doesn't affect you so much." But then not being able to get a driver's license and, especially, not being able to make plans to go to college, that was something big, a big separation. "It wasn't until senior year, when I found out I wouldn't be able to pay for college, that I learned it made all the difference in the world," she says.

In her AP English class, senior year, her teacher asked where she was going to college—would she apply to Chapel Hill? "I explained that my dad had a terrible accident," she says, "so I'm just going to work like my brothers do." (Sanchez's father had been hit by a drunk driver and suffered very serious brain damage.) But her teacher argued that going to college would be a better way to help take care of her family. "You are here to get a future and you get a future by getting an education," she said. "That way you can help your father the most," her teacher argued. Then, a little later, her high school guidance counselor asked, "Do you have a social security number, are you illegal?" "She used those exact words," Sanchez notes. "I asked what difference that made," she remembers. Her counselor said that's what you have to use to get financial assistance to go to school. "It was at that moment that it really stopped me and I realized what it meant to be 'illegal' in this country," she says.

Unwilling to give up without trying, Sanchez applied to UNC-Chapel Hill. She was admitted. But she soon realized it was impossible for her to actually go. Where would she get $40,000 or $50,000 a year? So she applied to Davidson County Community College and started writing to every scholarship granting entity she could discover. She applied to about ten a week, for many months. Almost all excluded her because she was undocumented. But she eventually received two scholarships that, with the much cheaper community college tuition, made it possible for her to go to school while working about twenty hours a week.

Davidson was Hispanic friendly. She got a lot of support from teachers and administrators. She graduated with high honors in the sciences, getting her associates degree in two years. She had become president of the Hispanic Culture Club and an officer in student government. She was even selected by the administration to speak to a national conference of higher education leaders held in California. She wowed the huge audience with a student keynote. She was the first Latina to be asked to give such an address to the conference and certainly the first person from Davidson County Community College to do so. Her speech was met with tears and ovations. They were particularly moved when she said she decided that she wasn't going to let a number, in this case a social security number, constrain her worth as a person: "A number doesn't define anyone as a human being, it doesn't show what you are capable of, what you can accomplish. It certainly doesn't define me. It doesn't show what I can do, what I'm able to get done. And I won't let it."

I asked Sanchez, some years later, what she had meant by that—not being fated by the number. She explained that when she was in high school, trying desperately to get to college, the social security number really did manage to define her. It decided what she could do and what she couldn't do. "It was like that number and life itself were deciding my destiny, but I decided I wasn't going to let that be the final word," she said. "It wasn't going to set my out my fate, it wouldn't stop me." So "I got scholarships and freed myself up to go to school so the number couldn't rule," she said. She got her degree with no debt, no government assistance. "I work, I pay for myself," she said; "I pay for my father's health care, I pay taxes. I'll do it myself."

She also told the California conference this:

> But I do have this fear. Every day I fear that I might wake up and find myself in some jail in a country I barely know. That happened to my brother. He'd been here for ten years. He never did anything wrong. Never got in any trouble. He just worked hard. But he came up on the immigration records. It happened two years ago. He was detained for no reason. I remember when he was deported he told me, "Ricsy, I'm glad it was me and not you, because I can defend myself." They tried to deport my dad too, but he is so badly injured we were able to fight it. The immigration people are extremely heartless. Every day I fear that I or a member of my family will be deported, though we've been here most of our lives. I also fear that I'll get a call saying my brother has been shot in Honduras because that happens there all the time.

The conference trip also meant Sanchez would have the chance to see her little sister for the first time in five years, since she had been required to move to Las Vegas. When they had last seen each other, they were fourteen and eighteen. Her sister had become a young woman. "It was wonderful, but bittersweet, we had missed so much, lost so much," she says.

After graduating, Sanchez was again accepted to Chapel Hill to finish her bachelor's degree. She scraped hard, wrote countless scholarship requests, but couldn't raise that kind of money. She had bills to pay and a disabled father to care for. So she went to work in a warehouse as a packer. Eventually her bosses realized she was capable of far more. So she began work as an auditor, later moving to a private company that helps people with representation before the Internal Revenue Service. She'll be certified as an enrolled representative in a year or so.

It's been four years since she gave the speech in California. She has a decent job. Looking back, she says she never expected to be where she is now when she came to the United States. The DACA program helped, at least for a while. She could work without being so scared. But it wasn't enough, because people still couldn't go to college. And a new president threatened to end it anyway. Most of her friends just sort of gave up. "They knew they couldn't really get an education, so what good would it do to try?" she says. They might take a course or two at a community college at night. But they knew it wasn't going to happen. They knew they wouldn't ever actually get a degree. So they quit.

"Now I feel stuck in a different way," she says. "I have a decent job in auditing, but what I really want is to finish my four-year degree at the university and go to law school," she says. But to finish, "I'll have to pay out-of-state tuition and fees and costs that will amount to about $50,000 a year for two years." It costs that much "because I don't have a social security number," she says. A nine-digit number sets the price and the possibilities. But she's determined to make it happen regardless. "Many things in life make you want to give up, but you have to choose just to make that next, single step." Just make it.

And there is more:

I love my mother for having the courage to make the decision to come. I don't regret it. I have a dream. I have a thousand of them. I'm not a Honduran; I don't even know that country. And to many, I'm not American, apparently, because I don't have a number. But in every other way, except on paper, I'm an American.

I think I could be sort of a symbol. To another boy or girl in my situation, they can say, look she did it. She didn't have documents. She didn't get any help from the government. She didn't take anybody's place in school. She just worked so hard that she made it. Maybe they have made some wrong decisions, like a lot of my friends did when they realized they weren't going to be given a fair chance. But now you can fix that. You can go get your GED. And you can start taking steps in the right direction instead of in the wrong ones. When I was in that spot in 2011, I didn't have anything going for me. There was no reason to think I could pull it off. But I did. You can do a lot. Then I graduated in the top ten of my high school class. And I got a college degree. And I graduated with high honors.

But I say, too, let me go to school. Put me at the back of the line if you want. Don't give me any help, if that's what you want. But don't make me pay out-of-state tuition, which you know is a ridiculous cost. An impossible one. I've saved up some money, even with all

I've been through and with needing to take care of my dad. I've saved enough that I think I can just barely make it with resident tuition. But don't pile on. I've gotten accepted twice to Chapel Hill. Just don't reach down and stop me from going. I've lived here more than half my life. How can you say I'm not a resident and never will be? In another twenty years, do you plan on still saying the same thing? That I'm not from here? Come on.

If I get shut out, like they seem to want, I'll still be here. I have a family. So in their view I should be a waitress or I should clean houses. I'd pay fewer taxes. Less money would be generated and spread around. It affects everyone. It is a lose, lose situation. There are, I think, 3 million undocumented young people in America. Why is it better for us to go uneducated? Do you just have something in your mind, in your ego, that says, "We won't give them anything, no matter what"? What good does that do? If you let me go to school, paying all my own way, just at a fair cost, I'll become a lawyer. I'll create my own firm. I'll generate jobs. I'll generate tax money. And then there's the other way, the darker side. If you close us out, lots of us make bad decisions. And that costs everybody. In jails, in welfare, in danger. You think what happens to me doesn't affect you, but it does. When you deny us an education, it costs us, surely it does. But it costs you too.

9

RACE AND POVERTY IN NORTH CAROLINA

If the disparities we see between blacks and whites in North Carolina were reversed, if those sorts of harms were experienced in the white community—it would lead to revolt, it would be seen as a crisis of the first order, leading to great economic and political and cultural mobilization. In our economic and political system, we expect to see lots and lots of poor people. If those poor people are black, all the better. Viewing intense poverty through a racial lens make it more tolerable. As long as it is black people who are down, we accept it.—Dr. Jarvis Hall, North Carolina Central University, Durham, North Carolina

A color-blind society does not exist in the United States and never has existed. Those who insist we should conduct ourselves as if such a utopian state already existed have no interest in achieving it and, indeed, would be horrified if we ever approached it.—Dr. John Hope Franklin, Duke University, Durham, North Carolina

It's obvious. It's planned. They want to think, here, that the world belongs to a certain race of people and they don't want the rest of us to be equal.—Rosanell Eaton, 94-year-old civil rights activist, Warrenton, North Carolina

No two characteristics of life in the state of North Carolina are as closely, consistently, and constantly linked as poverty and race. They are old, persistent, and unyielding companions. They have traveled together every day of the state's long history. They lock arms still.[1]

More than twice as many African American Tar Heels live in poverty as whites. The differential is even starker for children. Almost three times as many black kids as white ones live in poverty.[2] Two and a half times as many blacks are unemployed as whites. The ratio seems essentially to hold in robust economic times and bleak ones. Blacks experience much higher rates of hunger and are far more frequently uninsured than whites. Almost three times as many African Americans' home mortgages are underwater in the state.

The income and poverty disparities between the races are intense. But they pale compared with North Carolina's disparities in wealth— the accumulation of income and assets over time and, often, generations. Black North Carolina households have, astonishingly, only about one-sixteenth of the family wealth, on average, retained by white house-holds. Three times as many black families as white ones report negative net worth.[3]

Most of the state's counties experiencing brutal child poverty rates—Northampton (48.3 percent), Chowan (47.9 percent), Scotland (46.8 percent), Vance (44 percent) and Edgecombe (43 percent)—have high percentages of African Americans. The same is true of North Carolina's ten federally designated persistent-poverty counties. The state's congressional districts with the most stunning food insecurity rates have the highest percentage of African Americans.

Black children attend, very disproportionately, North Carolina's highest-poverty public schools. Under the state's A–F grading system, almost all high-poverty schools receive very poor grades, while almost all high-wealth schools excel. A 2015 study by the University of Pennsylvania determined that black students make up 26 percent of North Carolina public school enrollment but account for 51 percent of school suspensions.[4] The state, here, follows regional trends: thirteen southern states provide 55 percent of the nation's school suspensions. In Chapel Hill–Carrboro, where I live, black students make up 13.2 percent of school enrollment and 52.7 percent of the suspensions. About twice as many white Tar Heels have a college degree as African Americans.[5]

The North Carolina Department of Correction reports a prison population of about 38,000. A startling 57 percent of the inmates are African American, though 23 percent of the state's population is black. Thirty-five percent of the prison cohort is white, though whites make up over 70 percent of the overall populace. North Carolina incarcerates 357 whites and 1,665 blacks per 100,000.[6] A large portion of imprisoning convictions are based on drug offenses, hugely slanted toward blacks, though research indicates blacks and whites use and sell drugs at roughly the same rate. Of course, criminal convictions have potent and lasting collateral economic consequences for those who sustain them and for their families. A heavily racialized mass incarceration markedly affects the economic prospects of virtually every community in North Carolina.[7]

A broad study at UNC–Chapel Hill, reported on in 2015, reviewed 1.3 million Charlotte traffic stops over a twelve-year period. It found that although blacks make up less than a third of the driving-age population, more of them (in raw numbers) were pulled over, they received more tickets, and they were 77 percent more likely to be searched than white drivers.[8] A similarly broad study of Durham concluded that blacks were twice as likely as whites to be searched after a traffic stop and three times as apt to be arrested.[9] An expansive *New York Times* study examining tens of thousands of traffic stops and arrests in Greensboro revealed huge racial disparities.[10] Unsurprisingly, perhaps, other large empirical studies reveal dramatically disparate results for North Carolina whites and blacks in employment, contracting, housing, health care, education, and access to credit.[11]

In 2009, the North Carolina General Assembly enacted a pathbreaking Racial Justice Act that allowed capital defendants to challenge death penalty sentences if they could prove race was a significant factor in the decision to seek or impose the sentence at the time of the trial.[12] The initial hearings held under the statute were consistently successful and compelling, reflecting an adjudicatory process riven with racism, but the legislature promptly repealed the statute in 2013.[13] The repealing act, ironically, also made it easier to impose the death penalty.[14]

These massive polarizations, the chasms of racial disparity, are surprising to many, but likely not to the bulk of North Carolinians interviewed for this project. They, understandably, point to a cumulative effect that dispirits and diminishes the people affected. Shirley Edwards, whom I now think of as the guru of Goldsboro, explains:

You have to be willing to look at it from the broad sweep and the historical perspective. Most people aren't interested in doing that. And when I've gone into it, and when things have seemed a certain way to me, I try to substantiate what I think. To figure out what the root causes are. Not based on what I want to think, but on what is there. The largest cause of entrenched poverty in Wayne County, I'm certain, is the lack of a quality education being offered and directed to every child, black as well as white, easy as well as troubled. This is the county of Charles B. Aycock, the education governor of North Carolina. Of course he was also the racist and white supremacist governor of North Carolina. Poor and excluded black children in Wayne County have never had a high-quality education. Never. Not back then. Not now. That affects everything. It is layered year after year and generation after generation. We're also increasingly criminalizing our kids in the public schools. It used to be if kids got in a fight they would have some sort of in-school suspension. Now they're sent out and there's no real assurance about when and if they're going to come back. A lot of kids never really recover from it. The poor and people of color are segregated off, separated off, living in housing projects. It breeds discontent and disconnection. Crime multiplies because everyone around you is facing difficulty and desperation. There is a lot of abuse, a lot of child abuse, child sexual abuse, a lot of teenage pregnancy. And when you see that happen for four or five generations, it seems insurmountable. But it's not. There is also a perception in the schools and in the community that you can do anything you want to poor and marginalized people. They can't fight back. They won't be able to do anything about it. At least that's what people here think. So they really get pushed down. They get treated like they don't matter, because of who they are.

Melissa, whom we interviewed for months at Crisis Assistance Ministry in Charlotte, saw little doubt about the connection between the challenges visited on low-income, segregated-out workers and neighborhoods in the Queen City and racial bias:

I have a lot of things running in my mind right now. Some of the things in me make me angry. But I learn to deal with it and accept the things that I cannot change. Being "created equal" stands out big for me. Among us, among black people, there is no equal, you know? We're treated as "less than," if I can say that. And sometimes we'll feel that we don't matter. And I have felt that way. Where no matter what I say or how hard I work at my job, people see it—management sees it—but they will look over me and they'll pick someone else of a different color. And I'm not prejudiced, but we never were a people that, you know, felt created equal, or got treated as equals. Because of where we live, the places we work, the schools that our kids are going to, they're always at the bottom. I believe that we work just as hard as those people up in the offices that are making way more than us. I believe that we are the ones that are doing the job, and they're not. They're getting richer off of people like us—the very ones that they don't want to help. And that makes me angry. Very angry. And I just feel that we are created equal and we should get the same chances that they get.

I've seen it in the schools. The difference in the schools in east Mecklenburg County and north Mecklenburg County is something—the poor schools do not get the equipment, the academics, the new and different curriculums they get across town. Why not? And there is a big difference with black kids as opposed to white kids—how they are treated at school. My son would get in trouble for stuff the white kids got away with. If he acted real silly or laughed loud or misbehaved, he would get kicked out of class. But when another kid, who did not look like him, did the same thing, they just told him, "Go sit down and start being quiet." But we would get the suspensions and the phone calls.

A lot of the kids who got in trouble, they were decent kids. The only reason they did do a crime was because of their parents struggling. They realized that their mom and dad didn't make enough to support them so they would go out and steal to be able to bring stuff or to have certain things that they wanted and their parents couldn't afford to give them. A lot of the crime that is done is because they came up in a family that couldn't give them the things that they wanted or that they thought they needed. And then maybe they applied for a job and got turned down. I have met guys that apply for work over and over again just because the way they look they were turned down, they were being stereotyped, so when they couldn't get that job after trying for so many times, it made them angry, so sometimes they'll turn to crime. It's not a big surprise.

Danielle Baptiste, the inspiring educator at Dillard Academy in Goldsboro, sees the diminishing more directly linked to racial separation, isolation, and exclusion—a forced occupying and relegation to differing worlds:

The greatest issues in Goldsboro are poverty and separation, racial segregation. Period. Our kids can miss out on a lot of the possibilities of life that others enjoy almost automatically. They can miss out on relationships with all sorts of different kinds of people, from all sorts of different backgrounds. There are a lot of people who I know in town who will never come further than Ashe Street. For any purpose, at any time. So our students can be hurt by that. And when we go out across the county, people will sometime act like we don't belong. We won in the soccer league and people started demanding the kids' IDs and addresses, like we were cheating. So you can be cut off from the broader world—never really getting a full view of the world that's out there. We work hard to combat that at Dillard. It is a big part of our job, our mission. I was able to go to the University of North Carolina and I loved it. But a lot of these kids will not ever have that chance. They will just see what they see now. Unless we change things, they will just be relegated. I miss seeing black and white people walking around together. That is the segregation we try to break through, to push back against, every day. It is the hardest thing about Goldsboro. It does the most damage.

ANSWERING THE LITANY

The depressing cascade of statistics with which this chapter began is largely uncontroverted. It is also at least essentially reflective of broader national trends, though North Carolina's toll of racially disproportionate hardship can often exceed already demoralizing American norms. The Pew Research Center, for example, has recently again documented extraordinarily brutal and widespread disparities between blacks and whites in the United States, determining that "America remains two societies—one white and one black as measured by key demographic indicators of social and economic well-being."[15] Pew focused on potent racial distinctions in income, poverty, wealth, homeownership, foreclosure, unemployment, educational attainment, college attendance, marriage rates, and family structure.[16] Researchers concluded that "blacks, on average, are at least twice as likely to be poor or unemployed"; they earn, by household, little more than half of what white households claim, and they possess only about 8 percent of the net wealth enjoyed by white peers.[17]

When such daunting gulfs are examined or hinted at of course, heated arguments ensue about their causes, consequences, and cures. For some, the triggers are principally cultural: poverty results from the poor lacking virtue, middle-class norms, and decent moral codes. The problems of the economically disadvantaged, who are disproportionately racial minorities, are to be solved "through moral education and self-reliance, high quality relationships and strong family ties."[18] For others, crushing, dramatically unbalanced hardship springs from lingering foundational distinctions in class and race, rooted in current and continuing levels of discrimination, the character of local economies and communities, diminished opportunities and access, and cumulative generational disadvantage.[19] As Paul Krugman has put it, the racially disproportionate "poor don't need lectures on morality, they need more resources—which we can provide—and better opportunities, through everything from training and subsidies to higher minimum wages."[20]

No doubt sensibly, many scholars see shades of truth and shortcoming in both camps.[21] William Julius Wilson, for example, explores social structure (the way social positions, social roles, and networks of social relationship are arranged in our institutions) and culture (the sharing of outlooks and modes of behavior among individuals facing similar place-based circumstances) as driving causes of racial and economic inequality.[22] Ann Chih Lin and David Harris attempt to demonstrate, on the other hand, that racial inequality does not stem from a single, powerful socioeconomic driver but from multiple disadvantages that accumulate over time to undermine the life chances of impoverished racial minorities.[23] Untangling race and poverty, in North Carolina, in the South, and in the country at large, is a life's work. Or more.

Putting on my constitutional law professor hat for a moment, it is also true that American courts have made broad-ranging, systemic racial discrimination actions exceedingly difficult to present. Jurisdictional demands for distinct, concrete, and individualized injuries often pose insurmountable hurdles for generalized or aggregated constitutional claims.[24] And even more problematic, the U.S. Supreme Court has consistently rejected discrimination actions based on a law's or a program's disproportionate impact on racial minorities, requiring, instead, strong proof of intentional discrimination by a governmental defendant.[25] Plaintiffs must effectively demonstrate that challenged enactments or activities were undertaken in order, specifically, to harm various racial groups, rather than presenting mere incidental or ancillary burdens.[26] Taken together, these stringent legal standards mean, for example, that a state criminal justice system producing hideous racial disparities across the board can be challenged only by reviewing, one at a time, individual judicial determinations and that the challenge will prevail only if the plaintiff can reveal a subjective animus by the defendant. Almost nothing meets these tests. So the potent disparities reflected above are essentially, and wrongly, immune from judicial attack in either state or federal courts.

My point here is neither to solve the structure/culture debate nor to trace and seek to embrace new forms of overarching racial discrimination claims so that the courts might contribute more meaningfully to the defining American commitment to racial equality—though I would welcome progress on both fronts. I mean to make a smaller and, I think, less controversial claim. It is, simply, that unless we are to drain the term of all conceivable meaning, North Carolina experiences, at present, an intense, pervasive and systemic ("of or relating to the entire body of an organism") regime of racial subordination. Black North Carolinians, broadly considered, encounter dramatic and often debilitating differences in income, poverty, employment, housing, wealth, education, health care, law enforcement practice, criminal justice outcomes, and imprisonment—to name only the most obvious. The disparities have existed, in potent measure, every day of the state's long and often celebrated history. And though individual instances of racial discrimination or suppression or brutality may, on occasion, stir the attentions of the state and its leadership, this continuing, historic, overarching, and sys-

temic subordination triggers no ambitious state policy regimes or proposals. Brutal, widespread disparity is not derided in the statehouse or
probed in notable committee hearings. State leaders raise no alarms of
exigency. Pervasive, perennial racial subordination, it seems, is thought
to be as natural and as expected as the elevated temperatures of summer or the rise and fall of the North Carolina tides. I think it fair to add
a second corollary that, to someone contemplating the issue in candor,
seems equally uncontestable. If the roles were to be somehow reversed
and white North Carolinians were to experience, on virtually every conceivable front, a demonstrable and wounding subordination to Tar Heel
blacks, the state would deem the issue to present a crisis of unspeakable
and commonwealth-destroying urgency. The only acceptable response,
as Dr. Jarvis Hall has indicated, would be "revolt."

Of course this is hardly an insight of notable perceptiveness or creativity. Nor, in context, is it original or new. In 1967, ten days after he had
first spoken out forcibly against the Vietnam War, Martin Luther King
gave a speech at Stanford University titled "The Other America," address-
ing issues of race, poverty, and economic justice. In it, he contrasted the
nature of his organizing and demonstration efforts in Chicago and the
North with the earlier desegregation campaigns in Alabama, Mississippi,
and Florida. Much had been accomplished, he conceded, in those initial,
often brutal and heroic direct actions of civil disobedience, taking the
nation "back to those great wells of democracy dug deep by the Found-
ing Fathers." He then continued:

> But we must see that the struggle today is much more difficult. It's
> more difficult today because we are struggling now for genuine
> equality. It's much easier to integrate a lunch counter than it is to
> guarantee a livable income and a good solid job. It's much easier to
> guarantee the right to vote than it is to guarantee the right to live in
> sanitary, decent housing conditions. It is much easier to integrate a
> public park than it is to make genuine, quality, integrated education
> a reality. And so today we are struggling for something which says
> we demand genuine equality.
>
> It's not merely a struggle against extremist behavior toward
> Negroes. And I'm convinced that many of the very people who
> supported us in the struggle in the South are not willing to go
> all the way now. I came to see this in a very difficult and painful
> way, in Chicago, the last year where I've lived and worked. Some
> of the people who came quickly to march with us in Selma and

Birmingham weren't active around Chicago. And I came to see that so many people who supported morally and even financially what we were doing in Birmingham and Selma, were really outraged against the extremist behavior of Bull Connor and Jim Clark toward Negroes, rather than believing in genuine equality for Negroes. And I think this is what we've got to see now, and this is what makes the struggle much more difficult.

Actually, President Obama came close to saying something similar when the horrifying murders of black worshippers occurred at the Emanuel African Methodist Episcopal Church in Charleston, South Carolina, in the summer of 2015. Obama spoke movingly of the inspiration of the congregants and the families of the martyred victims and, beyond that, of "the reservoir of American goodness" that touched South Carolina leaders to remove the Confederate battle flag from the state capitol. But, he added, "I don't think God wants us to stop there." For too long, he claimed, noting the massive racial disparities that plague South Carolina and the nation, "we've been blind to the way that past injustices shape the present." In a sense, removing a flag after atrocity is the easier step. Facing a studied, pervasive, accepted, and debilitating subordination is the tougher challenge. Great numbers of us might be moved to action by Bull Connor, Jim Clark, and a white-supremacist mass murderer. We fall to silence when "all" that is presented is pervasive, system-wide racial subordination.

Of course the old equality lawyer in me is quick to concede that "equality" is a capacious, contested, ideological, question-begging, and some would claim, even empty term.[27] It is, perhaps, *the* most contested term. It triggers assumptions and life-altering battles and disagreements over its inevitable corollary: "equal in what?" In opportunity, in outcome, in education, in risk, in life chance, in condition, in health, in education, in subsistence, and in treatment according to race, sex, sexual orientation, citizenship, disability, age, legitimacy, and economic status—the list is long and ever evolving. It implicates, inevitably, many of the central questions of human existence. I make no pretense of easy demarcation.

That said, a nation that is the richest on earth and yet countenances greater poverty, child poverty, economic inequality, and income immobility and larger disparities in health care, education, housing, sustenance, and access to the civil justice system than almost any other major country is surely made nervous by a defining, constitutive commitment to equality. Or at least it ought to be. When those disparities are skewed into a regime of intense, systemic, racial subordination, any core semblance of human equality is further and decidedly challenged. When the massive transgression becomes accepted and routine, the commitment to equality, in any meaningful sense, is abandoned. In Melissa's words, there is no "created equal," there is only "less than."

Without pushing the acceptable intellectual boundaries of the commitment to equality, we could at least embrace the summary challenge of the late John Hope Franklin, long North Carolina's leading academic:

> The victories of the civil rights era did not wipe away three centuries of slavery, degradation, segregation, and discrimination. President Lyndon Johnson said in 1965 at Howard University that the battle for civil rights looked toward not just "freedom but opportunity, not just equality as a right and theory, but equality as a fact and as a result." We point with pride to Supreme Court decisions against racial discrimination. But racial discrimination and segregation continue in blatant as well as subtle forms. There is great racial imbalance in the schools, described now as reflecting parental preference, rather than inequity. The glass ceiling is intact when African-Americans seek employment or promotion. Discrimination in housing continues not only in upper-class neighborhoods but in low income [ones] as well. Low income neighborhoods, where the majority of African-Americans live, are without the agencies or organizations that encourage ambitions and nurture lofty goals. . . . The test of an advanced society is not in how many millionaires it can produce. But in how many law-abiding, hardworking, highly respected, and self-respecting loyal citizens it can produce. The success of such a venture is a measure of the success of our national enterprise.[28]

SUBMERGING POVERTY WITH RACE

Our economic system generates great inequality. We say we tolerate it because it is supposedly necessary in order to create appropriate incentives. Using a racial lens, as we do, makes the inequality more acceptable. We say the economic calculus justifies poverty because if you are black and you are poor, it's your own fault. You didn't work hard enough. As long as we think mainly black people are the ones who are down, we find it okay, even if, in reality, most poor people aren't black.
—Dr. Jarvis Hall, North Carolina Central University, Durham, North Carolina

If racial subordination mocks equality, racism also seems to submerge poverty as an overarching public challenge. At an event in South

Carolina during the 2016 Republican presidential primary, candidate Jeb Bush was asked how he planned to draw black voters to his campaign. He responded, "Our message is one of hope and aspiration." Continuing, he explained: "It isn't one of division and get in line and we'll take care of you with free stuff. . . . Our message is one that is uplifting, that says you can achieve success."[29] Governor Bush seemed to suggest that black American voters, or large numbers of them, are out to get "free stuff."

Americans are far more likely to be poor than citizens of other advanced industrial countries. And the United States does far less than other advanced nations to shield its citizens from poverty.[30] Yet we are also, by accounts, an immensely generous nation, donating hundreds of billions of dollars annually to charities. Why then, it might be asked, do Americans so strongly oppose welfare programs? Yale political scientist Martin Gilens sought to answer that puzzle in his landmark study *Why Americans Hate Welfare*, using evidence from opinion polls, analyses of public policy and welfare reforms, and a massive content study of media reports to probe the complex reasons for opposition to welfare in the United States.[31] Based on his empirical inquiries, Gilens concluded that negative feelings about welfare are related to the perception that such efforts are programs for African Americans bolstered by persistent media misrepresentations suggesting that most welfare recipients are black and undeserving. Americans dislike programs like food stamps and assistance to needy families not because they are too individualistic to believe in public social obligation or too self-interested to pay for them, but because they associate those programs with African Americans and, Gilens found, large numbers of whites fault the work ethic of blacks.

A massive subsequent study, conducted by Alberte Alesina, Edward Glaeser, and Bruce Sacerdote and published as "Why Doesn't the United States Have a European Style Welfare State?" reached similar demoralizing conclusions.[32] There, Harvard and Dartmouth professors sought to determine why the United States government is far less redistributive than its European counterparts, which deploy more progressive taxation schemes and more generous social programs. The authors concluded that explanations rooted in economic theory and distribution do not account for the differing European and American approaches to poverty programs or to exercises of progressive taxation. Nor do determinations of political or income stability, or distinctions in federalism, or structures of governmental organization provide the distinction. Instead, they concluded, "within the United States, race is the single most important predictor of support for welfare. . . . America's troubled race relations are clearly a major reason for the absence of an American welfare state."

> This history of American redistribution makes it quite clear that hostility to welfare derives in part from the fact that welfare spending in the United States goes disproportionately to minorities. Another important difference is that Americans dislike redistribution because they tend to feel that people on welfare are lazy, whereas Europeans tend to feel that people on welfare are unfortunate.

> [The] bottom line is that Americans redistribute less than Europeans for three reasons: because the majority of Americans believe that redistribution favors racial minorities, because Americans believe that they live in an open and fair society and that if someone is poor it is his or her own fault, and because the political system is geared toward preventing redistribution. In fact, the political system is likely to be endogenous to these basic American beliefs.[33]

Even if these studies could be said to border on being dated, the arguments are strong that their explanatory powers remain sadly undiminished. As Paul Krugman has argued, the same racial dynamic—leaving the United States unique among the advanced nations in its harsh treatment of the less fortunate and "its willingness to tolerate unnecessary suffering among its citizens"—has played out in the decisions by the states, over the last seven years, in choosing whether or not to accept Medicaid expansion under the federal Affordable Care Act.[34] The Supreme Court's principal decision validating the huge medical coverage reform law left individual states open to accept or to reject the statute's hefty expansion of Medicaid coverage, the main program providing health insurance for the poor. But the option was one that the U.S. Congress assumed would be accepted by any sensible state government. After all, states were offered an almost entirely federally funded program that would provide crucial benefits to millions of their most vulnerable citizens, pour billions into state economies, rescue struggling local hospitals, dramatically support health care providers, and of course, save thousands of lives in the process. Who would say no to such an offer?[35]

It turns out about twenty states have said no to Medicaid expansion, including, as previously discussed, North Carolina. What do the nonjoiners have in common? Mostly it is a history of slaveholding. Almost no members of the former Confederacy have chosen to embrace the enlarged poverty health care program. Over 80 percent of the population in states that have turned their backs on coverage hail from places that practiced slavery before the Civil War. They also tend to have much higher levels of poverty, more uninsured citizens, and more African Americans than the rest of the country. It seems clear that race has played a substantial role in the Medicaid refusal determinations.

Although I will examine recent legislative and policy decisions in North Carolina that make the immense challenges of poverty in the state far more trying in Chapter 10, it is important to add, even at this point, that the linkage between race and public policymaking is more direct and pervasive than even the Medicaid expansion example alone would suggest. Starting in 2012, North Carolina had large, veto-proof Republican majorities in both legislative houses. And though North Carolina is 21 percent African American, when the Republicans of each house repaired to their respective caucuses—where the entirety of the state's legislative decision-making occurs—no black member appeared.

In that posture of exclusion, since 2010 the General Assembly has repealed the state's pathbreaking Racial Justice Act (expanding available racial bases to challenge the operation of the death penalty); it has, the federal courts have concluded, racially gerrymandered the state's legislative electoral districts, racially gerrymandered congressional districts, racially gerrymandered local electoral districts, and imposed racially discriminatory voter identification and polling-access requirements. It has adopted policies increasing racial segregation in the public schools, protecting Confederate monuments, eliminating (state-based) race discrimination lawsuits in the local courts, and despite the Black Lives Matter movement, shielding police camera footage from public disclosure.[36]

ADDRESSING RACIAL SUBORDINATION

Facts cannot be denied, and in North Carolina today they can be stated simply. We must move forward as one people or we will not move forward at all. We cannot move forward as whites or Negroes. We can only move forward as North Carolinians.—Governor Terry Sanford, April 1963, receiving the Omega Psi Phi Citizen of the Year Award, North Carolina A&T

Dramatic differences in rates of poverty, child poverty, unemployment, median income, wealth, hunger, home foreclosure, health insurance coverage and outcomes, education, arrests, convictions, imprisonment, and the collateral consequences attendant to interaction with the criminal justice system reflect a social, legal, and economic structure that results, on average, in hugely disparate opportunities, expectations, and outcomes for black and white North Carolinians. The circumstances are unsurprisingly similar for Hispanics and Native Americans. The state began as and, on average, remains a commonwealth of tiered membership.[37]

And despite ringing endorsements of and pledges to equal citizenship and dignity, the chasms traceable to, or at least corollary to, race seem well accepted and, essentially, uncontested. North Carolina political campaigns almost never address them. We have, at bottom, become accustomed to a generalized polarization and separation—or at least white North Carolinians have. There can be little doubt that if three or four times as many white kids lived in poverty as black kids did, the state would declare cataclysmic exigency. As it is, we regard the reverse as essentially natural and nonproblematic. This regime leaves a defining commitment to equality, in actuality, largely empty. We avow compliance. We know better. Yet we are undisturbed. Our public demands and shared aspirations are untriggered. After all, we have always floundered on race, from our first day to this one.

It also seems true that as wrenching racial disparity demeans our constitutive commitment to equality, racial predisposition notably diminishes North Carolina's attention to poverty as a public challenge and concern. Immense economic distress and hardship, in a community of surpassing wealth, is removed from the arena of shared concern, in no small measure because it is assumed to be a black problem, not a North Carolina problem. Steps that might work to markedly abate the burdens of poverty are rejected largely because they are seen as principally benefiting racial minorities. What would otherwise likely be seen as a surpassing state challenge is submerged by legacies and traditions of racial subordination and presupposition. Race marks North Carolina's present as it has marred its past. It also radically handicaps its future.

North Carolina's boldest, most innovative and energetic attempt to struggle with the challenges of persistent poverty and race occurred from 1963 to 1968, under the leadership of Governor Terry Sanford, through the creation and implementation of the North Carolina Fund.[38] As I explain more fully in Chapter 10, Sanford turned to private philanthropy, innovative low-income community engagement initiatives, broad-ranging and idealistic volunteer support, and the beginnings of a national thrust to combat poverty to, in Sanford's words, "seek institutional, political, economic and social change to bring about a functioning, democratic society."[39] By late 1968, when the fund closed its doors, a resurgent politics of race had successfully prevailed against continued efforts to achieve civil rights and aid the poor. George Esser, the North Carolina Fund's executive director, explained that, with the fund's closing, "the challenge [of fighting racism and poverty] is to reinstate human freedom and human dignity and genuine justice as major goals of American society."[40] Almost a half-century later, Esser's word echo and haunt, unfulfilled.

10

FROM TARGETING POOR PEOPLE TO A POLITICS OF FULL MEMBERSHIP

A lot of us in North Carolina need to take the blinders off our eyes. There are real people here, by the hundreds of thousands, with real issues, facing real challenges and real burdens that are massively different than our own. They face barriers of income and of access that we never even dream of, that we simply do not imagine. We need to understand them, we need to work with them, shoulder to shoulder. We need to become an "us" rather than an "us" and a "them." And we need to learn, finally, that there is a difference between charity and justice.—Jill Staton Bullard, founder and former executive director, Inter-Faith Food Shuttle, Raleigh, North Carolina

Poverty is anything but new in North Carolina. The voices heard in these chapters are as fresh as they are wrenching. But their hardships are also often rooted in systems, structures, and practices that have existed for generations. In their book *To Right These Wrongs: The North Carolina Fund and the Battle to end Poverty and Inequality in 1960s America*, Robert Korstad and James Leloudis chronicle the history of what may be the last sustained effort to address broad-scale poverty in the state.[1] Fifty years ago, from 1963 to 1968, a public-private partnership called the North Carolina Fund attempted to break the crushing cycle of poverty that was at the time affecting some 450,000 poor people in the state.[2] As Korstad and Leloudis explain, the economic foundations upon which modern North Carolina was built originated in the aftermath of plantation slavery. After the Civil War, a revolutionary "fusion" politics, uniting Black Republicans and white populists, briefly held sway near the end of the nineteenth century. A determined and at least temporarily successful political platform capped interest rates, instituted progressive taxation, broadened educational opportunity, pursued racial cooperation and empowerment, and deepened democratic decision-making. It was met, however, by a ferocious campaign of white supremacy, culminating in a murderous "municipal coup d'état" in Wilmington in 1898. A hegemonic Democratic Party replaced the aspiring fusionists, instituting what was effectively single-party rule. Democrats at the turn of the twentieth century worked systematically to exclude African Americans and many poor whites from the polls. As these groups were disenfranchised, an enduring pattern of racial capitalism took hold, rooted in a monopoly of political power, brutal enforcement of segregation, and cheap, non-unionized labor.[3]

For generations, large agricultural and manufacturing interests saw little reason to invest in educational or social development. North Carolina, in turn, by the early twentieth century produced the highest illiteracy rates, the lowest worker productivity standards, and some of the worst personal income levels in the country. During World War II, North Carolina saw the highest percentage of its residents deemed physically unfit for military service. Franklin Roosevelt's "Report on the Economic Conditions of the South" characterized the wrenching deprivation in southern states like North Carolina as "the nation's number one economic problem," noting that millions lived "in poverty comparable to that of the poorest peasants in Europe."[4] Even by the late 1950s, North Carolina had more residents living in mobile homes than any other state, only half of its students graduated from high school, and well over a third of its households lived in torturous poverty. It had earlier, perhaps deservingly, been mocked broadly as the "Rip Van Winkle State."[5] As my colleague James Johnson has written: "Before World War II, poverty problems received limited public policy attention and that attention abated after the war. Poverty did not become a priority policy issue again until the early 1960s."[6]

Terry Sanford's pathbreaking North Carolina Fund, launched in 1962, promised, for the first time in the nation, an ambitious partnership sufficiently bold and idealistic to take aim at economic and racial conditions that crushed the "lives and livelihoods" of great numbers of Tar Heels. It sought to ameliorate a "poverty that withers the spirit of children who neither imposed it nor deserve it, and who lack the means to break out of it." Governor Sanford declared that "in North Carolina there remain tens of thousands whose family income is so low that daily subsistence is always in doubt." He saw the fund as an "all out assault on poverty" seeking "to find ways to break the cycle of [hardship] and dependency." A child, he wrote, "who goes to school with no breakfast under his belt does not have equal opportunity to learn, excel and move forward to adulthood"; neither does he have "an equal chance to learn if he happens to come from a home where reading is unknown and school is underappreciated."[7]

The fund was, purposefully, a five-year project, an "advance guard" for

Graph 20. United States and North Carolina poverty rates, 1960–2016

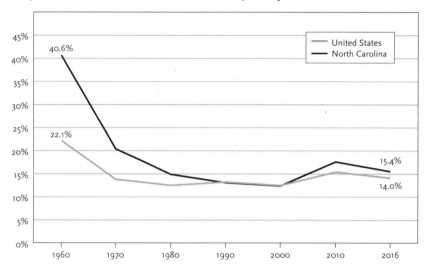

Sources: U.S. Census Bureau, 1960, 1970, 1980, 1990, and 2000 Decennial Census; 2010 and 2016 American Community Survey

anticipated federal antipoverty programs. It expended over $16 million in private and public funds. It saw both successes and failures—some economic and structural, others political and racial. When combined with the even more potent federal components of Lyndon Johnson's War on Poverty and Great Society programs, the impact on pervasive poverty was notable. In 1960, over a third of individual North Carolinians lived in poverty. By 1980, that number had been cut nearly in half, falling to about 15 percent, though the preceding decade had not been marked by dramatic economic growth.[8]

Since 1980, though, North Carolina's poverty rate has hovered in the 14 to 18 percent range. It has almost always exceeded federal standards, at times markedly. On the other hand, it has never been significantly lower than the national average. The elevated levels have continued under both Democratic and occasional Republican governors. And it has been difficult to find any modern-day equivalent of Terry Sanford or the sustained investments of the North Carolina Fund. Over the last three decades, political leaders in both parties have done relatively little to ensure that the plight of low-income people receives sustained attention. Meanwhile, as those whose voices are at the center of this volume have suggested, the challenges for hard-pressed North Carolinians have seemed to grow notably larger. If modest economic gains have appeared generally, stark levels of hardship have stubbornly persisted, and as these narratives have often revealed, the impact of deprivation has seemed only to increase. The polarization can echo periods in the first decades of the twentieth century, when the state's citizens struggled with the aftermath of profound economic crisis, single political parties held most power, and leaders wielded their clout in the interest of their principal benefactors. Then as now, the economic plight of poor Tar Heels did not significantly appear on the political radar screen.

Low-income residents of North Carolina began learning in 2012, though, that there are worse things than being ignored by their government. My conversations with impoverished Tar Heels frequently indicated a belief that they were being targeted by those who are supposed to represent their interests.

BURDENING THE IMPOVERISHED

Republicans took control of the General Assembly, for the first time in over a century, in 2010. Backlash to the election of President Barack Obama, the rise of the Tea Party nationally, a mounting antagonism to health care reform, and the near-collapse of the North Carolina Democratic Party were combining causes. The North Carolina Supreme Court had been securely in Republican hands for more than a decade. And in 2012, state government was captured completely with the election of Republican Pat McCrory, former mayor of Charlotte, as governor. A notable and historic alteration in governing philosophies surfaced almost immediately. Those who were struggling economically felt direct and sustained impact. The *New York Times* editorialized, in 2013, on "the decline of North Carolina," denouncing the "grotesque damage that a new Republican majority has [done] to a tradition of caring for the least fortunate."[9] National commentators began referring to North Carolina as a "conservative lab experiment."[10]

In 2013, the governor and the General Assembly quickly rejected the Medicaid expansion proffered by the federal government under the voluntary terms of the Affordable Care Act. As discussed in Chapter 4 above, the decision meant that 463,000 poor Tar Heels were denied health care coverage that would have been paid for almost entirely by the national government.[11] The choice was known to be a costly one. North Carolina would forgo tens of billions of health care dollars, hundreds of millions of state and local dollars in tax revenue, tens of thousands of jobs, and hundreds of millions of dollars in savings for uncompensated hospital care, and most telling, studies demonstrated that a thousand or more poor citizens would die annually as a result of the rejection.[12] Yet as in other, mostly southern states, North Carolina leaders pressed ahead, repeatedly declaring opposition to both the Affordable Care Act generally and Medicaid expansion specifically.

In the face of what were, at the time, soaring unemployment rates— the fifth highest in the nation—the General Assembly also swiftly enacted one of the steepest cuts to an unemployment compensation program in American history. Over 170,000 unemployed residents lost their federal unemployment benefits when North Carolina became the only state in the country to withdraw from central aspects of the national unemployment scheme. Again, in effect, the state rejected available federal funding to assist low-income Tar Heels—this time, those who had been unemployed for a significant period of time.[13] North Carolinians still able to receive benefits learned that their payments had been cut by a third. The maximum weekly benefit was reduced from $535 to $350. The length of time one could receive compensation was reduced from twenty-six weeks to twelve.[14] After the changes, only 11 percent of the state's unemployed residents received benefits, the lowest percentage in the country. The average duration for collecting benefits also fell to the bottom.[15] The cuts resulted in North Carolina's unemployment compensation program moving from the middle of the pack to the stingiest in America.[16]

The General Assembly also, in the same year, made North Carolina the only state to ever eliminate its earned income tax credit (EITC), thereby raising the taxes owed by nearly a million low-income taxpayers making about $35,000 to $40,000 a year.[17] Almost one out of four workers in North Carolina had qualified for the credit.[18] EITC programs have been widely heralded, on a bipartisan basis, as among the most effective and uplifting antipoverty programs. They were available only to people who work and earn income from wages, salary, or self-employment.[19] The state credit allowed employed, low-income families to keep a higher percentage of their income, thus becoming more readily able to support their children and avoid welfare and public assistance programs. The state EITC program also helped to offset the regressive aspects of sales and property tax regimes.[20] Research by the Center on Budget and Policy Priorities found that state EITC programs are "easy to administer, with nearly every dollar spent on the state credits going directly to the working families they were created to help. . . . They also [work] to reduce poverty, especially among children."[21] The North Carolina General Assembly, it concluded, had earned the "dubious distinction" of being the only American government to ever move, in this fashion, to make it harder for low-income working families to support their kids.[22]

But by late 2013 it had become clear that the elimination of the EITC was merely one component of a broader legislative strategy to shift the state's existing tax burden away from the wealthy and to lodge it more robustly on the poor.[23] The General Assembly first scrapped North Carolina's progressive income tax and replaced it with a flat tax,[24] markedly lowering the rate for wealthier taxpayers. It then eliminated the estate tax, a standard that already applied only to estates of $5 million or more.[25] It next cut the tax rate for corporations and worked to shield out-of-state businesses from paying taxes on some profits earned in North Carolina. Meanwhile, the legislature extended the sales tax to an array of new services, raising the relative burden on low-income taxpayers. In 2015, lawmakers again cut the income tax rate for personal and corporate taxpayers and expanded the regressive sales tax to more categories of goods and services, including car and appliance repairs, that fall more squarely on people with limited resources.[26]

A study by the North Carolina Budget & Tax Center exploring who had benefited from and who had been burdened by the flurry of tax changes from 2013 to 2015 revealed that the richest 1 percent of taxpayers enjoyed a cut of $14,977 per year. The next 4 percent got a decrease of almost $2,000. The fourth (highest) quintile received $465. The middle quintile saved $75. The bottom 40 percent received tax increases, not reductions, with the largest increases saved for the poorest 20 percent. Three-quarters of the total tax benefit went to the top 20 percent of earners. In 2015, North Carolinians making less than $20,000 a year paid 9.2 percent of their income in state and local taxes. Those making over $376,000 annually paid 5.3 percent.[27]

Lawmakers also dramatically cut or diminished the availability of an array of programs on which low-income Tar Heels had traditionally relied. Child care subsidies, essential to assure that many parents living at the edge of poverty can actually afford to work, were significantly reduced. Through changes in income eligibility, reductions in funding, and cuts to reimbursement rates, over 30,000 fewer children were given assistance in 2014 than had occurred in 2010 (dropping from 151,363 in 2010 to 121,113 in 2014). The state doesn't track what happened to the kids in question, but experts like Michele Rivest, director of the North Carolina Child Care Coalition, indicated that such cuts typically mean that either the parents had to quit their jobs, the children were cared for by neighbors or family members, or, too often, they were left home alone after school to fend for themselves.[28]

Despite rising demand, North Carolina's nationally recognized pre-K program, as a result of cuts enacted by the General Assembly, was able to serve 6,476 fewer low-income children in 2016 than it had in 2009. The cuts occurred as the Washington Center for Equitable Growth released a strong study finding that such programs are the most effective way to close the noted achievement gap between children from high- and low-income families and to improve the educational performance of students overall.[29] The state's Oral Health Department received a cascade of cuts that dropped the number of dental hygienists who provide examinations at elementary schools throughout the state and help to secure coverage for kids whose families cannot afford regular dental care from eighty-four a decade ago to thirty-six in 2015. The staff cuts left 35 (of 100) counties without dental services. Mary Oates, who coordinates the school nurse program in Lee County, which now receives no dental assistance from the state, indicated the reductions did not entail "a huge amount of money, but the benefits of [the dental program] across the state were tremendous for our children."[30]

Continuing the trend, in late 2015, the General Assembly passed a bill that cut off food assistance (SNAP benefits) to 105,000 impoverished Tar Heels in the state's seventy-seven most economically strapped counties. North Carolina, as discussed in Chapter 2, has one of the nation's highest food-insecurity rates. The SNAP benefits targeted provided, on average, $30 per week and were, again, completely funded by the federal government. Declining the assistance saved no dollars for the state treasury. Funding intended for poor Tar Heels, already having substantial difficulty making ends meet, was simply returned to Washington. Senator Norman Sanderson of Pamlico County explained that jobless recipients of food stamps needed a shove to go to work: "I think you are going to see a lot of them go and get that 20 hour a week job now," instead of sitting back, taking it easy.[31]

The North Carolina Senate attempted to expand the exclusionary move in 2017, voting to remove another 133,000 poor people from the SNAP program by eliminating "broad-based categorical eligibility" policies used in thirty-eight other states.[32] Such rules allow modestly higher economic eligibilities for food stamp applicants already qualifying for federal disability benefits, given additional care expenses incurred.[33] Senator Ralph Hise inserted the restriction on page 144 of the budget bill without hearings, debates, or notice during the allocation process. He claimed the restriction was crucial to allay recent "tremendous growth" in the SNAP program, though North Carolina food stamp participation rates had actually dropped to 13.9 percent in 2017, after peaking during the recession at 18.4 percent in 2011.[34] Hise explained that the change was "necessary to ensure benefits are delivered only to those who truly need them." Over 50,000 of those losing benefits under the proposal were children. The newly elected Democratic governor, Roy Cooper, protested that "this food makes a real difference for families who need it and it doesn't cost North Carolina any state tax money."[35] Fortunately, Senator Hise's 2017 proposal died in conference during budget reconciliation with the House.[36]

North Carolina's recent approach to food assistance reflects a longer trend. When the federal government temporarily shut down during budget deadlocks in 2013, North Carolina was the first (and only) state to suspend its Temporary Aid to Needy Families Program. The state Department of Health and Human Services instructed local offices that "no new approved applications for Work First should be processed because of the [possible] unavailability of federal funds."[37] The federal government assured state officials that any state dollars expended would be fully reimbursed. U.S. Congressmen David Price and G. K. Butterfield explained, in a letter to the governor, that the national assurances had been deemed sufficient "by 49 other states." Then–Health and Human Services spokesperson Julie Henry explained the commitment wasn't good enough for North Carolina.[38]

In October 2015, the General Assembly eliminated the state's appropriation for legal services. About a third of the already heavily burdened staff of Legal Aid of North Carolina had to be terminated, though they were able to meet only about 20 percent of the legal needs of poor Tar Heels even before the cuts were initiated.[39] In the 2017 session the legislature, without hearings, notice, or explanation, while enjoying an ample budget surplus, eliminated a remaining "legal access fee" attached to court filings that also had provided state assistance to legal service providers, approximating $1.7 million a year.[40] Another forty lawyers had to be terminated at Legal Aid of North Carolina, meaning more than half the staff had to be dismissed.[41] A couple of months after the imposing cuts were enacted, House Speaker Tim Moore explained that they were triggered because legal aid lawyers had become too zealous in representing poor tenants.[42] During the same session, the General Assembly passed a cumbersome procedural regime designed to make it immensely more difficult for state judges to waive court fees for indigent litigants.

It is likely unconstitutional under the Fourteenth Amendment,[43] but it echoed the legislators' apparent disdain for poor people's use of the justice system.[44] When the General Assembly called itself into special session to pass what came to be described as the noted "bathroom bill," HB2, in 2016, requiring that North Carolinians use the restroom facilities of the sex reflected on their birth certificates, it also included a provision making it illegal for any municipality to increase its minimum wage.[45] The list of measures removing benefits from or adding burdens to low-income Tar Heels from 2012 to 2017 is an imposing one. There is little reason to think it won't continue.

THE LIVES AND VOICES OF LOW-INCOME TAR HEELS

The North Carolina General Assembly also enacted a drug-screening requirement for Work First recipients in 2015.[46] The legislative sponsor of the new program indicated that it was rooted in the belief held, he said, by the bulk of his lawmaking colleagues "that a large segment of the population that receives welfare benefits either abuses the system or does not use the benefits for the purpose intended."[47] The Work First program offers short-term cash benefits, training, and support services to families in extreme exigency. In 62 percent of Work First cases only children get benefits. The drug tests are costly, administratively burdensome, and potentially humiliating to poor applicants. The legislature asked for a progress report on the new initiative in early 2016. Of the thousands tested, twenty-one came back positive, less than 0.3 percent of applicants screened. Of the twenty-one test failures, twelve were still approved for partial payments because children were the beneficiaries. The National Institute on Drug Abuse reports that illicit drug use among Americans age twelve or older, generally, is 9.4 percent.[48] To his credit, Representative Craig Horn, a driving force behind the testing requirement in the state house, admitted the results made him question whether he had made unfair assumptions about the behavior of poor people. "I was frankly surprised," he said. "I had expected different numbers; hopefully it's a good indicator." Nonetheless, the legislators opted to keep the humiliating testing scheme in place.[49]

Representative Horn's candor suggests that the actual lived experience of many poor North Carolinians may sometimes be at odds with the presuppositions of the government officials who, in theory, represent them. Legislators, like many of us, can simply turn their gaze away from the challenges, indignities, and depredations of North Carolina poverty and assume they don't really or significantly exist. Many of the low-income Tar Heels interviewed for the chapters above believe that this is precisely what occurs with their government decision-makers. Either little thought is given to the actual day-to-day challenges they face or inaccurate assumptions are made about their motivations and circumstance.

When Tonya Hall, interviewed for Chapter 4, read of the General Assembly's decision to reject Medicaid expansion, she said, "They must not understand what I'm going through." Her family's experiences with cancer mean that

> I live in fear. My kids deal with the constant worry that they're going to lose their mother. I've worked hard my whole life. I feel like I'm fighting for my life here and the state of North Carolina could care less. If I woke up tomorrow and got an email telling me I qualified for some type of insurance, it would change my life. It would be such a godsend to me and my family. It's disheartening now because my kids see I have to fight for every bit of medical care I get. I've got grandkids. I want to see them grow up. Surely no one would put me through this on purpose.

Dr. Arumugham, whom we also met in Chapter 4, echoes the notion: "I wish they would come to Kinston and meet my patients. Every day I see how we let people suffer, just because they don't have money and we won't let them have insurance. I know people say, 'I'm against giving them money they don't deserve,' but that's not what's happening. We're only saying, 'You are sick and we're going to try to fix you.'" Dr. Evan Ashkin similarly explained that his low-income patients do not match the stereotypes he hears coming from those who reject expanded health care coverage. The "notion that they are lazy freeloaders is possible only if you have never worked with anyone in this patient population." They are people "in excruciating circumstances, in intense distress arising from circumstances beyond their control." He thinks legislators might change their views "if they came down here to meet them."

During the weeks we were interviewing Yolanda and her colleagues at Crisis Assistance Ministry in Charlotte, North Carolina's child care subsidy program was significantly cut by the General Assembly. Yolanda has two young sons and goes to community college after a full day at work in health care. "I was told under the new rules passed by the legislature my income was now $100 too high, so I couldn't get any more help with child care at all." That meant her expenses would go up by several hundred dollars a month. They told her, at the agency, that she ought to quit her job, but that disgusted her: "I've had to quit jobs before to keep my child care and my kids are all that matters to me, but I wouldn't let them make me quit this time." You can't get anywhere, she said, if you aren't working. But "where in the world am I going to get another three hundred dollars a month?" While legislators may assume Yolanda is after a free ride, unwilling to work, she is actually desperate not to give up her career and the progress she has pressed so hard to secure. The inability to secure good child care, though, makes her employment prospects dramatically more challenging.

In the 2017 legislative session, as mentioned above, the General Assembly enacted a set of stringent procedural hurdles designed to make it inordinately difficult for state judges to waive an array of fines and user fees imposed increasingly upon even indigent criminal defendants.[50] Jill Shriver, whom my students interviewed in Orange County in November 2017, saw a different side of the sanctions. She pled guilty earlier in the year to misdemeanor larceny. Her public defender had convinced her it was the safest course. When the court accepted her plea, it assessed $560 in fees against her. She was told she would have six months to pay. If she failed to come up with the money, she would be held in violation of her probation. When my students asked if she could come up with the funds, Shriver replied, "Absolutely not, I don't have even $100 to spare." She had been jailed before for failure to pay an assessed court fee. The judge who imposed the costs never asked if she had any way to pay it, as the constitution demands. She said she lives in fear that she'll be incarcerated again and lose her job and her housing. "The whole thing leaves my family feeling hopeless, like we'll never get back on our feet, it's like a set-up, they know I won't possibly be able to pay." It reminds her, she says, of the old debtor prisons—you are put in jail just because you're poor.

Part of the North Carolina General Assembly's justification for its poverty policies is the oft-cited belief that there is no actual deep poverty in the state—that poverty data is manipulated to justify favored state and federal social programs.[51] That notion drives Daphany Hill, director of Jacksonville's Eastern North Carolina Human Services agency, over the top. She explained that in the winter of 2013 her agency opened up their potential wait-list for housing assistance. "We had people camped out, in the freezing weather, well before midnight." Over 300 folks lined up. "They came with blankets, their coffee, their tea, to make it through the brutally cold night." She recalled trying to get the elderly and frail inside, but there wasn't enough room in the building. The agency began taking applications at 9:00 A.M. They took potential enrollees for over four hours and had to shut the list back down. Many applicants explained, through tears, that they were desperate for help. Hill, holding back her own tears, said, "There may be some legislators who say we don't have any real poverty, but they should come down here and meet these people." It makes her furious, she explained. "There's plenty of deep poverty in Onslow County—you just have to be willing to see it."

Fayetteville police officer Stacy Sanders works directly with the ample homeless population in Cumberland County. The largest grouping lives, regularly, under the bridges in downtown Fayetteville at Person and Water streets. But Sanders says they're actually to be found all across the city—in empty buildings, in cars, in storage rooms, under overpasses, along woodlines. "I was shocked," she says, "when I first came across families with kids—mom, dad, baby." She had thought that would constitute abuse and neglect, but she was told the city thought that would be counterproductive. "It's a whole lot worse than it was when I started ten years ago," she reports. Lots of the homeless, especially in Fayetteville, are veterans, like Sanders is. Some are fresh from the nation's battlefields. And others just can't make ends meet. "I get tired of hearing people say we don't have these kinds of problems," she reminds me. "We have a lot of working homeless here, working at McDonald's or Taco Bell, doing landscaping on the side." They can't afford food, rent, and transportation on what they make. "We have to take the blinders off; people need to see what's actually going on and quit pretending it doesn't happen." Sometimes you don't see, she says, because you don't want to see.

The children of undocumented parents who have been treated roughly by the state of North Carolina would likely say their challenges, hardships, and exclusions are largely ignored no matter who is in power—Democrats or Republicans. The dreamers have been dismissed by them all. Ricsy Sanchez says,

I'm standing here. I hope that you can see me. I filed 5-10 applications for scholarships a week for months and months at a time. I'd always write my story. Hoping they would actually see me, not just a social security number. Or just a political debating point. I've lived here most all my life and I've always worked hard. How can you say I'm not a North Carolinian and that no matter how long I live here, where my family is, I never will be one? I wish the government here had more people whose eyes and minds were open. What do they actually want me to do? This is the only place I can live. I have a family. I have to take care of my disabled father. If I can only clean houses instead of being a lawyer, what good does that do anybody? I still think if you explain your story, people will open their hearts. So I always try to tell them. I always try. They may not listen, but I always try.

CIRCUMSCRIBING THE CONSTITUENCY: A NOTE ABOUT DEMOCRACY

Millions of North Carolinians live in families that don't enjoy a living wage or affordable housing or enough to eat or health insurance or safe neighborhoods or decent schools or access to transportation or higher education. Economic hardship and deprivation is widespread. It is not lodged in an isolated corner of the state or limited to an unfortunate, forgettable few. So, to the constitutional lawyer in me, it is modestly surprising that the reality of such barriers and degradations does not play a larger role in our state's political decision-making. The effect of poverty on individuals, families, and communities is intense and often debilitating. It alters people's prospects, happiness, and life chances on a broad-ranging basis. It restricts lots of people's opportunities and fortunes. I think James Madison would have believed it unlikely, or perhaps impossible, that such potently felt and widely shared interests would be all but excluded from the working agenda of a constitutional democracy.

Madison, of course, also would not have anticipated the role that money now plays in American government, at both state and federal levels. The broad swath of U.S. Supreme Court decisions that now are, perhaps collectively, referred to as "Citizens United" in our political and social discourse privilege economic power over political power in ways that test our actual claim to democracy. Much has been written on this front.[52] Even I have done some of it. I make no assertion that what I think of as "cash register politics" has anything other than an extraordinary, and extraordinarily negative, impact on low-income people in North Carolina.

Still, I think something even larger and more indefensible is at play as well in the dramatic political marginalization of poor people in North Carolina. Given the state's remarkable income disparity, its economic and racial segregation, its growing and potent concentrations of poverty amidst amazing plenty, and its gaping economic and social polarizations, for very large numbers of us the haunting challenges of North Carolina poverty, child poverty, hunger, health, and diminished dignity and opportunity can be, almost literally, invisible. Life is, as most of us see it, promising; horizons are potentially boundless, dreams are likely attainable, and prospects are typically appealing. And so, we assume, circumstances are basically similar for everyone, or at least almost everyone—this is, after all, the richest nation in human history. So why worry about problems that don't exist? Or if they do exist, it is only because people have brought them on themselves. The plight of the impoverished becomes, at best, an abstract problem. When the rest of us no longer see the poor, empathy is diminished. As Robert Putnam writes, "It constrains our sense of reciprocity. It constrains our sense of what we owe to one another. We are less and less a community."[53]

Then perhaps political presuppositions can go a step further. A 2014 poll conducted by the Pew Research Center for the People and the Press found that nearly half of all Americans and about 80 percent of self-identified political conservatives believe that "poor people today have it easy because they get government benefits without doing anything in return."[54] The notion that life is "easy" for low-income North Carolinians is impossible to square with their lived experiences and with the narratives captured in these chapters. It is not hard to imagine, though, that given such predispositions, many state leaders would move beyond ignoring the poor to actually targeting programs that are seen as aiding low-income people and increasing the costs and obligations the impoverished are expected to shoulder. When we actually do consider the poor, apparently many see them as "other"—plagued by flaws of character and resolution and mistaken incentive. They are not part of "us." They are not actual members of the constituency. They do not enter the political calculus.

A POLITICS OF FULL MEMBERSHIP:
BEING TREATED AS ENTIRE CITIZENS

There are many theories that seek to explain both the causes and cures of poverty in North Carolina. An array of political strategies, some reportedly liberal, some said to be conservative, have been developed to attack the scourge of poverty. Some platforms would deploy market-based solutions. Others would seek to intervene, assuming markets have obviously failed. Still others focus on the purported moral failures and shortcomings of low-income Tar Heels. And some try to embrace all or most of the alternatives above. Unsurprisingly, no consensus emerges. It likely never will. Money, human frailty, generosity, obligation, taxation, charity, freedom, equality, and hope are complicated and colliding notions.

It ought to be easy to conclude, though, that North Carolina's two dominant public policies of the past forty years—either ignoring or attacking the poor—are not only counterproductive but also powerfully at odds with our shared claims as a people. Targeting low-income people for political advantage or passively accepting wounding and brutal disadvantage for a quarter of Tar Heels is an unworthy stance for one of the most economically vibrant American states. It cannot be tenable to conclude that so many of our sisters and brothers simply don't matter. Our religions, our constitutions, our aspirations, our practical judgments, and our loathing of hypocrisy rail against it. None of us are invisible. None have disappeared. None are expendable.

Regardless of political predilection or economic theory, then, the first and most central step in dealing with poverty and marginalization is to embrace a politics of full membership. Ten million North Carolinians constitute the commonwealth we embrace. That total includes more than 2 million women, men, and children who live at or near the edges of poverty. There is no acceptable writing off of their challenging plight. The rights of dignity, participation, opportunity, and worth that attach to membership belong fully to each one of us. We have no invisible, partial, or disqualified members.

A politics of full membership, of course, includes shared and common opportunities of expression, participation, development, and engagement. It also means, when it comes to poverty policy, that the lives, challenges, and hardships of Tar Heels suffering from economic deprivation cannot be allowed to simply fade from sight. Separating and polarizing communities does not solve problems merely by making them seem to vanish. Instead, the problems are exacerbated. Problems don't evaporate just because they fall or are purposefully excluded from view.

Nor can the challenges of poverty be addressed through mere political ideology, philosophical speculation, economic calculation, or tribal predisposition. Meaningful confrontation with poverty must be rooted in the lived experiences of low-income and impoverished North Carolinians. No difficulties can be effectively understood except through the power of their descriptions and uplifted voices. No successes can be measured except by the actual impact of policies and practices on their day-to-day lives. No other voices can supplant theirs, even if the talkers purport to be learned or elevated. Rich and poor are full and equal members in their authority to call on our attentions and trigger our obligations of brotherhood. It is not permissible, consistent with our claims, to simply turn our gaze away.

And even in the private sector, full membership should mean that our foundational obligations to one another can't be allowed to recede just because the challenges have become increasingly unknown to us. If we have powers to mitigate hunger and destitution, and yet we still allow them to persist, it is not an effective answer to say, "I never saw it, no one I cared about told me, I didn't know."

As I have visited low-income communities in North Carolina over the past decade and listened to, written and spoken about, and studied the challenges they face, I have been reminded regularly of the state's deep, deep divisions over the social responsibilities that attach to poverty. Many North Carolinians, me among them, believe that our defining constitutive commitments to equal protection under law, full personal dignity and opportunity, and as we repeatedly pledge, "liberty and justice for all" bespeak a public, governmental obligation to secure the inherent "blessings of liberty" even to those at the bottom of the economic ladder. At present, with unacceptable doses of hardship, deprivation, and inequality, such adherents of publicly shared responsibility can scarcely feel satisfied.

But many North Carolinians reject such a vision of government. Injuries and burdens rooted in economic hardship are, generally speaking, not the concern or the accepted bailiwick of government, state or federal. The private sphere—religious, social, nonprofit, fraternal, eleemosynary, commercial, and corporate—shoulders the encumbrance of concern for "the least of these."[55] No shared obligation of generosity or attention to the plight of one's fellows can be mandated through the force of the state. We take up such virtue voluntarily. Compulsion defeats the dignity of both the receiver and the giver of care. The state appropriately assures only access to a leveled field of competition and participation. Charity resides at home, in private undertaking.

For me, the notion of a leveled field of opportunity and participation, when laid next to the realities of economic hardship and privation in North Carolina, defeats completely the underlying premise of the charity-alone model. But even if I am incorrect in that assessment and our obligations toward one another are merely private and religious or social, there seems little doubt that we are failing radically in our repeatedly asserted responsibilities to one another. Neither our religious nor our political attestations support being the richest, the poorest, and the most unequal society in the world. No matter where one lodges shared obligation, in other words, we don't seem to meet it. And it is no shield from obligation to choose to be unaware of the plight of our sisters and brothers.

I have been an equality lawyer for forty years. Since my earliest days on that path I have been taken with the words Thurgood Marshall spoke to the U.S. Supreme Court while arguing *Brown v. Board of Education*, the most important constitutional ruling in American history. As counsel for the poor, excluded black children pursuing the litigation, Marshall said to his future Supreme Court colleagues, "These infant appellants assert the most important claims that can be set forth by children. [They seek the right] to be treated as entire citizens of the society into which they have been born."[56]

Poor North Carolinians, too, are "entire citizens" of this commonwealth. They must be treated as if we fully understood and embraced that entirety.

ACKNOWLEDGMENTS

There are many people to thank on this project. The Z. Smith Reynolds Foundation and the A. J. Fletcher Foundation have provided essential support. A number of nonprofit leaders and social services providers generously opened doors to low-income communities that made deeper explorations possible. Raquel Lynch, Carol Hardison, and Daniel Valdez of Crisis Assistance Ministry in Charlotte; Heather Murphy of the Health Foundation in Wilkes County; Jessica Holmes in Raleigh; Roger Cornett of Open Door Ministry in greater Hickory; Danielle Baptiste of the Dillard Academy and Shirley Edwards, both of Goldsboro; Jill Staton Bullard of the Inter-Faith Food Shuttle in Wake County; and Clyde Fitzgerald of Second Harvest Food Bank in Winston-Salem are strong examples.

Many students have contributed their research efforts to the project through work with the North Carolina Poverty Research Fund: Rachel VanCamp, Matt Norchi, John Gibson, Rory Fleming, Will Graebe, Maya Waheed, Lashieka Hardin, and Kahlil Perine. Poverty Center fellows Joe Polich and Allison Demarco assisted as well. Daniel Horwitz provided strong editorial and research work.

But my most important partner, by far, was UNC Poverty Center and North Carolina Poverty Research Fund research associate Heather Hunt. Heather and I have worked together for almost a decade on North Carolina poverty issues. She is a master of census data and varied forms of empirical research, areas where my own shortcomings are difficult to even describe. (To hint, I don't have a smart phone.) She can also construct charts and graphs that I could never even attempt. So many parts of the book, especially the chapters on Charlotte, Wilkes County, and Goldsboro, could not have been developed, at least by me, without her. To call her a "research associate" is an understatement. She is also an immensely careful and solid scholar. I hope nothing here embarrasses her.

Finally, I am very grateful for the guidance of Mark Simpson-Vos of UNC Press. I'm not the easiest person in the world to edit. In every instance, Mark's interventions made this thin volume a better book.

A NOTE ON METHOD

There is, unsurprisingly, a good deal of U.S. Census Bureau and other federal agency income, poverty, inequality, wealth, and food insecurity data in these pages. I try my best throughout to use citations up to date as of December 2017. In Chapter 5, some state labor and workforce numbers and school district data are modestly older, 2014–16. Much of the book is comprised of narrative. Interviews reflected here occurred between 2013 and 2017. I conducted almost all of them, though my students and colleagues at the North Carolina Poverty Research Fund did a handful. Broadly speaking, for reasons of privacy and stigma, I have changed the names of the economically stressed, homeless, hungry, health care deprived, or otherwise impoverished and low-income people interviewed. There are a few exceptions to that. In one instance (in Chapter 7), I use an individual's real name to match a newspaper story I also discuss. In the Crisis Assistance Ministry Charlotte interviews, the Circles women interviewed debated and voted to use their first names only, so I comply with their request. In Chapter 8, the students or aspiring students opt to use their real names. The names of social service providers, doctors, teachers, community leaders, food bank workers, health and charitable care professionals, poverty workers, nurses, ministers, professors, and other advocates and activists are, of course, retained. Finally, Chapters 4, 5, 6, and 7 parallel longer, more data- and recommendation-laden reports by the North Carolina Poverty Research Fund. These reports have not been published in print but are listed and linked on the North Carolina Poverty Research Fund website. See http://www.law.unc.edu/centers/poverty/. The reports draw upon the same data, interviews, and research efforts as the corresponding chapters here, though I wrote these shorter, narrative-driven chapters before the longer poverty fund reports were compiled.

NOTES

PREFACE

1. National rating services indicate that Hickory's cost of living is well below the national average, scoring 87.4 based on a national average of 100. See *City-Data*, http://www.city-data.com/city/Hickory-North-Carolina.html#b (4 February 2018).

2. See *City of Hickory*, http://www.hickorync.gov (4 February 2018).

3. Peter Whoriskey, "Globalization Brings a World of Hurt to One Corner of North Carolina," *Washington Post*, 10 November 2009, http://www.washington post.com/wp-dyn/content/article/2009/11/09/AR2009110903705.html (4 February 2018).

4. Ibid.

5. See "America's Shrinking Middle Class: A Close Look at Changes within Metropolitan Areas," *Pew Research Center*, 11 May 2016, http://www.pewsocial trends.org/2016/05/11/3-the-middle-class-shrank-and-incomes-fell-in-most -metropolitan-areas-from-2000-to-2014/ (4 February 2018).

6. Charles B. Stockdale, "Ten Cities That Will Take a Decade to Recover from the Recession," *24/7 Wall St.*, 22 June 2011, http://247wallst.com/investing/2011 /06/22/ten-cites-that-will-take-a-decade-to-recover-from-the-recession/ (4 February 2018): "Once a major center for the production of textiles, many jobs have been sent overseas, causing textile mills to close down, and work to be lost."

7. Alexander E. M. Hess and Michael B. Sauter, "America's Most Content and Miserable Cities," *24/7 Wall St.*, 26 March 2013, http://247wallst.com/special -report/2013/03/26/americas-most-content-and-miserable-cities/5/ (4 February 2018): "Nowhere else in the nation did people have as negative an evaluation of their lives as in the Hickory metro area. A major reason was that the survey respondents were less optimistic about their life in five years than in almost all parts of the country. Many residents lacked the formal education necessary to work in higher paying jobs. Just 79 percent of residents had at least a high school diploma and 18 percent a bachelor's degree, versus 86 percent and 29 percent nationwide."

8. "America's Shrinking Middle Class."

9. Conversation with Roger Cornett.

10. I visited homeless camps in Hickory, often with Mr. Cornett, on eight occasions from 2012 to 2017. See Nation Hahn, "Homeless in Hickory," *EducationNC*, 13 January 2016, https://www.ednc.org/2016/01/13/homeless-in -hickory/ (5 February 2018); Nation Hahn, "Homeless in Hickory, Continued,"

EducationNC, 11 May 2016, https://www.ednc.org/2016/05/11/homeless-hickory
-continued/ (5 February 2018); Sharon McBrayer, "Number of Homeless Growing
in Catawba County," 30 January 2013, http://www.hickoryrecord.com/news
/number-of-homeless-growing-in-catawba-county/article_b70edb2a-6b53-11e2
-975e-0014bcf6878.html (5 February 2018); Gene Nichol, "Seeing the Invisible:
'What Are We Doing for the Least of These?,'" *Raleigh News & Observer*, 23
February 2013, http://www.newsobserver.com/opinion/op-ed/article10345121
.html (4 February 2018); Gene Nichol, "The North Carolina Poor Our State
Officials Refuse to See," *Raleigh News & Observer*, 19 February 2015, http://www
.newsobserver.com/opinion/op-ed/article10880423.html (4 February 2018).

11. McBrayer, "Number of Homeless Growing in Catawba County."

12. See the discussion on targeting poor people in North Carolina in Chapter 10.

13. Christopher Hale, "St. Augustine's Restlessness and MLK's 'Dream,'"
Sojourners, 26 August 2016, https://sojo.net/articles/keeping-feast/st-augustines
-restlessness-and-mlks-dream (5 February 2018).

CHAPTER 1

1. "Transcript of Johnson Address on Voting Rights," *New York Times*, 16 March
1965, http://www.nytimes.com/books/98/04/12/specials/johnson-rightsadd.html
(5 February 2018).

2. Jessica L. Semega, Kayla R. Fontenot, and Melissa A. Kollar, *Income and
Poverty in the United States: 2016*, U.S. Census Bureau, Current Population Reports
(Washington, D.C.: U.S. Government Printing Office, 2017), 43, https://www
.census.gov/content/dam/Census/library/publications/2017/demo/P60-259.pdf
(27 February 2018).

3. Ibid., 13.

4. Ibid.

5. Ibid.

6. "Federal Data Summary, School Years 2012–13 to 2014–15: Education
for Homeless Children and Youth," *National Center for Homeless Education,
University of North Carolina at Greensboro*, December 2016, https://nche.ed.gov
/downloads/data-comp-12-13-14-15.pdf (5 February 2018).

7. Alisha Coleman-Jensen, Matthew P. Rabbitt, Christian A. Gregory, et al.,
Household Food Security in the United States in 2016, Economic Research Service,
USDA, September 2017, https://www.ers.usda.gov/webdocs/publications/84973
/err-237.pdf (5 February 2018).

8. Jesse Bricker et al., *Changes in US Family Finances from 2013 to 2016:
Evidence from the Survey of Consumer Finances*, Federal Reserve Bulletin, 13
September 2017, 10, https://www.federalreserve.gov/publications/files/scf17.pdf
(7 February 2018).

9. Ibid.

10. Steve Hargreaves, "How Income Inequality Hurts America," *CNN Money*,

25 September 2013, http://money.cnn.com/2013/09/25/news/economy/income
-inequality/index.html (7 February 2018).

11. Chuck Collins and Josh Hoxie, "The Forbes 400 and the Rest of Us," *Institute for Policy Studies*, December 2015, http://www.ips-dc.org/wp-content/uploads
/2015/12/Billionaire-Bonanza-The-Forbes-400-and-the-Rest-of-Us-Dec1.pdf
(7 February 2018); Robert Frank, "Billionaires Own as Much as the Bottom Half of Americans?," *Wall Street Journal*, 7 May 2011, https://blogs.wsj.com/wealth/2011
/03/07/billionaires-own-as-much-as-the-bottom-half-of-americans/ (7 February 2017); Richard Fry and Rakesh Kochhar, "America's Wealth Gap between Middle-Income and Upper-Income Families Is Widest on Record," *Pew Research Center*, 17 December 2014, http://www.pewresearch.org/fact-tank/2014/12/17/wealth
-gap-upper-middle-income/ (7 February 2018); Emily Horton, Chad Stone, Danilo Trisi, and Arloc Sherman, "A Guide to Statistics on Historical Trends in Income Inequality," *Center on Budget and Policy Priorities*, 11 October 2017, https://www
.cbpp.org/research/poverty-and-inequality/a-guide-to-statistics-on-historical
-trends-in-income-inequality#_ftn1 (7 February 2018); Carrie Wofford, "'Inequality for All' Is Killing the Economy," *U.S. News and World Report*, 27 September 2013, https://www.usnews.com/opinion/blogs/carrie-wofford/2013/09/27/robert-reichs
-inequality-for-all-explains-our-major-economic-problems (7 February 2018).

12. Elise Gould and Hilary Wething, "U.S. Poverty Rates Higher, Safety Net Weaker Than in Peer Countries," *Economic Policy Institute*, 24 July 2012, http://www.epi.org/publication/ib339-us-poverty-higher-safety-net-weaker/
(7 February 2018).

13. Christian Belanger, "Sanders: Child Poverty Is Higher in America Than Any Other Major Country," *Politifact*, 8 July 2015, http://www.politifact.com/truth
-o-meter/statements/2015/jul/08/bernie-s/sanders-child-poverty-higher
-america-any-other-maj/ (7 February 2018); Max Fisher, "How 35 Countries Compare on Child Poverty: The US Is Ranked 34th," *Washington Post*, 15 April 2013, https://www.washingtonpost.com/news/worldviews/wp/2013/04/15/map
-how-35-countries-compare-on-child-poverty-the-u-s-is-ranked-34th/?utm
_term=.035b6313114b (7 February 2018); Gould and Wething, "U.S. Poverty Rates Higher."

14. Brooks Stokes, "US Stands Out as Rich Country Where a Growing Minority Say They Can't Afford Food," *Pew Research Center*, 14 May 2013, http://www
.pewresearch.org/fact-tank/2013/05/24/u-s-stands-out-as-a-rich-country
-where-a-growing-minority-say-they-cant-afford-food/ (7 February 2018); Jordan Weissman, "America May Have the Worst Hunger Problem of Any Rich Nation," *Slate*, 4 September 2014, http://www.slate.com/business/2018/02/why-rising
-wages-scare-the-heck-out-of-stock-market-investors.html (7 February 2018).

15. Drew Desilver, "U.S. Income Inequality, On Rise for Decades, Is Now Highest since 1928," *Pew Research Center*, 5 December 2013, http://www
.pewresearch.org/fact-tank/2013/12/05/u-s-income-inequality-on-rise-for

-decades-is-now-highest-since-1928/; see also OECD, "Income Inequality" (indicator), *Organisation for Economic Co-operation and Development*, 2017, http://www.oecd-ilibrary.org/social-issues-migration-health/income-inequality /indicator/english_459aa7f1-en (7 February 2018).

16. "Country Comparison, Distribution of Family Income—Gini Index," *The World Factbook, Central Intelligence Agency*, https://www.cia.gov/library /publications/resources/the-world-factbook/rankorder/2172rank.html (7 February 2018).

17. Erik Sherman, "America Is the Richest, and Most Unequal, Country," *Fortune*, 30 September 2015, http://fortune.com/2015/09/30/america-wealth -inequality/ (7 February 2018).

18. See Maureen Berner, Alexander Vazquez, and Meagan McDougall, "Documenting Poverty in North Carolina," *UNC School of Government*, March 2016, https://www.sog.unc.edu/sites/www.sog.unc.edu/files/reports/2016-03 -31%2020151227%20Documenting%20Poverty%202016-final.pdf (7 February 2018); Tazra Mitchell, "North Carolina's Greatest Challenge," *NC Budget & Tax Center*, 2016, http://www.ncjustice.org/sites/default/files/POVERTY%20REPORT%20 2016—final.pdf (7 February 2018); U.S. Census Bureau, 2016 American Community Survey 1-Year Estimates, S1701.

19. U.S. Census Bureau, 2016 American Community Survey 1-Year Estimates, S1701.

20. U.S. Census Bureau, 2016 American Community Survey 1-Year Estimates, S1903. Dollar amounts are in 2016 dollars.

21. Brian Kennedy, "Working Poor Make Up One Third of North Carolina Workforce," *NC Budget & Tax Center*, 13 September 2016, http://www.ncjustice .org/?q=budget-and-tax/prosperity-watch-issue-65-no-1-working-poor-make -one-third-north-carolina-workforce (7 February 2018).

22. U.S. Census Bureau, 2011–2015 American Community Survey 5-Year Estimates, S1701 (40 of North Carolina's 100 counties have a poverty rate of 20 percent or more).

23. Alexandra F. Sirota, "The Legacy of Hardship: Persistent Poverty in North Carolina," *NC Budget & Tax Center*, 2012, http://www.ncjustice.org/sites/default /files/BTC%20Brief%20-%20Persistent%20Poverty_0.pdf (7 February 2018); Sarah Willets, "Report: Poverty Entrenched," 15 April 2016, http://www.robesonian.com /news/86584/report-poverty-entrenched (7 February 2018).

24. Berner, McDougal, and Vasquez, "Documenting Poverty in North Carolina."

25. U.S. Census Bureau, 2016 American Community Survey 1-Year Estimates, S1701.

26. Men who work year-round, full time, earn $45,180 at the median; women earn $36,987. See U.S. Census Bureau, 2016 American Community Survey 1-Year Estimates, DP03.

27. U.S. Census Bureau, 2016 American Community Survey 1-Year Estimates, S1702.

28. U.S. Census Bureau, 2016 American Community Survey 1-Year Estimates, S1701.

29. U.S. Census Bureau, 2016 American Community Survey 1-Year Estimates, B17024.

30. U.S. Census Bureau, 2015 American Community Survey 5-Year Estimates, B17001I, B17001B, and B17001C.

31. See ibid.; Berner, McDougal, and Vasquez, "Documenting Poverty in North Carolina," 6–7.

32. Berner, McDougal, and Vasquez, "Documenting Poverty in North Carolina," 8–10.

33. Gene Nichol and Jeff Diebold, "Racial Wealth Disparity in North Carolina," *UNC Center on Poverty, Work and Opportunity*, 1 September 2010, http://www.law .unc.edu/documents/poverty/publications/racial_wealth_disparity_in_nc_unc _cpwo.pdf (7 February 2018).

34. Gene Nichol, "Tracing the Causes of Racial Wealth Disparity in North Carolina," *UNC Poverty Center*, 31 May 2011, http://www.law.unc.edu/documents /poverty/publications/tracingcauses_povertycenter.pdf (7 February 2018).

35. U.S. Census Bureau, 2016 American Community Survey 1-Year Estimates, S1701.

36. Ibid.

37. "Three North Carolina Cities Ranked among Nation's Poorest," *ABC 11 Eyewitness News*, 10 October 2013, http://abc11.com/archive/9281906/ (7 February 2018).

38. Food and Nutrition Service, USDA, Supplemental Nutrition Assistance Program (SNAP), State Level Participation & Benefits, Persons, July 2017, https:// www.fns.usda.gov/pd/supplemental-nutrition-assistance-program-snap (7 February 2018).

39. Brian Kennedy, "SNAP and Hunger Rates in North Carolina," *NC Budget & Tax Center*, July 2015, http://www.ncjustice.org/?q=budget-and-tax/chartbook -snap-and-hunger-north-carolina (7 February 2018).

40. "Hunger in North Carolina," *Feeding the Carolinas*, http://ncfoodbanks.org /hunger-in-north-carolina/ (7 February 2018).

41. Raj Chetty et al., "Where Is the Land of Opportunity? The Geography of Intergenerational Mobility in the United States," *National Bureau of Economic Research*, 2014, http://www.nber.org/papers/w19843 (7 February 2018). Chetty's research suggests that variation in mobility is correlated with five factors: (1) racial and income segregation, (2) income inequality, (3) school quality, (4) social capital, and (5) family structure.

42. Allen Smith, "The 15 US Cities Where Poor Neighborhoods Are Expanding Fastest," *Business Insider*, http://www.businessinsider.com/concentrated-poverty

-in-america-2014-8?op=1/#colorado-springs-colorado-14 (7 February 2018); David Perlmutt, "Poverty Spreads across Charlotte, North Carolina," *Charlotte Observer*, 2 August 2014, http://www.charlotteobserver.com/news/local/crime/article 9146654.html (7 February 2018) (reviewing census data findings).

43. Gene Nichol, "Deep Pockets of Urban Misery Masked," *Raleigh News & Observer*, 29 September 2013, 23A.

44. Ashley Williams Clark, "Study: More Than 4,000 Homeless Students in Mecklenburg County," *UNC Charlotte Urban Institute*, 13 March 2017, https:// ui.uncc.edu/story/studycharlotte-mecklenburg-schools-students-homeless (7 February 2018).

45. Bernadette D. Proctor, Jessica L. Semega, and Melissa A. Kollar, "Income and Poverty in the United States: 2015," *U.S. Census Bureau*, 2015, https://www .census.gov/content/dam/Census/library/publications/2016/demo/p60-256.pdf (7 February 2018).

46. U.S. Census Bureau, 2016 American Community Survey 1-Year Estimates, S1701.

47. Alex Kotch, "Amid Deepening Child Poverty in the South, Glimmers of Hope," *Facing South*, 24 July 2015, https://www.facingsouth.org/2015/07/amid -deepening-child-poverty-in-the-south-glimmers.html (7 February 2018); "Children in Extreme Poverty (50 Percent Poverty)," *Kids Count Data Center*, 2016, http://datacenter.kidscount.org/data/tables/45-children-in-extreme-poverty -50-percent-poverty?loc=1&loct=2#ranking/2/any/true/870/any/326 (7 February 2018); "The State of America's Children, 2014," *Children's Defense Fund*, http:// www.childrensdefense.org/library/state-of-americas-children/2014-soac.pdf (7 February 2018).

48. Jessica Dillinger, "US Poverty Level by State," *WorldAtlas*, 25 April 2017, https://www.worldatlas.com/articles/us-poverty-rate-by-state.html (7 February 2018); Katherine Peralta, "What's Wrong with the South?," *US News & World Report*, 18 September 2014, https://www.usnews.com/news/blogs/data-mine /2014/09/18/whats-wrong-with-the-south (7 February 2018).

49. Rep. George Cleveland, Republican from Onslow County (Jacksonville), claimed on the floor of the statehouse in 2012 that there was "no extreme poverty" in North Carolina, missing the fact that 10 percent of the children in his own district live, according to the federal government, in extreme poverty— on incomes below 50 percent of the federal poverty standard. See Lynn Bonner, "N.C. Republican Lawmaker Claims 'Extreme Poverty' Doesn't Exist in State," *Raleigh News & Observer*, 2 March 2012, http://www.mcclatchydc.com/news /politics-government/article24725242.html (7 February 2018).

50. Chapter 10 outlines these changes in detail.

CHAPTER 2

1. "A New Majority Research Bulletin: Low Income Students Now a Majority in the Nation's Public Schools," *Southern Education Foundation*, January 2015, http://www.southerneducation.org/getattachment/4ac62e27-5260-47a5-9d02 -14896ec3a531/A-New-Majority-2015-Update-Low-Income-Students-Now.aspx (7 February 2018).

2. Christian Bellanger, "Child Poverty in America Higher Than Any Advanced Country," *Politico*, 8 July 2015, http://www.politifact.com/truth-o-meter /statements/2015/jul/08/bernie-s/sanders-child-poverty-higher-america-any -other-maj/ (9 February 2018); Max Fisher, "How 35 Countries Compare on Child Poverty: The US Is Ranked 34th," *Washington Post*, 15 April 2013, https://www .washingtonpost.com/news/worldviews/wp/2013/04/15/map-how-35-countries -compare-on-child-poverty-the-u-s-is-ranked-34th/?utm_term=.25bbef0fc76e (9 February 2018); Elise Gould and Hilary Wething, "U.S. Poverty Rates Higher, Safety Net Weaker Than in Peer Countries," *Economic Policy Institute*, 24 July 2012, http://www.epi.org/publication/ib339-us-poverty-higher-safety-net-weaker/ (9 February 2018). The OECD study cited in Fisher's *Washington Post* article is now somewhat dated. Newer versions of the study have the United States about 27th or 28th of 32 OECD countries for child poverty. See OECD (2018), "Poverty rate" (indicator), doi:10.1787/0fe1315d-en (9 February 2018). See also Gonzalo Fanjul, "Children of the Recession," *UNICEF Office of Research*, September 2014, https:// www.unicef-irc.org/publications/pdf/rc12-eng-web.pdf (9 February 2018).

3. "Maternal and Infant Mortality," OECD.Stat, 2014, https://stats.oecd.org/# (9 February 2018). See also Christopher Ingraham, "Our Infant Mortality Rate Is a National Embarrassment," *Washington Post*, 29 September 2014, http://www .washingtonpost.com/blogs/wonkblog/wp/2014/09/29/our-infant-mortality -rate-is-a-national-embarrassment/ (9 February 2018); M. F. MacDorman, T. J. Mathews, A. D. Mohangoo, and J. Zeitlin, "International Comparisons of Infant Mortality and Related Factors: United States and Europe," *National Center for Health Statistics*, 2014, https://www.cdc.gov/nchs/data/nvsr/nvsr63/nvsr63_05.pdf (9 February 2018).

4. "Children in Extreme Poverty (50 Percent Poverty)," *Kids Count Data Center, a Project of the Annie E. Casey Foundation*, http://datacenter.kidscount.org/data /tables/45-children-in-extreme-poverty-50-percent-poverty?loc=1&loct=1#detailed /2/35/false/870,573,869,36,868/any/325,326 (9 February 2018).

5. "Notable Numbers: Election Spending, Airline Prices, Homeless Children," *Raleigh News & Observer*, 21 November 2014, http://www.newsobserver.com /opinion/editorials/article10140353.html (9 February 2014).

6. U.S. Census Bureau, 2015 American Community Survey 5-Year Estimates, B17001B, B17001C, and B17001I. Forty-five percent of black, Hispanic, and Native American children under five are poor.

7. U.S. Census Bureau, 2015 American Community Survey 5-Year Estimates, S1701.

8. U.S. Census Bureau, 1990 and 2000, and 2016 American Community Survey 1-Year Estimates.

9. See U.S. Census Bureau, 2016 American Community Survey 1-Year Estimates, C17014.

10. U.S. Census Bureau, 2015 American Community Survey 5-Year Estimates, S0901.

11. Ibid.

12. Laura Gerald, "Social Determinants of Health," *North Carolina Medical Journal* 73, no. 5.

13. Caroline Ratcliffe and Signe-Mary McKernan, "Child Poverty and Its Lasting Consequences," *The Urban Institute*, September 2012, https://www.urban.org/sites/default/files/publication/32756/412659-Child-Poverty-and-Its-Lasting-Consequence.PDF (9 February 2018).

14. David T. Burkam and Valerie E. Lee, *Inequality at the Starting Gate: Social Background Differences in Achievement as Children Begin School* (Washington, D.C.: Economic Policy Institute, 2002).

15. See Joan Luby et al., "The Effects of Poverty on Childhood Brain Development," *JAMA Pediatrics*, 2013, https://jamanetwork.com/journals/jamapediatrics/fullarticle/1761544 (10 February 2018). See also Guy Boulton, "Growing Up in Severe Poverty Affects Brain Size," *Journal Sentinel*, 29 August 2015, http://archive.jsonline.com/business/growing-up-in-severe-poverty-affects-brain-size-uw-madison-study-shows-b99560996z1-323318361.html (10 February 2018); Michelle Castillo, "Children Who Grow Up Poor Shown to Have Smaller Brain Volume," *CBSNews*, 28 October 2013, https://www.cbsnews.com/news/children-who-grow-up-poor-shown-to-have-smaller-brain-volume/ (10 February 2018); Diana Kwon, "Severe Poverty Affects Brain Size, Study Finds," *Scientific American*, 22 July 2015, https://www.scientificamerican.com/article/poverty-disturbs-children-s-brain-development-and-academic-performance/ (10 February 2018). Researchers found that children growing up in families with incomes below the federal poverty line had gray matter volumes 8 to 10 percent below normal development levels.

16. Quoted in Emily Badger, "The Surprising Cost of Growing Up Poor in the Shadow of Wealth," *Washington Post*, 23 January 2015, https://www.washingtonpost.com/news/wonk/wp/2015/01/23/the-surprising-cost-of-growing-up-poor-in-the-shadow-of-wealth/?utm_term=.e406a4e1ddbf (10 February 2018).

17. See Sean F. Reardon, "The Widening Income Achievement Gap between the Rich and the Poor: New Evidence and Possible Explanations," *Stanford University*, July 2011, https://cepa.stanford.edu/sites/default/files/reardon%20whither%20opportunity%20-%20chapter%205.pdf (10 February 2018).

18. Emma Garcia and Elaine Weiss, "Early Education Gaps by Social Class and

Race Start U.S. Children Out on Unequal Footing," *Economic Policy Institute*, 17 June 2015, http://www.epi.org/publication/early-education-gaps-by-social-class -and-race-start-u-s-children-out-on-unequal-footing-a-summary-of-the-major -findings-in-inequalities-at-the-starting-gate/ (10 February 2018).

19. Emma Garcia, "Inequalities at the Starting Gate: Cognitive and Noncognitive Skills Gaps between 2010–2011 Kindergarten Classmates," *Economic Policy Institute*, 17 June 2015, http://www.epi.org/publication/inequalities-at-the -starting-gate-cognitive-and-noncognitive-gaps-in-the-2010-2011-kindergarten -class/ (10 February 2018).

20. Ibid.

21. See Helen F. Ladd, "Education and Poverty: Confronting the Evidence," Sanford School of Public Policy, Duke University, Working Paper Series, SAN 11-01, 4 November 2011; Helen Ladd and Ted Fiske, "Class Matters. Why Won't We Admit It?," *New York Times*, 11 December 2011, http://www.nytimes.com/2011/12/12 /opinion/the-unaddressed-link-between-poverty-and-education.html (10 February 2018). See also Garcia, "Inequalities at the Starting Gate."

22. Ladd, "Education and Poverty."

23. See ibid. and Ladd and Fiske, "Class Matters."

24. Reardon, "Widening Income Achievement Gap between the Rich and the Poor."

25. Ibid.

26. Martin Carnoy and Richard Rothstein, "What Do International Tests Really Show about US Student Performance?," *Economic Policy Institute*, 28 January 2013, http://www.epi.org/publication/us-student-performance-testing/ (10 February 2018).

27. Emma Swift Lee and Joe Ableidinger, "Local School Finance Study," *Public School Forum of North Carolina*, 2017, https://www.ncforum.org/wp-content /uploads/2017/03/2017-Local-School-Finance-Study.pdf (10 February 2018).

28. Lynn Bonner and T. Keung Hui, "North Carolina Public School Grades Reflect Wealth of Students' Families," *Raleigh News & Observer*, 5 February 2015, http://www.newsobserver.com/news/local/article10255961.html (10 February 2018). See also "Notable Numbers: School Grades, Zika Infections and Confidence in Trump," *Raleigh News & Observer*, 9 September 2016, http://www.newsobserver .com/opinion/editorials/article100898867.html (10 February 2018).

29. T. Keung Hui, "Teachers Are Bailing Out of High Poverty Schools: Some Say That Needs to Change," *Raleigh News & Observer*, 16 June 2017, http://www .newsobserver.com/news/local/education/article156539969.html (10 February 2018).

30. Ta-Nehisi Coates, *Between the World and Me* (New York: Spiegel & Grau, 2015).

31. See Jerry McBeath, Maria Elena Reyes, and Mary Ehrlander, *Education Reform in the American States* (Charlotte, N.C.: Information Age, 2008), 115–30.

32. Ibid.

33. See Mark Barrett, "North Carolina's 'War on Public Education Debate': Rounds 2 and 3," *Citizen Times*, 26 August 2015, http://www.citizen-times.com /story/news/politics/elections/2015/08/26/war—education-north-carolina -general-assembly/32403227/ (10 February 2018); Valerie Strauss, "North Carolina's Step by Step War on Public Education," *Washington Post*, 8 August 2015, www.washingtonpost.com/news/answer-sheet/wp/2015/08/07/north-carolinas -step-by-step-war-on-public-education/ (10 February 2018).

CHAPTER 3

1. See "Food Insecurity in the United States," *U.S. Department of Agriculture*, https://www.ers.usda.gov/topics/food-nutrition-assistance/food-security-in-the -us/measurement.aspx (10 February 2018).

2. "How Hungry Is America?," *Food Research and Action Center*, June 2016, http://www.frac.org/wp-content/uploads/food-hardship-2016-1.pdf (10 February 2018).

3. "Poverty and Hunger Fact Sheet," *Feeding America*, September 2017, http:// www.feedingamerica.org/assets/pdfs/fact-sheets/poverty-and-hunger-fact-sheet .pdf (10 February 2018).

4. "Hunger in North Carolina, the Latest Scandalous Numbers," *NC Policy Watch*, http://www.ncpolicywatch.com/2016/10/05/hunger-north-carolina -latest-scandalous-numbers/food-insecurity-chart/ (10 February 2018); Brian Kennedy, "Putting a Face on Hunger in North Carolina," *NC Policy Watch*, 24 May 2017, http://pulse.ncpolicywatch.org/2017/05/24/putting-face-hunger-north -carolina/#sthash.mnobRo1X.TV0qJfHN.dpbs (10 February 2018).

5. See "Map the Meal Gap 2017," *Feeding America*, 2017, http://www.feeding america.org/research/map-the-meal-gap/2015/2015-mapthemealgap-exec -summary.pdf (10 February 2018). See also "Food Hardship in America: Households with Children Especially Hard Hit," *Food Resource and Action Center*, September 2017, http://frac.org/wp-content/uploads/food-hardship-report -households-with-children-sep-2016.pdf (10 February 2018); "Food Security Status of U.S. Households in 2016," *U.S. Department of Agriculture*, 4 October 2017, https://www.ers.usda.gov/topics/food-nutrition-assistance/food-security-in-the -us/key-statistics-graphics.aspx (10 February 2018); "Hunger in North Carolina, the Latest Scandalous Numbers"; Rob Christensen, "A Magazine Ranked All 50 States: How Did North Carolina Do?" *Raleigh News & Observer*, 11 March 2017, http://www.newsobserver.com/news/politics-government/politics-columns -blogs/rob-christensen/article137766828.html (10 February 2018).

6. "Map the Meal Gap 2017: Overall Food Insecurity in North Carolina by County in 2015," *Feeding America*, 2017, http://www.feedingamerica.org /research/map-the-meal-gap/2015/MMG_AllCounties_CDs_MMG_2015_2/NC _AllCounties_CDs_MMG_2015.pdf (10 February 2018).

7. "How Hungry Is America?"

8. Bertrand M. Gutierrez, "Hunger Study Calls Area Worst in US," *Winston-Salem Journal*, 16 August 2011, http://www.journalnow.com/news/local/hunger-study-calls-area-worst-in-u-s/article_136ce0c7-6763-5cb9-9e39-3f23dd0113ec.html (10 February 2018).

9. "Food Insecurity in the United States," *Feeding America*, 2017, http://map.feedingamerica.org/congressional/2015/overall (10 February 2018).

10. Ibid., North Carolina.

11. See "History of the Food Bank of Central & Eastern NC," *Food Bank of Central and Eastern North Carolina*, 2017, http://fbnc.convio.net/site/PageServer?pagename=about_history (10 February 2018).

12. Beth Walton, "Hunger Activists Say Change Is Needed," *Asheville Citizen Times*, 21 April 2014, http://www.citizen-times.com/story/news/local/2015/09/17/hunger-activists-want-reform-summer-feeding/32517427/ (10 February 2018).

13. "Food Banks Devoured by Demand after State Federal Cuts," *WRAL.com*, 13 September 2013, http://www.wral.com/nc-food-banks-devoured-by-demand-after-state-federal-cuts/12880663/?comment_order=forward (10 February 2018).

14. A team led by neuroscientists Kimberly Noble from Columbia University in New York City and Elizabeth Sowell from Children's Hospital in Los Angeles examined the biological underpinnings of these effects. See Sara Reardon, "Poverty Shrinks Brains from Birth," *Nature*, 30 March 2015, http://www.nature.com/news/poverty-shrinks-brains-from-birth-1.17227 (10 February 2018).

CHAPTER 4

1. Jon Greenberg, "Bernie Sanders Says U.S. the Only Major Country Not to Guarantee Health Care," *Politifact*, 29 June 2015, http://www.politifact.com/truth-o-meter/statements/2015/jun/29/bernie-s/bernie-sanders-us-only-major-country-doesnt-guaran/ (10 February 2018); Sean Gorman, "U.S. Only Major Country without Health Care Guarantee," *Politifact*, 1 September 2015, http://www.politifact.com/virginia/statements/2015/sep/01/dan-gecker/dan-gecker-says-us-only-wealth-nation-without-univ/ (10 February 2018).

2. See OECD, *Society at a Glance 2014: OECD Social Indicators* (OECD Publishing, 2014), http://www.oecd-ilibrary.org/docserver/download/8113171e.pdf?expires=1518319881&id=id&accname=guest&checksum=78E66886F0BD5F8E6A1D1E30B24522E4 (10 February 2018).

3. U.S. Census Bureau, 2016 American Community Survey 1-Year Estimates, S2701.

4. Reena Flores, "Report: America's Uninsured Rate Falls Below 10%," *CBS News*, 12 August 2015, https://www.cbsnews.com/news/report-americas-uninsured-rate-falls-below-10 (10 February 2018).

5. U.S. Census Bureau, 2016 American Community Survey 1-Year Estimates, S2701.

6. Ibid.

7. 2016 data: ibid.; 2010 data: U.S. Census Bureau, 2010 American Community Survey 1-Year Estimates, GCT-2702.

8. See "America's Health Ranking: Annual Report," *United Health Foundation*, December 2016, https://assets.americashealthrankings.org/app/uploads/ahr16 -complete-v2.pdf (10 February 2018).

9. "Current Status of State Medicaid Expansion Decisions," *Kaiser Family Foundation*, 16 January 2018, http://kff.org/health-reform/slide/current-status -of-the-medicaid-expansion-decision/ (10 February 2018).

10. Leighton Ku et al., *The Economic and Employment Costs of Not Expanding Medicaid in North Carolina: A County Level Analysis*, Center for Health Policy Research (Washington, D.C.: George Washington University School Of Public Health, 2014).

11. See Matt Broadus, "Census Data: States Not Expanding Medicaid Lag Further on Health Coverage," *Center on Budget and Policy Priorities*, 12 September 2017, https://www.cbpp.org/blog/census-data-states-not-expanding-medicaid -lag-further-on-health-coverage (10 November 2018). See also Karen Garloch, "In North Carolina, Thousands Still Lack Health Insurance and Health Care: What Should the State Do?," *Raleigh News & Observer*, 14 October 2016, https:// insurancenewsnet.com/oarticle/in-nc-thousands-still-lack-insurance-and -health-care-what-should-the-state-do (10 February 2018).

12. See Rachel Garfield and Anthony Damico, "The Coverage Gap: Uninsured Poor Adults in States That Do Not Expand Medicaid," *Henry J. Kaiser Family Foundation*, 1 November 2017, https://www.kff.org/uninsured/issue-brief/the -coverage-gap-uninsured-poor-adults-in-states-that-do-not-expand-medicaid/ (10 February 2018); "How Will the Uninsured in North Carolina Fare under the Affordable Care Act," *Henry J. Kaiser Family Foundation*, 6 January 2014, https:// www.kff.org/health-reform/fact-sheet/state-profiles-uninsured-under-aca -north-carolina/ (10 February 2018); Gene Nichol, Heather Hunt, and Matt Norchi, "Putting a Face on Medicaid Expansion in North Carolina," *NC Poverty Research Fund*, October 2016, http://www.law.unc.edu/documents/poverty /publications/medicaid_report_final.pdf (10 February 2018).

13. Eric C. Schneider et al., "Mirror, Mirror 2017: International Comparison Reflects Flaws and Opportunities for Better U.S. Health Care," *Commonwealth Fund*, July 2017, http://www.commonwealthfund.org/~/media/files/publications /fund-report/2017/jul/schneider_mirror_mirror_2017.pdf (10 February 2018).

14. See David Squires and Chloe Anderson, "U.S. Health Care from a Global Perspective," *Commonwealth Fund*, October 2015, http://www.commonwealth fund.org/publications/issue-briefs/2015/oct/us-health-care-from-a-global -perspective (1 March 2018). See also Dan Mangan, "US Health Care Spending High, Results Are Not So Good," *CNBC*, 18 October 2015, https://www.cnbc

.com/2015/10/08/us-health-care-spending-is-high-results-arenot-so-good.html (10 February 2018).

15. "Per Capita Healthcare Costs—International Comparison," *Peter Peterson Foundation*, 3 May 2016, https://www.pgpf.org/chart-archive/0006_health-care -oecd (11 February 2018).

16. Bradley Sawyer and Cynthia Cox, "How Does Health Spending in the U.S. Compare to Other Countries?," *Peterson-Kaiser Health System Tracker*, 22 May 2017, https://www.healthsystemtracker.org/chart-collection/health-spending -u-s-compare-countries/ (11 February 2018).

17. Dan Munro, "U.S. Healthcare Spending On Track to Hit $10,000 per Person This Year," *Forbes*, 4 January 2015, https://www.forbes.com/sites/danmunro /2015/01/04/u-s-healthcare-spending-on-track-to-hit-10000-per-person-this -year/#161c84026dea (11 February 2018); Ricardo Alonso Zaldivar, "New Peak for US Health Care Spending: $10,345 per Person," *Associated Press*, 13 July 2016, https://www.apnews.com/dd6612ead1a14cd39bcca0be8758ef79 (11 February 2018).

18. "Health System Dashboard," *Peterson-Kaiser Health System Tracker*, https:// www.healthsystemtracker.org/dashboard/#health-well-being (11 February 2018).

19. Bradley Sawyer and Selena Gonzales, "How Does Infant Mortality in the U.S. Compare to Other Countries?," *Peterson-Kaiser Health System Tracker*, July 7, 2017, https://www.healthsystemtracker.org/chart-collection/infant-mortality-u-s -compare-countries/ (1 March 2018).

20. David U. Himmelstein and Steffie Woolhandler, "The Current and Projected Taxpayer Shares of U.S. Health Costs," *American Journal of Public Health*, March 2016, http://ajph.aphapublications.org/doi/abs/10.2105/AJPH .2015.302997 (11 February 2018).

21. "Government Funds Nearly Two-Thirds of U.S. Health Care Costs: American Journal of Public Health Study," *Physicians for a National Health Program*, 21 January 2016, http://www.pnhp.org/news/2016/january/government-funds-nearly -two-thirds-of-us-health-care-costs-american-journal-of-pub (11 February 2018).

22. Ibid.

23. See Squires and Anderson, "U.S. Health Care from a Global Perspective."

24. *See* OECD, *Health at a Glance 2011: OECD Indicators* (OECD Publishing, 2011), https://www.oecd.org/els/health-systems/49105858.pdf (11 February 2018).

CHAPTER 5

1. Allen Serkin and Stephen Whitlow, "State of North Carolina Urban Distressed Communities," *Center for Urban and Regional Studies*, February 2005, http://digital.ncdcr.gov/cdm/ref/collection/p249901c01122/id/10689 (12 February 2018); William High and Todd Owen, "North Carolina's Distressed Urban Tracts," *Center for Urban and Regional Studies*, February 2014, https://curs.unc.edu/files /2014/02/NC-Distress-Update-final.pdf (12 February 2018).

2. High and Owen, "North Carolina's Distressed Urban Tracts."

3. Joe Polich, "The Other Durham: Poverty Up in Poorest Areas," *Durham Herald-Sun*, 22 October 2013; "Exploring Economic Distress in N.C.—Other Locations," *UNC School of Law, N.C. Poverty Research Fund*, http://www.law.unc.edu/centers/poverty/distress/other.aspx (2 February 2018).

4. High and Owen, "North Carolina's Distressed Urban Tracts."

5. "Charlotte Overview," *Charlotte Chamber of Commerce*, https://charlottechamber.com/eco-dev/charlotte-overview/ (3 February 2018).

6. "Charlotte," *Visit Charlotte*, 6 May 2015, http://www.charlottesgotalot.com/national-tourism-week-spotlights-travel-industrys-economic-impact-charlotte (12 February 2018).

7. "Tracking Growth, Prosperity, and Inclusion in the 100 Largest U.S. Metropolitan Areas," Metropolitan Policy Program, *Brookings Institution*, January 2016, http://www.brookings.edu/~/media/research/files/interactives/2016/metro-monitor/metromonitor.pdf; Elizabeth Kneebone, "The Growth and Spread of Concentrated Poverty, 2000 to 2008–2012," *Brookings Institution*, http://www.brookings.edu/research/interactives/2014/concentrated-poverty (11 May 2016); Raj Chetty et al., "Where Is the Land of Opportunity? The Geography of Intergenerational Mobility in the United States," *National Bureau of Economic Research*, 2014, http://www.nber.org/papers/w19843 (7 February 2018).

8. Gene Nichol and Heather Hunt, "Economic Hardship, Racialized Concentrated Poverty and the Challenges of Low-Wage Work: Charlotte, North Carolina," *UNC School of Law, N.C. Poverty Research Fund*, Spring 2016, http://www.law.unc.edu/centers/poverty/distress/charlotte/ (12 February 2018).

9. David Erickson, Carolina Reid, Lisa Nelson, Anne O'Shaughnessy, and Allen Berube, eds., "The Enduring Challenges of Concentrated Poverty in America, U.S. Federal Reserve," *Federal Reserve System* and the *Brookings Institution*, 2008, https://www.brookings.edu/wp-content/uploads/2016/06/1024_concentrated_poverty.pdf (12 February 2018).

10. Motoko Rich, Amanda Cox, and Matthew Bloch, "Money, Race and Success: How Your School District Compares," *New York Times*, April 29, 2016, http://www.nytimes.com/interactive/2016/04/29/upshot/money-race-and-success-how-your-school-district-compares.html (18 April 2018); N.C. Department of Public Instruction, "2014–15 School Report Cards," *NC School Report Cards*, http://www.ncpublicschools.org/src/ (18 April 2018); N.C. Department of Public Instruction, "Free and Reduced Meals Application Data, 2014–2015," *Financial and Business Services*, Data and Reports, http://www.ncpublicschools.org/fbs/resources/data/ (18 April 2018).

11. "Interactive Metro Monitor 2017 Dashboard," *Brookings Institution*, 23 February 2017, https://www.brookings.edu/interactives/metro-monitor-2017-dashboard/#V0G16740 (13 May 2016).

CHAPTER 6

1. Michael B. Sauter, Evan Comen, Samuel Stebbins, and Thomas C. Frohlich, "America's Richest and Poorest Cities," *24/7 Wall St.*, 8 October 2015, https://247wallst.com/special-report/2015/10/08/americas-richest-and-poorest -cities/11/ (11 February 2018).

2. Gregor Aisch, Eric Buth, Matthew Bloch, Amanda Cox, and Kevin Quealy, "The Best and Worst Places to Grow Up: How Your Area Compares," *New York Times*, 4 May 2015, https://www.nytimes.com/interactive/2015/05/03/upshot/the -best-and-worst-places-to-grow-up-how-your-area-compares.html (11 February 2018).

3. "America's Shrinking Middle Class: A Close Look at Changes within Metropolitan Areas," *Pew Research Center*, 11 May 2016, http://www.pewsocial trends.org/2016/05/11/americas-shrinking-middle-class-a-close-look-at-changes -within-metropolitan-areas/ (11 February 2018).

4. Ibid.

5. Ibid.

6. "Welcome to Our City," *City of Goldsboro*, 2018, http://www.goldsboronc.gov /mayor-of-goldsboro/about-goldsboro/ (11 February 2018).

7. "2012 Wayne County Community Health Assessment," *East Carolina University, Wayne County, and Wayne Memorial Hospital*, 2012, https://www .waynegov.com/ArchiveCenter/ViewFile/Item/78 (11 February 2018), 15.

8. Ibid., 11.

9. "Children in Poverty," *Kids Count Data Center*, September 2015, http:// datacenter.kidscount.org/data/tables/2238-children-in-poverty#detailed/5 /4910-5009/false/36,868,867,133,38/any/12873,4680 (11 February 2018).

10. Aisch, Buth, Bloch, Cox, and Quealy, "Best and Worst Places to Grow Up."

11. Ibid.

CHAPTER 7

1. Robert E. Scott, "NAFTA's Impact on the States," *Economic Policy Institute*, 10 April 2001, http://www.epi.org/publication/briefingpapers_nafta01_impactstates/ (11 February 2018).

2. Jule Hubbard, "Wilkes 2nd in U.S. in Income Loss," *Wilkes Journal-Patriot*, http://www.journalpatriot.com/news/wilkes-nd-in-u-s-in-income-loss/article _c83dbd82-d732-11e5-9eca-773f01f3e4f8.html; Stateline, "Fewer Manufacturing Jobs, Housing Bust Haunt Many U.S. Counties," *Pew Charitable Trust*, http:// www.pewtrusts.org/en/research-and-analysis/blogs/stateline/2016/01/22/fewer -manufacturing-jobs-housing-bust-haunt-many-us-counties. According to the N.C. Department of Health and Human Services, Wilkes County had the third highest overdose death rate in the country in 2007, attributed primarily to opioids. See also "North Carolina Communities Work Together to Combat Opioid Crisis,"

Daily Tar Heel, 29 January 2018, http://www.dailytarheel.com/article/2018/01 /opioid-epidemic-0129; "County May File Lawsuit over Opioids," *Wilkes Journal-Patriot*, 5 January 2018, http://www.journalpatriot.com/news/county-may-file -lawsuit-over-opioids/article_3bac24b0-f221-11e7-8dce-23c153c6182d.html; Richard Fausset, "Feeling Let Down and Left Behind with Little Hope for Better," *New York Times*, 15 May 2016, https://www.nytimes.com/2016/05/26/us/feeling -let-down-and-left-behind-with-little-hope-for-better.html; U.S. Census Bureau, 2016 American Community Survey 5-Year Estimates, B01001.

3. "QuickFacts North Carolina," *U.S. Census Bureau*, 1 July 2017, https://www .census.gov/quickfacts/fact/table/NC/PST045217 (11 February 2018).

4. Stateline, "Fewer Manufacturing Jobs, Housing Bust Haunt Many U.S. Counties."

5. "Mapping America's Rental Housing Crisis," *Urban Institute*, 27 April 2017, http://apps.urban.org/features/rental-housing-crisis-map/ (11 February 2018).

6. Laura Mitchell, "Providing Shelter and Hope," *Wilkes Journal-Patriot*, 17 August 2016.

7. Ibid., http://www.journalpatriot.com/news/providing-shelter-hope/article _7b498834-64a5-11e6-8adf-1b291c41166c.html (11 February 2018).

8. "Success Stories from 2014 Class," *Wilkes Circles of Care*, 24 May 2016, http:// www.wilkescirclesofcare.org/new.html (11 February 2018).

CHAPTER 8

1. Jeffrey S. Passel and D'vera Cohn, "A Portrait of Unauthorized Immigration in the US," *Pew Research Center*, 14 April 2009, http://www.pewhispanic.org/2009 /04/14/a-portrait-of-unauthorized-immigrants-in-the-united-states/ (11 February 2018); Alexandra Sirota and Tazra Mitchell, "Tuition Equity: Expanding College Opportunity and Paving the Way for North Carolina's Economic Future," *NC Budget & Tax Center*, June 2014, http://www.ncjustice.org/sites/default/files/BTC %20Brief%20-%20Tuition%20Equity_0.pdf (11 February 2018).

2. See Hannah Gill, *The Latino Migration Experience in North Carolina: New Roots in the Old North State* (Chapel Hill: University of North Carolina Press, 2010), 164.

3. *Plyler v. Doe*, 457 U.S.202 (1982).

4. See Gill, *Latino Migration Experience in North Carolina*, 165–69.

5. See Emily Starbuck Crone, "5 Facts You Need to Know about the DREAM Act," *USA Today*, 26 February 2015, http://college.usatoday.com/2015/02/26/5 -facts-you-need-to-know-about-the-dream-act/ (11 February 2018).

6. Letter from Attorney General Roy Cooper to Honorable Marcus Brandon, January 22, 2014, "Advisory Letter—Undocumented Students," Alexander Peters and Kimberley Potter; see also Craig Jarvis, "Cooper Sides with UNC: No In-state Tuition Rate for DACA Students," *Raleigh News & Observer*, January 23, 2014, http://www.newsobserver.com/news/local/article10290989.html (15 April 2018).

7. See Gill, *Latino Migration Experience in North Carolina*, 170–73.

8. "Demographic Profile of Hispanics in North Carolina," *Pew Research Center*, 2014, http://www.pewhispanic.org/states/state/nc/ (11 February 2018); see also Sejal Zota, "Immigrant in North Carolina: A Fact Sheet," *Popular Government*, Fall 2008, http://sogpubs.unc.edu/electronicversions/pg/pgfa108/article4.pdf (11 February 2018), 38–45.

9. Frank Bruni, "Emilio's Great Race," *New York Times*, 27 January 2014, https://www.nytimes.com/2014/01/28/opinion/bruni-emilios-great-race.html?_r=0 (11 February 2018).

CHAPTER 9

1. See Lucian Reed, dir., *America Divided: Democracy for Sale* (2016); Ari Berman, "The 94-Year-Old Civil-Rights Pioneer Who Is Now Challenging North Carolina's Voter-ID Law," *Nation*, 25 January 2016, https://www.thenation.com/article/the-92-year-old-civil-rights-pioneer-who-is-now-challenging-north-carolinas-voter-id-law/ (11 February 2018).

2. Bernadette D. Proctor, Jessica L. Semega, and Melissa A. Kollar, "Income and Poverty in the United States: 2015," *U.S. Census Bureau*, 2015 https://www.census.gov/library/publications/2016/demo/p60-256.html (11 February 2018). See also Tazra Mitchell and Alexandra Forter Sirota, "North Carolina's Greatest Challenge—Elevated Poverty Hampers Economic Opportunity for All," *North Carolina Justice Center*, October 2016, http://www.ncjustice.org/?q=budget-and-tax/btc-report-north-carolinas-greatest-challenge%E2%80%94elevated-poverty-hampers-economic (11 February 2018).

3. Maureen Berner, Alexander Vazquez, and Meagan McDougall, "Documenting Poverty in North Carolina," *UNC School of Government*, March 2016, https://www.sog.unc.edu/sites/www.sog.unc.edu/files/reports/2016-03-31%2020151227%20Documenting%20Poverty%202016-final.pdf (11 February 2018); see also Gene Nichol and Jeff Diebold, "Racial Wealth Disparity in North Carolina," *University of North Carolina Center on Poverty, Work and Opportunity, Z. Smith Reynolds Foundation*, June 2013, https://www.zsr.org/sites/default/files/documents/Racial%20Wealth%20Disparity%20in%20NC.pdf (11 February 2018); Gene Nichol, "Being Repulsed by Charleston Shootings Is the Easy Part," *Raleigh News & Observer*, 11 July 2015, http://www.newsobserver.com/opinion/op-ed/article26999395.html (11 February 2018).

4. Edward J. Smith and Shaun R. Harper, "Disproportionate Impact of School Suspensions," *Center for Race and Equity in Education*, 2015, https://equity.gse.upenn.edu/sites/default/files/publications/Smith_Harper_Report.pdf (11 February 2018); T. Keung Hui, "Report Finds NC Black Students Disproportionately Suspended," *Raleigh News & Observer*, 25 August 2015, http://www.newsobserver.com/news/politics-government/politics-columns-blogs/under-the-dome/article32310816.html (11 February 2018).

5. See Gene Nichol, "Documenting Poverty in North Carolina," *UNC Poverty Center, Z. Smith Reynolds Foundation*, 2009, http://www.law.unc.edu/documents /poverty/publications/documentingpoverty_finalreport.pdf (11 February 2018).

6. "North Carolina Profile," *Prison Policy Initiative*, 2016, https://www .prisonpolicy.org/profiles/NC.html (11 February 2018); Joseph E. Kennedy and Mika W. Chance, "Collateral Damage: How Mass Incarceration Increases Poverty and Crime in North Carolina's Poorest African American Communities," *Trial Briefs*, August 2011, http://www.law.unc.edu/documents/faculty/kennedy -trianglebriefs.pdf (12 February 2018); Ashley Nellis, "The Color of Justice: Racial and Ethnic Disparity in State Prisons," *Sentencing Project*, 2016, http://www .sentencingproject.org/wp-content/uploads/2016/06/The-Color-of-Justice -Racial-and-Ethnic-Disparity-in-State-Prisons.pdf (12 February 2018); Gene Nichol, "'Current Conditions' and the Voting Rights Act," *Progressive Populist*, 1 September 2015, http://www.populist.com/21.15.nichol.html (12 February 2018).

7. See Kennedy and Chance, "Collateral Damage."

8. See Observer Editorial Board, "Are Charlotte Police Stopping, Searching Motorists Just Because They Are Black?," *Charlotte Observer*, 27 October 2015, http://www.charlotteobserver.com/opinion/editorials/article41611026.html #storylink=cpy (12 February 2018).

9. Nicole Flatow, "North Carolina Police Three Times More Likely to Arrest Blacks after Seat Belt Violation, Study Finds," *ThinkProgress*, 30 September 2013, https://thinkprogress.org/north-carolina-police-3-times-more-likely-to-arrest -blacks-after-seat-belt-violation-study-finds-f9e67221e784/ (12 February 2018). The data, which N.C. Central University's Scott Holmes called evidence that "as an empirical fact . . . we have a culture in our law enforcement for unconscious institutional racism," comes as the Department of Justice is filing a lawsuit alleging the state's new restrictive voting law is discriminatory and will disenfranchise minority voters.

10. See Sharon Lafraniere and Andrew W. Lehren, "The Disproportionate Risks of Driving While Black," *New York Times*, 24 October 2015, https://www.nytimes .com/2015/10/25/us/racial-disparity-traffic-stops-driving-black.html?_r=0 (12 February 2018). Here in North Carolina's third largest city, officers pulled over African American drivers for traffic violations at a rate far out of proportion to their share of the local driving population. Police used their discretion to search black drivers or their cars more than twice as often as white motorists—even though they found drugs and weapons significantly more often when the driver was white. See also William R. Smith, Donald Tomaskovic-Devey, Matthew T. Zingraff, H. Marcinda Mason, Patricia Y. Warren, and Cynthia Pfaff Write, "The North Carolina Highway Traffic Study," *North Carolina State University*, January 2004, https://www.ncjrs.gov/pdffiles1/nij/grants/204021.pdf (12 February 2018).

11. Matt Shipman, "Study Shows That, in Restaurants, Race Matters," *NC State*

News, 23 April 2012, https://news.ncsu.edu/2012/04/wms-rusche-restaurants/ (12 February 2018). "Many people believe that race is no longer a significant issue in the United States," says Sarah Rusche, a Ph.D. candidate in sociology at N.C. State and coauthor of a paper describing the study. "But the fact that a third of servers admit to varying their quality of service based on customers' race, often giving African-Americans inferior service, shows that race continues to be an issue in our society." See, generally, "North Carolina Department of Transportation Racial Disparity Study," *Colette Holt & Associates*, 2014, https://www.ncdot.gov/download /about/regulations/ncdotdisparitystudy2014.pdf (12 February 2018); George Gonzalez, "Racial and Ethnic Minorities Face More Subtle Housing Discrimination: HUD Study Finds Decline in Blatant Discrimination While Unequal Treatment Persists," *U.S. Department of Housing and Urban Development*, 11 June 2013, https://archives.hud.gov/news/2013/pr13-091.cfm (12 February 2018); Paul A. Buescher and Jack Leiss, "Race, Education, and Mortality in North Carolina," *North Carolina Department of Health and Human Services*, April 1994, http:// digital.ncdcr.gov/cdm/ref/collection/p249901co1122/id/158346 (12 February 2018).

12. "North Carolina Racial Justice Act," *American Civil Liberties Union*, 2018, https://www.aclu.org/north-carolina-racial-justice-act (12 February 2018).

13. Kim Severson, "North Carolina Repeals Law Allowing Racial Bias Claim in Death Penalty Cases," *New York Times*, 3 June 2013, http://www.nytimes.com/2013 /06/06/us/racial-justice-act-repealed-in-north-carolina.html?_r=0 (12 February 2018).

14. Andrew Cohen, "Racial Bias in Death Penalty Cases: A North Carolina Test," *Atlantic*, 23 April 2012, https://www.theatlantic.com/national/archive/2012/04 /racial-bias-in-death-penalty-cases-a-north-carolina-test/256197/ (12 February 2018).

15. See "On Views of Race and Inequality, Blacks and Whites Are Worlds Apart," *Pew Research Center*, 27 June 2016, http://www.pewsocialtrends.org/2016 /06/27/on-views-of-race-and-inequality-blacks-and-whites-are-worlds-apart/ (12 February 2018).

16. Ibid.

17. Ibid.; Dedrick Asante-Muhammed, Chuck Collins, Josh Hoxie, and Emanuel Nieves, "The Ever Growing Gap," *Institute for Policy Studies* and *CFED*, August 2016, http://www.ips-dc.org/wp-content/uploads/2016/08/The-Ever-Growing -Gap-CFED_IPS-Final-1.pdf (12 February 2018).

18. See David Brooks, "The Nature of Poverty," *New York Times*, 1 May 2015, https://www.nytimes.com/2015/05/01/opinion/david-brooks-the-nature-of -poverty.html?smid=tw-share&_r=0 (12 February 2018). But see also Sean Illing, "Why David Brooks Shouldn't Talk about Poor People," *Slate*, 1 May 2015, http:// www.slate.com/technology/2018/02/study-facebooks-plan-to-rate-the-media -could-actually-work.html (12 February 2018). See also Maggie Habberman,

"Newt: Fire the Janitors, Hire Kids to Clean Schools," *Politico*, 18 November 2011, https://www.politico.com/story/2011/11/newt-fire-the-janitors-hire-kids-to-clean-schools-068729#ixzz306Bz8bZU (12 February 2018).

19. Daniel Tovaskovic Devey and Vincent Roscigno, "Race and Economic Subordination in the US South," *American Sociological Review* 61, no. 565 (August 1996). Higher differences in racial wealth and income disparity reflect fundamental factors—the class and racial character of the local economies and continuing current levels of discrimination, not educational attainment and opportunity.

See also Ann Chih Lin and David R. Harris, eds., "The Colors of Poverty: Why Racial and Ethnic Disparities Persist," *University of Michigan*, January 2009, http://www.npc.umich.edu/publications/policy_briefs/brief16/ (12 February 2018); Cecily R. Hardaway and Vonnie C. Mcloyd, "Escaping Poverty and Securing Middle Class Status: How Race and Socioeconomic Status Shape Mobility Prospects for African Americans during the Transition to Adulthood," *Journal of Youth and Adolescence*, 11 November 2008, https://www.ncbi.nlm.nih.gov/pmc/articles/PMC4108157/ (12 February 2018):

> Historical and present-day institutional racism and discrimination have contributed greatly to the disadvantaged status of African Americans. The effects of past racial discrimination and economic marginalization are seen in the high rates of poverty and in the difficulty each generation has in assuring that the next generation achieves greater success. African Americans face especially tough challenges to upward mobility and are particularly susceptible to downward mobility (Hertz, 2005; McBrier & Wilson, 2004; South & Crowder, 1997). The research reviewed here highlights some of the factors that contribute to upward mobility. It suggests that parenting practices and structured activities can be used to foster the accumulation of social and cultural capital to facilitate upward mobility. It further suggests that cultural, economic, and social resources both impede and facilitate mobility.

See also David Leonhardt, "The Complex Story of Race and Upward Mobility," *New York Times*, 25 July 2013, https://economix.blogs.nytimes.com/2013/07/25/the-complex-story-of-race-and-upward-mobility/?mtrref=undefined (12 February 2018): "The metropolitan areas with the highest percentage of African-Americans are clustered in the southeast and the industrial Midwest. So are the metropolitan areas where low-income children have the longest odds of making it into the middle class."

See also Paul Krugman, "Race, Class, and Neglect," *New York Times*, 4 May 2015, http://www.nytimes.com/2015/05/04/opinion/paul-krugman-race-class-and-neglect.html?_r=0 (12 February 2018).

20. Krugman, "Race, Class, and Neglect."

21. See Ann Lin, *The Colors of Poverty: Why Racial and Ethnic Disparities*

Exist (New York: Russell Sage Foundation, 2010); Robert Putnam, *Our Kids: The American Dream in Crisis* (New York: Simon & Schuster, 2015); William Julius Wilson, *More Than Just Race: Being Black and Poor in the Inner City* (New York: Norton, 2006).

22. Wilson, *More Than Just Race*, 3–7.

23. See Lin, *Colors of Poverty*.

24. See *City of Los Angeles v. Lyons*, 461 U.S. 95 (1976); *Rizzo v. Goode*, 423 U.S. 362 (1973).

25. See *Washington v. Davis*, 426 U.S. 229 (1976); *Feeney v. Massachusetts*, 442 U.S. 256 (1979).

26. See *Feeney v. Massachusetts*, 442 U.S. 256 (1979).

27. See Peter Westen, "The Empty Idea of Equality," *Harvard Law Review* 95 (1982).

28. John Hope Franklin, *Mirror to America: The Autobiography of John Hope Franklin* (New York: Farrar, Straus & Giroux, 2005) 378–81.

29. See Charles Blow, "Jeb Bush, 'Free Stuff' and Black Folks," *New York Times*, 28 September 2015, https://www.nytimes.com/2015/09/28/opinion/charles-m -blow-jeb-bush-free-stuff-and-black-folks.html (12 February 2018); Max Ehrenfreund, "Jeb Bush Suggests Black Voters Get 'Free Stuff.' So Does He," *Washington Post*, 30 September 2015, https://www.washingtonpost.com/news /wonk/wp/2015/09/30/jeb-bush-says-black-voters-get-free-stuff-so-does-he /?utm_term=.ef229513f4cf (12 February 2018).

30. See Robert Lieberman, "Why Americans Hate Welfare," *American Prospect*, 30 November 2000, http://prospect.org/article/why-americans-hate-welfare (12 February 2018).

31. See Martin Gilens, *Why Americans Hate Welfare: Race, Media, and the Politics of Anti-Poverty Policy* (Chicago: University of Chicago Press, 1999). See also Lieberman, "Why Americans Hate Welfare."

32. Alberte Alesina, Edward Glaeser, and Bruce Sacerdote, "Why Doesn't the United States Have a European Style Welfare State?," *Harvard Institute of Economic Research*, November 2001, https://scholar.harvard.edu/files/glaeser/files /why_doesnt_the_u.s._have_a_european-style_welfare_state.pdf (12 February 2018).

33. Ibid.

34. See Paul Krugman, "Slavery's Long Shadow," *New York Times*, 22 June 2015, http://www.nytimes.com/2015/06/22/opinion/paul-krugman-slaverys-long -shadow.html (12 February 2012).

35. Ibid. See also Paul Krugman, "Obamacare in Retrospect," *Raleigh News & Observer*, 4 August 2017, http://www.newsobserver.com/opinion/op-ed/article 165495487.html (12 February 2018).

36. See Dan Carter, "North Carolina: A State of Shock," *Southern Spaces*, 23 September 2013, https://southernspaces.org/2013/north-carolina-state-shock (12

February 2018); Vann R. Newkirk II, "The Battle for North Carolina," *Atlantic,* 27 October 2016, https://www.theatlantic.com/politics/archive/2016/10/the-battle -for-north-carolina/501257/ (12 February 2018); "Altered State: How Five Years of Conservative Rule Have Redefined North Carolina," *NC Policy Watch,* December 2015, http://www.ncpolicywatch.com/wp-content/uploads/2015/12/NC-Policy -Watch-Altered-State-How-5-years-of-conservative-rule-have-redefined-north -carolina-december-2015.pdf (12 February 2018); Vann R. Newkirk II, "The Supreme Court Finds North Carolina's Racial Gerrymandering Unconstitutional," *Atlantic,* 22 May 2017, https://www.theatlantic.com/politics/archive/2017/05 /north-carolina-gerrymandering/527592/ (12 February 2018); Charles Pierce, "Our Democracy Is at a Crossroads," *Esquire,* 10 January 2018, http://www.esquire.com /news-politics/politics/a15054112/gerrymander-north-carolina-voter-purge-ohio/ (6 February 2018).

37. See Robert R. Korstad and James L. LeLoudis, *To Right These Wrongs: The North Carolina Fund and the Battle to End Poverty and Inequality in 1960s America* (Chapel Hill: University of North Carolina Press, 2010), 54–55.

38. Ibid.

39. Ibid., 1–2.

40. Ibid., 10.

CHAPTER 10

1. See Robert R. Korstad and James L. Leloudis, *To Right These Wrongs: The North Carolina Fund and the Battle to End Poverty and Inequality in 1960s America* (Chapel Hill: University of North Carolina Press, 2010), 1–13.

2. Ibid., 1–13, 16–19.

3. Ibid., 9–16.

4. Ibid.

5. See "The Rip Van Winkle State," *Learn NC,* http://web.archive.org/web /20170207200810/http://www.learnnc.org/lp/editions/nchist-newnation/4.0 (12 February 2018).

6. James H. Johnson Jr., "The Changing Face of Poverty in North Carolina," *Popular Government,* Spring/Summer 2003, 14–19.

7. Aidan Smith, "The North Carolina Fund," *Learn NC,* http://web.archive.org /web/20180203194719/%20http://www.learnnc.org/lp/editions/nchist-postwar /6010 (12 February 2018).

8. Johnson, "Changing Face of Poverty in North Carolina," 14–19.

9. The Editorial Board, "The Decline of North Carolina," *New York Times,* 9 July 2013, http://www.nytimes.com/2013/07/10/opinion/the-decline-of-north-carolina .html (12 February 2018).

10. Jonathan M. Katz, "In North Carolina, Some Democrats See Their Grim Future," *Politico,* 27 December 2016, https://www.politico.com/magazine/story

/2016/12/in-north-carolina-some-democrats-see-the-future-214553 (12 February 2018).

11. "Federal Medical Assistance Percentage (FMAP) for Medicaid and Multiplier," *Henry J. Kaiser Family Foundation*, 2018, https://www.kff.org /medicaid/state-indicator/federal-matching-rate-and-multiplier/?currentTime frame=0&sortModel=%7B%22colId%22:%22Location%22,%22sort%22:%22asc %22%7D (12 February 2018); Rachel Garfield and Anthony Damico, "The Coverage Gap: Uninsured Poor Adults in States That Do Not Expand Medicaid," *Henry J. Kaiser Family Foundation*, 1 November 2017, https://www.kff.org/uninsured /issue-brief/the-coverage-gap-uninsured-poor-adults-in-states-that-do-not -expand-medicaid/ (12 February 2018); "How Will the Uninsured in North Carolina Fare Under the Affordable Care Act?," *Henry J. Kaiser Family Foundation*, 6 January 2014, https://www.kff.org/health-reform/fact-sheet/state-profiles -uninsured-under-aca-north-carolina/ (12 February 2018); Leighton Ku, Brian Bruen, Erika Steinmetz, and Tyler Bysshe, "The Economic and Employment Costs of Not Expanding Medicaid in North Carolina: A County-Level Analysis," *George Washington University Center for Health Policy Research*, December 2014, https:// www.conehealthfoundation.com/app/files/public/4202/The-Economic-and -Employment-Costs-of-Not-Expanding-Medicaid-in-North-Carolina.pdf (12 February 2018).

12. Benjamin D. Sommers, Robert J. Blendon, and E. John Orav, "Changes in Utilization and Health among Low-Income Adults after Medicaid Expansion or Expanded Private Insurance," *JAMA Internal Medicine* 176 (2016): 1501–9; Sam Dickman, David Himmelstein, Danny McCormick, and Steffie Woolhandler, "Opting Out of Medicaid Expansion: The Health and Financial Impacts," *Health Affairs*, 30 January 2014, https://www.healthaffairs.org/do/10.1377/hblog2014 0130.036694/full/ (12 February 2018); Adam Searing and Jack Hoadley, "Beyond the Reduction in Uncompensated Care: Medicaid Expansion Is Having a Positive Impact on Safety Net Hospitals and Clinics," *Georgetown University Health Policy Institute*, June 2016, http://ccf.georgetown.edu/wp-content/uploads/2016/05 /Medicaid_hospitals-clinics-June-2016.pdf (12 February 2018); Mark A. Hall And Edwin Shoaf, "Medicaid Expansion Costs in North Carolina: A Frank Discussion," *Wake Forest University, Health Law & Policy Program*, January 2016, http://hlp.law .wfu.edu/files/2016/01/Expansion-Issues-final-2b.pdf (12 February 2018).

13. Justin Wolfers, "North Carolina's Misunderstood Cut in Jobless Benefits," *New York Times*, 26 July 2014, https://www.nytimes.com/2014/07/27/upshot/north -carolinas-misunderstood-cut-in-jobless-benefits.html?_r=0 (12 February 2018).

14. See Editorial Board, "Decline of North Carolina"; Jeff Linville, "Gov. McCrory and His Great Triumph," *Mount Airy News*, 15 December 2016, http:// www.mtairynews.com/opinion/46756/gov-mccrory-and-his-great-triumph (12 February 2018).

15. Kevin Rogers, "North Carolina's Unemployment Program Experiment Is a Failure," *Charlotte Observer*, 23 February 2016, http://www.charlotteobserver.com /opinion/op-ed/article62016117.html (12 February 2018).

16. Mike Evangelist, "One-Two Punch: As States Cut Unemployment Benefit Weeks, Jobless Also Lose Federal Aid, Even as Jobs Remain Scarce," *National Employment Law Project*, February 2013, http://www.nelp.org/content/uploads /2015/03/Policy-Brief-States-Cut-UI-Weeks.pdf (12 February 2018); Editorial Board, "Decline of North Carolina"; Catherine New, "North Carolina Unemployment Benefit Cuts Harshest in the Nation," *Huffington Post*, 2 November 2013, https://www.huffingtonpost.com/2013/02/11/north-carolina -unemployment-benefits-cuts_n_2662511.html (12 February 2018).

17. Tazra Mitchell, "First in Flight from the EITC—Low-Income Working Families Bid Farewell to NC's Earned Income Tax Credit," *NC Budget & Tax Center*, March 2014, http://www.ncjustice.org/?q=budget-and-tax/btc-brief-first-flight -eitc-low-income-working-families-bid-farewell-ncs-earned (12 February 2018).

18. Ibid.

19. See Tazra Mitchell, "North Carolina's Earned Income Tax Credit," *NC Budget & Tax Center*, February 2013, http://www.ncjustice.org/sites/default/files /BTC%20Brief-%20A%20Modest%20But%20Vital%20Boost%20to%20Low-Paid %20Workers%20across%20the%20State.pdf (12 February 2018).

20. John Frank, "Legislation Would Repeal NC Credit for Low Income Taxpayers," *Raleigh News & Observer*, 14 February 2013, http://www.newsobserver .com/news/weather/article10344959.html (12 February 2018).

21. Michael Leachman, "Unhappy New Year: North Carolina Eliminates Its EITC," *Center on Budget and Policy Priorities*, 13 January 2014, https://www.cbpp .org/blog/unhappy-new-year-north-carolina-eliminates-its-eitc (13 February 2018).

22. Ibid.

23. Colin Campbell, "NC Budget: More Sales Taxes in 2016, Income Tax Cuts in 2017," *Raleigh News & Observer*, 19 September 2015, http://www.newsobserver .com/news/politics-government/state-politics/article35825601.html (13 February 2018).

24. "Altered State: How 5 Years of Conservative Rule Have Redefined North Carolina," *North Carolina Policy Watch*, December 2015, http://www.ncpolicy watch.com/wp-content/uploads/2015/12/NC-Policy-Watch-Altered-State-How -5-years-of-conservative-rule-have-redefined-north-carolina-december-2015.pdf (13 February 2018), 5; Alexandra Forter Sirota, "House's Flat Income Tax a Windfall for the Wealthy," *NC Budget & Tax Center*, June 2013, http://www.ncjustice.org /?q=budget-and-tax/btc-brief-houses-flat-income-tax-windfall-wealthy (13 February 2018).

25. "Altered State," 5.

26. Chris Fitzsimon, "The Ways Regressive Tax Hikes Will Harm the Poor," *Raleigh News & Observer*, 18 September 2015, http://www.newsobserver.com /opinion/op-ed/article35727654.html (13 February 2018); The Editorial Board, "Behind NC Tax Surge Is a Tax Shift," *Raleigh News & Observer*, 16 January 2016, http://www.newsobserver.com/opinion/editorials/article55101605.html (13 February 2018).

27. See Alexandra Sirota, "State Budget Agreement Doubles Down Once More on Regressive Tax Policies," *NC Policy Watch*, 29 June 2016, http://www.ncpolicy watch.com/2016/06/29/state-budget-agreement-doubles-down-once-more -on-regressive-tax-policies/ (13 February 2018); Colin Campbell, "NC Legislators Consider Expanding Sales Taxes, Cutting Income Taxes," *Raleigh News & Observer*, 12 January 2016, http://www.newsobserver.com/news/politics-government/state -politics/article54351470.html (13 February 2018).

28. "Altered State," 9–10.

29. The Editorial Board, "NC Would Save By Expanding Pre-K," *Raleigh News & Observer*, 4 February 2015, http://www.newsobserver.com/opinion/editorials /article10253654.html (13 February 2018).

30. "Altered State," 8.

31. Rob Schofield, "Cutting Off Food Assistance to the Poor? Really??," *NC Policy Watch*, 6 October 2015, http://www.ncpolicywatch.com/2015/10/06/cutting -off-food-assistance-to-the-poor-really/ (13 February 2018); Jessica Murrell, "SNAP Truly a Lifesaver for Many North Carolinians," *Raleigh News & Observer*, 24 February 2016, http://www.newsobserver.com/opinion/op-ed/article62267887 .html (13 February 2018).

32. Colin Campbell, "133,000 Would Lose Food Stamps under NC Senate Budget," *Raleigh News & Observer*, 18 May 2017, http://www.newsobserver.com /news/politics-government/state-politics/article151063487.html (13 February 2018).

33. Brian Kennedy, "Senate's Bill to Strip Food Assistance Is Based on Faulty Reasoning and Misinformation," *NC Policy Watch*, 19 May 2017, http://pulse .ncpolicywatch.org/2017/05/19/senates-bill-strip-food-assistance-based-faulty -reasoning-misinformation/#sthash.UHLPLjJn.pBLyfeWC.dpbs (13 February 2018).

34. Ibid.

35. Campbell, "133,000 Would Lose Food Stamps."

36. Colin Campbell, "No Food Stamp Cuts for 133,000 In Final Budget Bill," *Raleigh News & Observer*, 22 June 2018, http://www.newsobserver.com/news /politics-government/state-politics/article157587259.html (13 February 2018).

37. Laura Leslie, "North Carolina Shutting Down Work First," *WRAL.Com*, 14 October 2013, http://www.wral.com/nc-shutting-down-work-first/12994151/ (13 February 2018).

38. Ibid.

39. Kirk Warner, "NC Missing Good Investment by Cutting Civil Legal Aid," *Raleigh News & Observer*, 2 October 2015, http://www.newsobserver.com/opinion/op-ed/article37238517.html (13 February 2018).

40. Melissa Boughton, "Final Budget Delivers Hits to Legal Services, Emergency Judges, Department of Justice," *NC Policy Watch*, 21 June 2017, http://pulse.ncpolicywatch.org/2017/06/21/final-budget-delivers-hits-legal-services-emergency-judges-department-justice/#sthash.9SAMdTF6.dHItsmSE.dpbs (13 February 2018).

41. Ibid.

42. Gary D. Robertson, "N Carolina Speaker Blames Lawyers' Zeal for Legal Aid Cuts," *Associated Press*, 11 August 2017, https://www.usnews.com/news/best-states/north-carolina/articles/2017-08-11/moore-blames-overzealous-lawyers-for-legal-aid-money-cuts (13 August 2018).

43. *See Bearden v. Georgia*, 461 U.S. 660 (1983).

44. Travis Fain, "Budget Language Targets Court Fee Waivers for Poor Defendants," *WRAL.Com*, 25 June 2017, http://www.wral.com/budget-language-targets-court-fee-waivers-for-poor-defendants/16781429/ (13 February 2018); Melissa Boughton, "House and Senate Differ over Budget Provision Making It Harder for Judges to Waive Fees for Poor Defendants," *NC Policy Watch*, 1 June 2017, http://www.ncpolicywatch.com/2017/06/01/house-senate-differ-budget-provision-making-harder-judges-waive-fees-poor-defendants/ (13 February 2018).

45. "HB2: A Timeline for North Carolina's Controversial Law," *Raleigh News & Observer*, 10 May 2016, http://www.newsobserver.com/news/politics-government/state-politics/article76726392.html (13 February 2018); Colin Campbell, "Four Things to Remember about House Bill 2," *Raleigh News & Observer*, 13 September 2016, http://www.newsobserver.com/news/politics-government/state-politics/article101602642.html (13 February 2018).

46. Lynn Bonner, "NC Begins Drug Tests for Welfare Applicants," *Raleigh News & Observer*, 10 February 2016, http://www.newsobserver.com/news/politics-government/state-politics/article59389341.html (13 February 2018).

47. Ned Barnett, "Drug Tests Dispel a Myth about North Carolina's Poor," *Raleigh News & Observer*, 13 February 2016, http://www.newsobserver.com/opinion/opn-columns-blogs/ned-barnett/article60097156.html (13 February 2018).

48. "Nationwide Trends," *National Institute on Drug Abuse*, June 2015, https://www.drugabuse.gov/publications/drugfacts/nationwide-trends (13 February 2018).

49. Barnett, "Drug Tests Dispel a Myth about North Carolina's Poor."

50. Boughton, "House and Senate Differ over Budget Provision"; Fain, "Budget Language Targets Court Fee Waivers for Poor Defendants."

51. Representative George Cleveland of Onslow County stated in a committee

hearing concerning poor kids, "There is no extreme poverty in North Carolina." Federal poverty figures are just "government agency efforts to justify what they want as a poverty level." See Lynn Bonner, "N.C. Republican Lawmaker Claims 'Extreme Poverty' Doesn't Exist in State," *Raleigh News & Observer*, 2 March 2012, http://www.mcclatchydc.com/news/politics-government/article24725242.html (13 February 2018).

52. *Citizens United v. Federal Election Commission*, 558 U.S. 310 (2010).

53. Robert Putnam, *Our Kids: The American Dream in Crisis* (New York: Simon & Schuster, 2015).

54. "Beyond Red vs. Blue: The Political Typology," *Pew Research Center*, 26 June2014, http://www.people-press.org/2014/06/26/section-3-fairness-of-the -economic-system-views-of-the-poor-and-the-social-safety-net/ (13 February 2018), 4.

55. I cite the common Christian refrain from the book of Matthew: "Truly I tell you, whatever you did for one of the least of these, you did for me" (Matthew 25: 40, 45).

56. *Brown v. Board of Education*, 347 US 473 (1954); Gene Nichol, "Richmond Bar Association Law Day Address," *William & Mary*, 1 May 2007, http://www .wm.edu/about/administration/president/history/twentyone/nichol/addresses /richmondbar/index.php (13 February 2018).

INDEX

Page numbers in italics refer to illustrations.